THE PARACLETE.

THE PARACLETE:

AN ESSAY ON
THE PERSONALITY AND MINISTRY OF

THE HOLY GHOST,

WITH

SOME REFERENCE TO CURRENT DISCUSSIONS.

BY

JOSEPH PARKER, D.D.,
Author of "Ecce Deus," "Ad Clerum," etc.
Minister of the City Temple, Holburn Viaduct, London.

Wipf & Stock
PUBLISHERS
Eugene, Oregon

Wipf and Stock Publishers
199 West 8th Avenue, Suite 3
Eugene, Oregon 97401

The Paraclete
An Essay on the Personality and Ministry of the Holy Ghost
By Parker, Joseph
ISBN: 1-57910-083-X
Publication date 11/12/1997
Previously published by Scribner, Armstrong & Co., 1997

Veni, CREATOR SPIRITUS,
Mentes Tuorum visita,
Imple supernâ Gratiâ
Quæ Tu creasti pectora.
Qui Paracletus diceris,
Donum Dei Altissimi,
Fons vivus, Ignis, Charitas,
Et Spiritalis Unctio.
Tu Septiformis munere,
Dextræ Dei Tu Digitus,
Tu rite promissum Patris,
Sermone ditans guttura.
Accende Lumen sensibus,
Infunde Amorem cordibus,

Infirma nostri corporis
Virtute firmans perpeti.
Hostem repellas longius,
Pacemque dones protinus,
Ductore sic Te prævio,
Vitemus omne noxium.

Per Te sciamus da Patrem,
Noscamus atque Filium,
Te utriusque Spiritum
Credamus omni tempore.
Sancto simul Paracleto
Nobisque mittat Filius,
Charisma Sancti Spiritus.

INTRODUCTION.

How far is it possible to divest the Christian doctrine of the Holy Ghost of such mystery as is superstitious rather than religious? Christian theology affirms the existence of a Ghost—a spiritual Person—who is the highest Teacher of truth and the supreme Minister of comfort: does that dogma carry with it such a quality of mystery as resents the investigations of reason, or is it possible so to use reason as to see, even with considerable distinctness, that the word *Ghost* is the proper development of the word *Person*, and that without such progress and consummation the word "Person" would become a limited and self-exhausting term?

This inquiry will receive some elucidation from two admissions which an instinct common to humanity has never failed to act upon, though they have not been allowed to pass without obstinate controversy upon their boundaries and liberties :—(1) It is universally admitted, in practice if not in theory, that altogether apart from religion there is an invisible world; a world of thought and feeling, as distinguished from a world of fact and activity,—a sphere of ideas, schemes, purposes, desires, vows, fancies, from which the most importunate curiosity may be excluded though the veil of defence is apparently so unsubstantial: (2) It is also universally admitted that the forces which are invisible and impalpable, and on that account regarded by Christian thinkers as spiritual, are undoubtedly the mainsprings of human energy. Thought, Hope, Faith, Ambition, are within the veil, yet the meanest industries and the most imposing projects are moved by their pulsation. So well is this known, that even flippant men have occasionally been sobered as they have been reluctantly constrained to consult probabilities and quantities whose full proportion and consequence have been disguised or obscured by a concealing cloud.

In view of these two admissions, how far does the doctrine of the personality and ministry of the Holy Ghost become, at least upon its revealed and practical side, a doctrine comprehensible by reverential reason? Do they help us in any degree towards self-control when speculative impatience threatens to avenge itself by scepticism? For example, when Religion says, No man hath seen God at any time, may not Reason, reflecting upon these two admissions, reply—That is not improbable, seeing that in reality no man has seen *himself* at any time; he has seen a fleshly figure which he identifies as himself, but his spiritual self, the self that thinks, dreams, vows, and creates his behaviour, he has never seen. Thus the invisible world, which each man owns as a secret and private dominion, and which is already accepted by mankind as the most assured of realities, may supply some help towards the recognition of that most mysterious of all life which is revealed in Scripture as the Holy Ghost.

The following inquiry is, in the first place, theological and expository, occupying the Christian standpoint, and endeavouring to trace the outline and establish the argument of a positive faith. In the next place, the inquiry is almost wholly critical and controversial, dealing frankly with objectors and objections, and examining in a fearless but equitable way the pretensions of many Sadducees. Christian criticism may have been too lenient in assigning the proper value to the moral authority of ostensible destroyers of spiritual Christianity, and possibly some objectors may have mistaken forbearance for weakness. In the second part of this work an endeavour has been made to show the moral issues which have always proceeded from a Sadducean creed, and also to point out the worthlessness of its science and logic when applied to moral questions. A great battle as between Faith and Unbelief has yet to come. There have long been wars and rumours of wars, but Armageddon itself is now evidently in the near distance. The struggle will probably relate not so much to the mere facts of Christian history, as to the reality of Spiritual existence; man's personal spirituality will be denied; thought itself will be still more emphatically pronounced but a form or expression of matter; and as a logical necessity, so far as these things are supposed to be proved, Christianity will be regarded as the outcome of a tragical mistake, and the entire theological idea be classed with the nightmares of paganism. This is the manifest course of the controversy which is immediately impending. Christian men therefore are bound to show cause why they insist upon retaining their old theological landmarks, and unless they give some answer to the persistent and boastful Sadduceeism of the times, they may place themselves in a false position, and lose, in respect to young and inexperienced Christians, the reward of being a tongue to the dumb.

CONTENTS.

PART I. EXPOSITORY AND AFFIRMATIVE.

		PAGE
I.	Personality and Manifestation	1
II.	The Historic Movement towards Spirituality	10
III.	Inspiration as a Doctrine	19
IV.	Inspiration as a Fact	31
V.	Inspiration of Christ's Biography	43
VI.	The Holy Spirit as the Interpreter of Scripture	78
VII.	The Ministry of the Comforter	96
VIII.	The Convictive Work of the Holy Ghost	113
IX.	Regeneration	136
X.	Pentecost	150
XI.	The Witness of the Spirit	167
XII.	The Human Spirit limited by the Human Body	178
XIII.	The Gift of the Holy Ghost considered as the Culmination of the Gospel	190
XIV.	The Miracles of the Holy Ghost	220
XV.	Holiness	234
XVI.	Incidental Testimony	247

PART II. CRITICAL AND CONTROVERSIAL.

		PAGE
XVII.	THE COLLATERAL SPIRITUAL ARGUMENT	269
XVIII.	MATERIALISM AND SPIRITUALISM	288
XIX.	THE SPIRITUAL ORGAN	347

EPILOGUE 369

PART I.

EXPOSITORY AND AFFIRMATIVE.

THE PARACLETE.

I.

PERSONALITY AND MANIFESTATION.

EVERYWHERE in the Bible—which in the meantime is the one field of Christian evidence—the Holy Ghost is described as a person, and never as a mere influence separable from personality. Poetic licence, indeed, allows natural objects, and even objects of human contrivance, to be spoken of in a limited sense as living creatures, as, for example, when personal pronouns of masculine and feminine gender are used in speaking of the sun and moon; but this is wholly different from the varied and precise expressions which are constantly employed by biblical writers in referring, however fully or incidentally, to the ministry of the Holy Ghost. According to the doctrine of those writers, the Holy Spirit "teaches," "comforts," "reproves," "guides," and "sanctifies" mankind; He "leads into all truth"; He "testifies of Christ"; He quickens the memory, so that all things taught by Jesus Christ are brought to remembrance; He "searches all things, yea the deep things of God." It would certainly appear, therefore, that so far as it is possible for language to escape indistinctness when applied to purely spiritual subjects, such terms must be taken as settling decisively the fact that the biblical writers themselves did, rightly or wrongly, believe in the proper personality of the Holy Ghost; and all the more so in the light of the further fact, that precisely the same terms are applied to the Holy Spirit as are applied to the Father, so that the personality of the one stands or falls with the personality of the other.

But how to escape the danger of bodily manifestation and at the same time secure the consciousness and comfort of divine personality? How to have heaven without the risk and pain of earth? Such is the problem which awaits solution. Think of the danger of any form of personality which is comprehensible by bodily vision. First of all that vision is itself imperfect, and must therefore come to erroneous conclusions respecting the objects of its observation. What two men ever saw exactly alike? Vision is affected by critical training, by taste, by skill in delicate comparison, also by physical and atmospherical conditions, so much so that not only do no two men see alike, but the same man corrects the observations of his own vision as he grows in judgment or changes his point of observation. The eye takes note of figure, attitude, colour, magnitude, so that whatever may be inward and spiritual in humanity is necessarily approached in the first instance through physical appearances; and appearances are proverbially deceptive. Who can say with unquestioning certitude that he ever saw anything as it really is? The eye is probably the least reliable of the senses, though amply sufficient for noting the rough outlines and magnitudes of objects. But the *hand* is too quick for the eye. The skilled conjuror will make a fool of any man who insists that seeing is believing; yet it *is* so, only that "seeing" is something other than the ordinary use of the visual organs. Seeing is believing, let us say, but what is *seeing?* The young look for beauty of form; the mature look for beauty of character. In early life we inquire for outward charms; we say this is lovely and that is grand, our meaning simply being that in our estimation the outline is perfect, the colour is exquisite, or the proportions are noble. By-and-by however, when we are disciplined and mellowed, we know that there is no satisfaction but in moral excellence alone, and, indeed, a reluctant distrust of all ephemeral charms begins to affect our estimates of life. Out of this experience has come the homely proverb "handsome is that handsome does," a proverb full of almost painful meaning when traced to its philosophy,—the outward and the formal having befooled or misled us, and the neglected excellence (without form or comeliness) having only slowly come to recognition and honour. We say of some persons that the more they are known the more they are beloved, or we vary the expression by saying that such and such persons will "bear knowing;" and on the other hand we say of certain persons that the more they are known the less do they justify either confidence or esteem. In both cases the risks of merely bodily or physical manifestation are illustrated; thus: in the former case there was perhaps something of ungainliness or unattractiveness to be got over before the real quality of the character was ascertained; very little perhaps, yet there it was,—a frown, an occasional expression, apparent coldness or even pride, want of ease and frankness, indisposition to speak, and unconcealed objection to confide;—in the latter case there were marked personal advantages, a winning smile, frankness, geniality, beauty of face, elegance of carriage, but farther acquaintance with the life dispelled the charm of mere appearances. Wise men know how much better it is that the difficulty, if any, should present itself in physical appearances rather than in moral features. Yet it is not easy to begin the world successfully without physical attractions, for the world is much given over to the lust of the eyes. The plain man must stand aside until the gainly man has had his full turn; the gold ring first, the mean raiment last, everywhere,—perhaps even in the house of God! In Jesus Christ's own case the most serious dangers arose from the physical and local aspect of His life and ministry. His contemporaries could not get over the appearances, and they had no lack of various expression of disappointment and disgust. A few of their contemptuous utterances will prove this : " Can any good thing come out of Nazareth ?" " Are not His sisters with us ?" " Whence hath this man this wisdom?" " Thou art not yet fifty years old." " Thou art a Samaritan and hast a devil." " Search and look, for out of Galilee ariseth no prophet." Clearly, then, the contention turned upon nativity, relationship, locality,—in a word, upon all the accidents of merely bodily manifestation. The acknowledged " wisdom " could not subdue the prejudice arising out of " Nazareth," " Galilee," and " Samaritanism." A great risk, therefore, in a human point of view, was the incarnation of Godhead. Even to apostolic faith it presented itself as the great mystery of godliness.

Why does this difficulty, in all its varying forms and degrees arise, in connection with every presence, and especially every living presence that appeals to the eye ? Because of the limitation of such presence. When men can see what they suppose to be the boundaries of a figure, they instinctively compare it with other bodies ; its probable force can be calculated, its relative value can be appraised, and the discrepancy between its capacity and its purpose can be exaggerated or decried according to the bias of the observer. The consequence is that before spiritual questions can be approached, the temptation which is always presented by appearances must be encountered, and at that point spiritual inquiry may be perverted or arrested.

Where, as in the case of Jesus Christ, the instrument is considered to be evidently weak, there is a temptation to contemn and distrust it; and where to all human appearance it is obviously equal to the task which has to be fulfilled, there is a counter temptation to forget that after all it is but an instrument. On account, therefore, of this limitation, bodily presence is often detrimental to spiritual influence. We know, for example, how perilous it often is to be admitted to familiar intercourse with the men who have stimulated us by their thoughts and thrown upon our intellectual life the spell of their genius. So long as such men stand afar off, clothed with their spiritual house, and working with their spiritual functions, we give them homage; but when they come near us they invite criticism upon points which did not enter into their original mastery of our admiration and confidence; some weakness of the flesh, some conceit of manner or feebleness of expression, or other more or less trifling peculiarity, may impair their spiritual dominion, and cause us to regret that the god of our early love ever came down from Olympian invisibility.

An argumentative difficulty may be here interposed. If no two men can *see* alike, can any two men *think* alike? If a man has to correct his own observation, has he not also to correct his own thinking? If so, is not mental incompetency as great an objection to spiritual personality as visual defect is to bodily manifestation? Imaginatively

Personality and Manifestation. 7

it is, but substantially it is not. Because whilst physical vision cannot be perfected, and is at best but temporary in its uses, spiritual faculties are not only susceptible of the highest refinement, but are the only powers by which men can lay hold upon immortality,—without them there can be no manhood. Whilst, therefore, in the one case the difficulty is inherent, in the other it is a continually decreasing quantity. We shall always, as a matter of happy necessity, have diversity and conflict of thinking, yet the thinking powers are by this very opposition being trained to the strength and precision out of which will come vital reconciliation and harmony.

From the beginning the danger of a visible manifestation of the godhead was foreseen and guarded against : " Ye saw no manner of similitude on the day that the Lord spake unto you in Horeb out of the midst of the fire, lest ye corrupt yourselves, and make you a graven image, the similitude of any figure, the likeness of male or female." Man has always wanted to *see* God, and God has always refused to be seen. So we have no image of God. Mythological deities we have in galleries of marble cunningly cut, but the God that made the heavens is nowhere to be found amongst all the ambition and daring of the most audacious art. And what have we even of the Man Christ Jesus in sculpture or painting ? Much, yet nothing. Do any two heads of His correspond ? Does any head of His satisfy the observer, filling up all his dreams and desires, and turning all his holy prayers into visible and enrapturing answers? It would seem, indeed, as if one or two Christs had actually been painted under the direct inspiration of the Holy Ghost, and yet as if the hand of the painter had failed the Inspirer himself. And as if the painter too had reeled just as he was about to add the touch that would have shown divinity. There is a better Christ in every broken heart than can be found amongst the artistic treasures of men,— a Christ full of sympathy, very pitiful and gracious stooping with infinite condescension, and counting no service mean. Who would have only a portrait of Christ when he can have in his heart the Son of God Himself?

This is the point towards which we have been moving throughout these collateral reflections. How needful soever to escape the perils of bodily manifestation (a need whose importance cannot be exaggerated), yet the comfort of divine *personality*, as distinguished from abstract infinitude, must be secured. In his highest aspirations man requires, and indeed demands, distinct, individual, companionable life,—he must have pathos as well as augustness, or he will be overpowered and discouraged; his progress will be an advancement into solitude, and loneliness will kill him. We have now to find out, by an honest exposition of scripture and a fair interpretation of human consciousness, how far this necessity is provided for in the revelation of the Holy Ghost. That is precisely our work in this argument. Is the Holy Ghost a person? Is it true that he can be the Guest of the heart, the Teacher of the understanding, the Revealer of Christ? Is the Holy Ghost a *Comforter*, and as such will He come to the bruised and aching heart with solaces not earthly but heavenly? These inquiries are of some consequence to men who already see the coming sunset, having first felt the disappointment and bitterness of life. One word may be a key to our reasoning, viz., God is a spirit, —so is man. Man *has* a body, but he *is* a spirit.

II.

THE HISTORIC MOVEMENT TOWARDS SPIRITUALITY.

THE succession which is indicated by the words—Father, Son, and Holy Ghost, is neither nominal nor accidental, it is a philosophical progress and culmination. Any transposition of this order would be felt to be irregular and impossible,—violent, unnatural, and self-destructive. When we think ourselves back towards the origin of things, we are conscious of the keenest dissatisfaction with all mere terms that get no farther than the approbation of the strictly critical faculty; we want something more; something for which we cannot hit the exact word, but for want of which the heart often aches and cries. Then is suggested the biblical word, *Father*, and with it comes at least a promise of satisfaction; it is *felt* to be the true start-point, having difficulties of its own no doubt, but difficulties that may be overcome. The Fatherhood is not emotional, but causative and sovereign paternity. Logic can do but little towards its explanation; the mind must accept this idea of fatherhood as the mind accepts itself, a mystery certainly, but not greater except in degree than the silent, invisible, spiritual *life* that is in every man. But fatherhood is a plural or inclusive term: immediately it suggests the idea of childhood, and childhood is realised most conspicuously and impressively in the sonship of Jesus Christ; but sonship such as this, involving manifestation or visible expression, is, as we have just urged, beset with peculiar risks; provided, therefore, that it go barely far enough to establish itself as an indisputable fact in human history, the sooner it is withdrawn from ocular criticism, the less will the world be tantalised and distracted by the exercise of its own imperfect physical senses. This manifestation and withdrawment are exclusively characteristic of Jesus Christ. He was here long enough to remove all doubt as to His personal identity, yet He withdrew Himself immediately that He had secured for His personality an unquestioned place in human history. Nothing more was to be gained by His visible continuance on earth; His bodily mission had been wholly fulfilled, and therefore He "vanished out of the sight" of men. But what of the future of His work? Then, according to Christian teaching, was to come manifestation without visibility; instead of bodily presence, there was to be a new experience of life, spirituality, insight, sensibility, and sympathy almost infallible in holy instinct. In one word, the Holy *Man* was to be followed by the Holy *Ghost*.

This idea of a philosophical rather than a merely arbitrary succession, is strictly consistent with the fact that *the whole movement of history, in all that is vital and permanent, is a movement from the outward and visible to the inward and spiritual:* this we claim to be true of all history, not merely of any particular section or bias,—it is true of civilization in all its enduring elements. A brief indication of facts will make this clear.

1. The order of *Creation,* as detailed in the account given in Genesis, is a movement towards the spiritual. The succession runs thus : Light, firmament, dry land, seas, the fruit-tree yielding fruit, sun, moon, and stars, the moving creature that hath life, and fowl flying in the open firmament of heaven, cattle, creeping thing, and beast of the earth ; if we pause here we shall be dissatisfied, because of a sense of incompleteness : there has, indeed, been an onward movement, but expectation will be mortified if the scene close at this point. We know the rest : " God said, Let us make MAN in our image and in our likeness,"—*that* was the highest point of spirituality attainable within the first idea of creation ; yet it was but a promise.

2. The biblical order of *human recovery* (apart altogether from any theological construction of it) is also a movement towards spirituality. Beginning with the Levitical ritual, what could be more objective, or more thoroughly penetrated with all the elements of the most violent tragedy ? Exaction follows exaction, as if the uttermost farthing alone would mitigate the severity of the inexorable demand. The sin-offering, the trespass-offering, the burnt-offering, the peace-offering ; the baptisms, the incenses, and the eternal flow of blood, represent

the most sensuous and exhausting system of mediation. Could aught be farther from the point of spirituality? Every day opening with fire and blood; every evening darkening around an altar specially consecrated for its quiet and solemn hours; the Sabbath having its double sacrifice; the new moon to have its sacrifice of bullocks and rams; until it was made plain that in God's estimate of sin, Lebanon itself was not sufficient to burn, nor the beasts thereof sufficient for a burnt offering. In moving forward to the Incarnation, we take an immense step along the line whose final point is spirituality, yet even there we are still distinctly upon the carnal line. How to escape it? How to pass to the highest homage? The answer is as full of pathos as of truth: the final Representative of sensuous worship must Himself be the Revealer of *spiritual life.* Jesus Christ did not pass away as a figure complete in itself; He *ascended* that He might conduct His work from a higher level and by a more energetic and universal agency. Henceforth we know not even Jesus Christ "after the flesh," for the fleshly Christ has Himself placed mankind under the tuition of a spiritual monitor.

3. The order of *written testimony*, though in some respects apparently accidental, moves in precisely the same direction. From picture and symbol we pass to spiritual meanings; through the noise and fury of war we pass into the quietness and security of moral civilization; through the porch of miracles and mighty signs and wonders we enter the holy

place of truth and love; from the erratic and most startling course of Matthew's genealogical table we pass into John's gospel, where the WORD meets us without one stain of earth upon its robe of light. The quality of John's gospel requires the very place that has been assigned to it in the New Testament. It is infinitely better that it should be preceded by the synoptic gospels, in which the attention of the world is boldly challenged by activity, spectacle, and a quickly-moving scene of divers strange things, such as had never been seen even in Israel. In the gospel by John, spiritual teaching, promise, devotion, comfort, and sanctification, are dominant, though publicity and mighty deed are certainly not wanting. John interprets and completes his predecessors. He seems to say, "You have heard what the evangelists have had to tell, and have seen the wonderful things which they remember of their Master's ministry, now let me explain the deep meaning of the whole." Thus he comes in his proper place. From Malachi to Matthew is but a step; but to get from Malachi to John, you have to cross the universe. John's gospel is waiting until the Church becomes mature enough to understand it. It waits without perturbation. Meanwhile there is no lack of interest in Matthew and Mark and Luke; yet they are but the genesis of which the fourth gospel is the apocalypse. Matthew shows the *fact;* John reveals the *truth:* Matthew pourtrays on canvas; John puts his word into the heart. Only relatively so, of course; for in Matthew there is a mystery of godliness, as in John there is a panorama of activity.

4. The whole *law* is a movement towards spirituality. From the minuteness of microscopic bye-laws men have passed to a spiritual sense of moral distinctions. Every moment of the Jew's time, and every act of the Jew's life, was guarded by a regulation. Amidst our spiritual light, such regulations could not be re-established without awakening the keenest resentment. The great tables of bye-laws have been taken down, because the Spirit of Order and of Truth has been given. What is true of law is equally true of all *institutionalism*,—its progress is from a crude outline towards completeness of purpose and critical accuracy of statement, with a due reserve of defensive reply in the event of a serious assault. The original scheme was probably very imperfect, open to hostility at every point, and inadequate to the occasion to which it primarily addressed itself; then came criticism and re-consideration; modification and re-adjustment came quickly afterwards; the very wording of the purpose was more keenly set, with a view to unexpressed opposition or distrust; in short, the crude outline was wrought out into intellectual and spiritual completeness and beauty; so much so, that a comparison between the first prospectus and the last is like a comparison between a rough pencil sketch and a fully coloured picture. And this very word "picture" suggests that even in the department of art the law of progression towards spiritu-

ality prevails; the best pictures and statuary do all but *live;* though standing out with startling independence from all other earthly things, they seem to have around them somewhat of the mystery of eternity, now tender, now awful, connected by invisible threadlets with the Infinite, and abounding inexhaustibly with suggestion to the observer, whose eye is alight with true life.

Probably these illustrations of the doctrine that the whole movement of history has gone persistently in the direction of spirituality, will be accepted or rejected according to the theological prejudices of the reader; but their practical value will be determined by the fact that *precisely the same movement takes place in the consciousness and experience of every progressive life.* Every man can test this doctrine for himself,—the doctrine, namely, that the growth of manhood is a growth towards spirituality. The child grows towards contempt of its first toys; the youth reviews the narrow satisfactions of his childhood with pity; the middle-aged man smiles, half-sneeringly, as he recalls the conceits of his youth; and the hoary-haired thinker lives already amid the peace and joy of invisible scenes, or if he go back, living in memory rather than in expectation, it is so ideally as to divest his recollections of all that was transient and unlovely. It is worth while to halt a moment that we may see the bearing of this common fact upon the special doctrine under examination. In approaching the mystery of the Holy Ghost, we may be but approaching the highest expression of a mystery which is continually ruling the whole economy of human progress. Whatever we may believe about the personality of the Holy Ghost, we cannot get away from the fact of *spirituality* in our own consciousness. The spiritual world of the wise man increases every day; and, strangely enough, in point of coincidence, that very increase becomes to him what the Holy Ghost becomes to the Church, namely, a *Comforter;* so much so, that the wise man is never desolate, nor can any fool trouble the depths of his peace. This is the first testament between man and God; is it not meant to introduce a higher covenant? To the intellectual man, the Christian appeal is this: You have a spiritual *consciousness,* to which Jesus Christ would add a spiritual *personality;* you have the spirit of interpretation, add to it the spirit of sanctification; you have received the preliminary baptism, receive also the Holy Ghost.

These suggestions point to the conclusion that the Holy Ghost is the *reasonable* completion of theological revelation, and as such His ministry is an impregnable proof of the reasonableness of Christianity. In the person of Jesus Christ truth was outward, visible, and most beautiful: in the person of the Holy Ghost truth is inward, spiritual, all-transfiguring. By the very necessity of the case the bodily Christ could be but a passing figure; but by a gracious mystery He caused Himself to be succeeded by an eternal Presence, "even the Spirit of Truth, which abideth for ever." It is claimed, then, on behalf of Christianity, that there is a Holy Ghost, and to this doctrine is invited not only the homage of the heart but the full assent of the most robust and dispassionate understanding.

III.

INSPIRATION AS A DOCTRINE.

According to the teaching of both Testaments, a few men seem to have been divinely inspired either to speak, or to put into a written form, what was communicated to them as the truth of God. This inspiration was, we are led to believe, accorded to but a few, not one of whom, however, so far as we can learn, ever brought moral discredit upon his solemn and august vocation. Some of them had been even profligate in iniquity *before* their inspiration; but having spoken the word of God, they appear to have been purified as by a holy fire. That their number was but small, is rather an argument in favour of their claim than otherwise, when we consider what is evident in all the highest energy and form of life known amongst ourselves. Few men, for example, have been inspired (qualified) to write the intermediate bible of civilisation,—that exciting and often tragical book which interposes between the volume of nature and the volume of spiritual testimony. There are but few historians, few poets, few aphorists. Yet the few do not speak for themselves alone: they represent human nature, and establish their right to supremacy and homage in proportion as they speak not the jargon of a class but the universal language of humanity. Inspiration does not separate David and Paul from the human race: it lifts the human race to a high pinnacle of honour and expectation. The divine inspiration of one man presupposes a corresponding degree of divine inspiration (actual or possible) in all other men. Few, indeed, may have been inspired to *speak* the word, but all have been inspired to *feel* it. Is inspiration, as commonly understood, given to but a few? So is wealth, so is poetry, so is courage, so is art, so is wisdom. The key of the chamber is given to one keeper, but the chamber itself is to be opened for the entrance of the whole world. "Why should David or Paul have been more inspired than I am?" is a peevish inquiry, wanting as much in reason as in dignity, and finding its natural completion in the profane inquiry—"Why is *God* more divine than I am?" It is the kind of question which vexes human life with the most pitiful discontent. It brings with it a brood worthy of itself. Why should Homer have been more poetical? Why should Plato have been more philosophical? Why should Euclid have been more mathematical? It will be answered that their supremacy is held only until a higher genius can successfully dispute it, and that Moses and John should be allowed to hold theirs on the same condition. Be it so! Where do Moses and John deprecate a challenge of their personal supremacy? Yet common justice will insist that if the inspiration of the biblical writers be challenged, *the rival inspiration must cover the whole of the original ground;* for it must be borne in mind that not only do the biblical writers touch upon some subjects which may be treated by ordinary sagacity and learning, but they distinctly touch subjects which are connected with the innermost life and secret of the universe. It will not be enough, then, to limit the competition to the production of felicitous proverbs or artistic parables; there must be a moral purity, an intellectual grasp, a spiritual insight and sympathy, which shall so combine as to represent the same mastery and familiarity in relation to the invisible and supernatural which are to be found in the inspired testaments. Then will arise a farther question. Supposing something like an equality in the breadth and tone of the rival revelations, we must know in what direction they respectively move in affecting the practical life of mankind. Does the one move towards reverie, self-content, spiritual isolation? Does the other impel in the direction of philanthropy, sacrifice, worship? These are inquiries which can be definitively settled.

But the complaint is not so much that a *few* writers should have claimed divine inspiration, as that their authority should bind the religious faith of all men through all time. It is the idea of apparent despotism in doctrine that is strongly resented. Is the grievance substantial or imaginary? It should be observed that the Bible opens its revelation without any preliminary contract with the reader either as to a limit of faith or a degree of authority. The believers in inspiration may possibly have themselves to charge with a grave mistake upon this important point; for it might be supposed by any one who has attended to the controversy without carefully reading the Bible itself, that the book has upon its very forefront a distinct statement of its divine inspiration and authority, which must be accepted without question or murmur. Nothing can be farther from the fact. As to a formal claim of inspiration, there is no more of it in the opening of Genesis than there is in the opening of the Metamorphosis. Were the Bible put into the hands of a scholarly and critical pagan, without one word of introduction or comment, he would be a long time in discovering any tittle of a formal claim on the part of the book to be considered inspired and authoritative. He would at once be struck by the loftiness and firmness of its tone, and might be led so far as to say, "This man could not have spoken more boldly had the very gods themselves addressed him from the heavens"; or he might attribute the boldness to the quality of a language peculiar for pomp and sublimity; but he would not be either humbled or embarrassed by a preliminary demand for the surrender of his judgment or his life. The inspiration of the Bible grows upon a man much as a consciousness of his own intellectual and spiritual life grows upon him. This higher consciousness is often sudden in its development. It would seem that in a moment—preceded it may be by a long, though more or less unconscious, preparation—an initial lifetime is thrown off and a new spiritual citizenship is established. In this way the slave of dictionaries sometimes rises into a master of languages, the slow cipherer into a philosophical arithmetician, and the cautious student of politics into a sagacious statesman. The line of separation is invisible, almost imaginary, yet it divides experiences that are most diverse. In some such way the Bible has suddenly elevated itself from a schoolbook to a revelation, and men have felt that they could not set it again in the rank of common writings without a sense of serious moral loss. They have not foreseen the result of their reading. At first they yielded to a merely literary fascination; by-and-by moral sympathy was touched in some degree; curiosity was excited; then came wonder, and after wonder came uncertainty, like a keen pain in the heart; then came a sentence like this to test the faith and to ripen the strange experience into Christian joy,—"holy men of old spake as they were moved by the Holy Ghost"; and with that sentence came a responsibility which put the reader into a new and solemn relation to the Book.

If the Bible is divinely inspired, it follows that it is divinely authoritative. Inspiration and authority must stand or fall together. Consider what it is that is professedly revealed. What is it? It is not history; it is not cosmogony; it is not ethnology; it is not even a code of morals. It is worth while, then, to pause a moment, that we may get the full emphasis of the answer. The supreme revelation that is made in the Bible is the revelation of GOD. Everything else belongs to the region of detail. The divine personality is the vital and all-embracing revelation. Creation may suggest it; the curious interweaving and combination of daily events may point towards it as towards a possibility; but the Bible distinctly reveals it as the secret of all things. But the Bible having made this revelation cannot stop there. The term *God* includes all other terms. It is not a high symbol in abstract reasoning, or the almost aërial line which the metaphysician is content to begin with: it is the all-controlling factor in regions visible and invisible,—it is this, or it is nothing. The moment, therefore, that the question of divine Fatherhood or Rulership is raised, all the great questions covered by the term "humanity" are raised along with it, and by their very urgency they may easily create a clamour unfavourable to the consideration of their most important bearings. It is better, therefore, to reason downward from the quiet and solemn heights of the divine personality, than to struggle upwards through all the controversy and bewilderment of human interests. If the Bible declares the true idea of God, it must presumptively give the true doctrine of human nature. God must be self-declared. Man has no instruments that can measure the divine power, or search out the divine wisdom. But *how* is God to grant a revelation of Himself? Christian theology answers,—By the inspiration of chosen men who shall be His instruments for this special purpose. Instantly that inspiration becomes thus individualised a great difficulty arises,—the very difficulty which has been pointed out in the divine incarnation: we look at the divine mystery through the human medium, and instead of fixing the mind upon the inspiring Spirit we fix it upon the inspired man. It is thus that loss is incurred, and that disadvantage is inflicted upon the subjects of inspiration. To speak, for example, of the inspiration of *David*, is to limit a divine quantity by a human personality; and the danger (almost inevitable) is that the mind be fixed upon the term *David* rather than upon the term *inspiration*. We must enlarge the minor term if we can; and how is this to be done but by speaking, not of the inspiration of Moses or David, Ezekiel or John, but of the inspiration of *humanity*, the individuals themselves being nothing but the points of contact at which a divine action is set up. Much is gained by this elimination of the personal element. Inspiration is greater than personality. Instead of speaking of the authority of ***Paul***, we are to speak of the authority of *truth:* Paul may, indeed, have been chosen as the medium of utterance, but the utterer is God. It is mere peevishness, or perhaps defiance, which chafes at the authority of a *man:* that is not the question at all; assent is sought to the proposition that the eternal authority of God has been declared through human instrumentality. In what other way could it have been declared? Is there any other way so free from the vulgarity of sensationalism, so rational, so philosophical, so ennobling, so sublime? No homage is offered to Moses, to David, or to Paul. The Bible, in all its divine elements, would be unimpaired were the names of its human penmen removed. Yet those names are of peculiar value in humanising a volume which requires softening shadows to mitigate its unique glories. The writers never obtrude their personal dignity; they never conceal their personal weaknesses; the word of the Lord is a burden to them, and is often accepted with hesitation and misgiving. But what if there be slips or other faults in the work of the inspired men? In one sense, so much the better; in the sense, for example, that these are imperfections which actually beget confidence,—superficial imperfections which give all the advantage of contrast to work that is known to be solid and enduring. The musician is limited by his instrument. Though he may have ravished a world by his strains, he could be almost angry with the instrument which has failed to express the still finer tones which madden him with indescribable joy. In the matter of inspiration the Almighty proposed to dwell in houses of clay, what wonder if they were unequal to such a Presence?

We have said that the divine inspiration of one man presupposes a corresponding degree of divine inspiration (actual or possible) in all other men. The inspiration of speech presupposes the inspiration of hearing, true listening being much more than an exercise of a merely physical function. If few men know how to speak, fewer still know how to listen. Men are preoccupied; voices of prejudice, interest, self-worship, never cease to besiege the ear of the soul: add to these a drowsiness hardly distinguishable from a temptation, and a persistent appeal from the whole external estate of life, and the difficulty of spiritual hearing will be no longer a mystery. The universal inspiration comes through a quickening and sanctifying action upon the *moral sense* of mankind. The one thing which that moral sense never did accomplish is *the discovery of God*. In its most exalted and energetic moods it got no farther than an inscription to the Unknown Power, —a long way, too,—a sublime distance, verily,—still, not a Bible, but a marble slab.

That the biblical revelation of God does not instantly satisfy every mind, and bring into unanimity the religious sentiment of the world, is a self-destructive argument as applied against the doctrine of divine inspiration. It proves too much. Where is there unanimity upon any subject which challenges alike the intellectual and moral attention of mankind? Not only so, the Bible itself anticipates the very difficulty, and mourns with pathetic lamentation that the disclosure of God has been received with incredulity or resentment. If it be suggested that such a revelation should have been given as would at once, by its copiousness and brilliance, have established itself in the confidence of the world, the suggestion proceeds in forgetfulness of the fact that that very confidence itself has been warped and vitiated, and is no longer the simple and honest love which is the secret of spiritual sympathy and interpretation. How to recover the idea of God was the problem. The Bible distinctly undertakes its solution, and in so doing claims authoritatively to be known, not as a volume of history, a code of morals, a treatise on philosophy, but as the one written Book of *God.*

Inspiration had at the very outset to encounter the difficulty of *language,* inasmuch as there was no speech common to the whole world.* The world

---

* "And while thus the characteristic excellences of the Greek language invite us to the investigation of the likenesses and differences between words, to the study of the words of the New Testament there are reasons additional inviting us. If by such investigations as these we become aware of delicate variations in an author's meaning, which otherwise we might have missed, where is it so desirable that we should miss nothing, that we should lose no finer intention of the writer, as in those words which are the vehicles of the very mind of God Himself? If thus the intellectual riches of the student are increased, can this anywhere be of so great importance as there, where the intellectual may, if rightly used, prove spiritual riches as well? If it encourage thoughtful meditation on the exact forces of words, both as they are in themselves, and in their relation to other words, or in any way unveil to us their marvel and their mystery, this can nowhere else have a worth in the least approaching that which it acquires when the words with which we have to do are, to those who receive them aright, words of eternal life; while in the dead carcases of the same, if men suffer the spirit of life to depart from them, all manner of corruptions and heresies may be, as they have been, bred. The *words* of the New Testament are eminently the στοιχεῖα of Christian theology, and he who will not begin with a patient study of those, shall never make any considerable, least of all any secure, advances in this; for here, as everywhere else, sure disappointment awaits him who thinks to possess the whole without first possessing the parts of which that whole is composed."—ARCHBISHOP TRENCH on *New Testament Synonyms.*

has a common heart, a common nature, a common instinct, but not a common tongue. Even in the same language words constantly vary in expressiveness and value : not only does time change their application and their limits, but they actually convey different meanings to different minds ; and there is not always an interpreter at hand to draw the line of exact signification and prevent confusion and controversy. A word may not mean precisely the same thing to any two men, though it may be well known to both of them in a rough sense, which may suffice for ordinary purposes. How to express an eternal quantity through a mutable language! This is in another form the precise difficulty of the Incarnation ; for what flesh is to spirit speech is to thought. The difficulty has never been wholly overcome,— certainly not in the Incarnation, for Jesus Christ was despised and rejected of men ; and certainly not in the Bible, for it has provoked more controversy, fiercer and bitterer too, than any other book in all literature. It should be noted, too, that the very objections which from the beginning have been urged against Christ, have also been pressed against the Bible ; objections relating to form, to structure, to origin, to apparent contradiction, and to manifest insufficiency to meet the demands of the situation. In both cases human expectation was set at naught, and something was offered which could not but mortify the pride of the receiver. We must, then, go beyond forms, symbols, and measurable quantities, and find the meaning of inspiration in elevation and purity of thought, in the scrupulousness and magnanimity of moral instinct, in the ennobling and all-hoping charity by which our best life is distinguished; and ceasing all pedantic strife about mere *words*, must cast ourselves with reverence and holy joy upon the eternal *Word*.

IV.

INSPIRATION AS A FACT.

So far we have looked at Inspiration as a *doctrine;* if we are to estimate its value as a *fact*, we must get at least a general notion of the principal characteristics of the particular book on behalf of which inspiration is claimed. In this and the succeeding chapter we shall move within what may be called extra-theological limits; for a purpose which will be disclosed as we proceed. At the outset, we must strongly deny that any man could *a priori* have told the proper scope and tone of a book divinely inspired. It is one thing to have the book, and to reason backwards; it is another to be called upon, in its absence, to say exactly what an inspired revelation should be. We have to found an opinion upon a particular book; and it will be entirely for the book itself to prove its own inspiration. The Bible must do, what every other book must do, that is to say, it must make its own place in the world; let it prove its inspiration by inspiring its readers; let it show its heavenliness by the amount of heaven which it sets up on earth; if it fail by these tests, any attempt to uphold it by organised authority is absurd and hopeless. The object of this chapter is to gather into one view three or four marked characteristics of the book, simply regarded as a literary composition, and to ask the reader to assign them some value in the argument. At first, we open the Bible for critical, and not for theological purposes, and at once we encounter the difficulty arising from a profusion of peculiar and startling characteristics,—

1. The Bible is undoubtedly marked by *a wonderful reserve of power.* Its writers nowhere betray any sign of exhaustion, nor do they display the slightest wish to make the most of their materials in a literary point of view. There are single chapters which any writer could easily have elaborated into a volume. The rule seems to have been to say everything in the fewest possible words. The Bible abounds in indications, brief, vivid, and multitudinous, and is, hence, pre-eminently a text-book. We wonder that the writers do not say more, yet we feel that even in their brevity they have said more than any other men have ever said. They have marvellous skill in perspective. They excite the greatest expectations, and then teach the readers whom they have thus almost frenzied, that such expectations are to be held as a discipline, and not to be pushed to a premature fulfilment. The great ambition of other sacred books seems to be to do everything: they put a key into every lock; under every enigma they write at least a conjectural answer; they determine the attitudes and services proper to every hour of the day; and whatever intellectual energy they have is apparently expres-

sible in letter and symbol. They resemble the finite in an ambitious determination to represent the infinite; whereas the Bible represents the infinite in a condescending endeavour to find expression in the finite. The Bible is a perpetual beginning, rich in its immediate satisfactions, but richer still in its promises. Through every revelation there is a hint of another revelation yet to come. The Bible has a wonderful firmament, out of which the light comes, and the rain, and from which the key of heaven may at any moment drop. Its earth is very legible: its firmament is an eternal mystery. Is this, then, the kind of book which is presumably worthy of a high origin? In this reserve of power has it any resemblance to the book of physical nature? In Bashan are there not more acorns than oaks? Under quiet exteriors are there any fierce energies? Is there anywhere a sign of exhaustion, as if the creation were almost equal to the Creator? Completeness may be a sign of weakness. Omnipotence has no final line. When the artist says that he can add nothing further to his picture, he confesses the limitation of his power: the attainment of his ideal is the signature of his weakness. The Bible is full of gaps, of unfinished pictures, of jagged and broken outlines; in the artistic sense of the word there is no perfection,—the question is whether there is sufficient astronomic force to overcome all surface inequalities, and to secure the velocity which is rest, and the friction which is light. The theologian must determine this, rather than the critic.

2. The Bible grapples with *the highest subjects* which can engage the attention of mankind. A professedly inspired book treating of mere trifles, or of points which are but of secondary interest, would have been the very cruelty of irony. The Bible advances instantly to the highest lines of spiritual inquiry : God, creation, invisible worlds, sin, death, immortality, are its familiar themes. But more important than the fact of its grappling with such subjects, is its peculiar method of treating them. Its approach (so to speak) is invariably from the higher side : the Bible *reveals*, it does not *suggest;* it *declares*, it does not *investigate;* all the surprise is on the side of the reader, never on the side of the writer. Looked at in the light of presumptive inspiration, this is precisely the proper result. If God has spoken at all, He must have spoken positively and authoritatively. The *tone* of the Bible is emphatically immodest and exaggerated, if it is the tone of mere inquirers or speculators ; on the other hand it is the only tone (so far as we can judge) that befits the supremacy and condescension of God. The imperative mood which is seemly in a king, is brusque in an equal and impertinent in an inferior. This is the mood of the Bible. Though its subjects are innumerable there is no incertitude in its statement of any one of them ; more, indeed, might have been stated as it appears to our impatience, but more may mean less, as excess of light is equivalent to darkness. The Bible tone is such as befits inspiration ; but it is an obvious and fatal

mistake if it is *vox et preterea nihil*. Even ordinary men may secure respect when they speak subjunctively; but when they speak imperatively they become ridiculous and contemptible. It is not difficult to distinguish between a bray and a roar.

The precision and weight of the tone will be seen to be the more remarkable when the peculiarity of the revelation is considered. The Bible seems to have a line without a limit. In nature, we seem to be bounded by the horizon; yet who has measured its diameter, or laid his hand upon the sky-line? We move towards it, yet we never get away from the centre. It is the same with the divine revelation. Its sky-line recedes as we advance. The limit is visible yet unapproachable. We can get to the end of the chapters, yet we never get to the end of the book. The Bible combines a wide liberty with a conspicuous and sacred law of trespass. Its words of promise are rich in incentive and solace; thus:—"I have many things to say unto you, but ye cannot bear them now;" "We know in part, and we prophesy in part, but when that which is perfect is come, then that which is in part shall be done away;" "It doth not yet appear what we shall be;" "Hereafter ye shall see;" "When Christ, who is our life, shall appear, then shall ye also appear with Him in glory." By such words (were there no other) the Bible separates itself from all other books which claim to convey such sacred communications.

3. Not only does the Bible grapple with the great-

est subjects, and pronounce upon them with dogmatic precision and emphasis, *it so discloses its subjects as to demand the interest of all nations through all time.* The Bible insists upon being the book of the whole world. It does this, too, in a very wonderful manner. At first it makes no claim as to circulation. By-and-by it becomes a book of much importance to a particular people. Farther on, its language increases in copiousness and boldness. Finally, it declares its leaves to be for the healing of the nations. The change of tone as between the Old Testament and the New is one of the most remarkable phenomena in all literature. There is a steady, though often imperceptible, movement from the local to the universal : in the Old Testament there is an antiquity which makes one solemn ; so gigantic, so silent, so irreparable, are the ruins of empire, ritual, and fortune ; there we find the thick moss, the biting canker, the seal of death ; and all this strangely interspersed with beauty which must live for ever: in the New Testament there is all the stir of modern life,—enterprise, revolution, progress ;—men are moving from land to land, speaking all languages, publishing one name, and bearing one grim symbol. Is such a movement in keeping with the presumptive inspiration of the book ? The Old Testament having reached the height of sublimity, what eminence remained for the New ? After thunder and pomp, resounding trumpets and tramp of mailed men, there came gentleness and beauty, purity and nobleness, pardon and love. Is such a line of development in keeping with the presump-

Inspiration as a Fact.

tive inspiration of the book ? What could be more daring than to displace a soldier by a missionary ? This is an anti-climax in history, unless, indeed, it be " the foolishness of God."

Looking at great breadths of history it is evident that the believers in the Abesta, the Veda, and even the Koran, have not been careful to create a system of world-wide propagation of their respective faiths. Little beyond a military spasm in the case of the last of them has been attempted in this direction. But the believers in the Bible have been impelled to translate it into all languages and to send it into all regions. The Bible has, as a mere matter of fact, forced its way where no other book has ever gone ; and as for the variety of intellect which it has interested in its fortunes, no other writing can bear comparison with it. The coldest and the most ardent temperaments have alike sought to extend its influence : the richest learning and the most splendid eloquence have felt honoured in its service ; and the most valorous men have hazarded their lives to publish its contents in hostile lands. They have done this because of the effect of Bible teaching upon their hearts ; necessity was laid upon them ; and out of this necessity came their highest joy. Such facts, which can be verified without trouble, show how true it is that the Bible so discloses its subjects as to claim the homage of all nations through all time. This consideration is evidently of some value as a practical test of the presumptive inspiration of the book. If nature be recalled as a witness, we shall be told that *universality* characterises all the great gifts of God, and *therefore* will probably mark any revelation which professes to have been indited by His Spirit.

4. The Bible contains *the most startling proposition as to the destruction of sin.* In some respects this is its supreme peculiarity. The action which the Bible proposes is infinitely more remarkable on the *divine* side than on the human. How to take *sin* out of the world, is the problem. Let the mind dwell upon the terms for a moment that their import may be felt. *How* is sin to be met, overcome, ultimately and for ever destroyed? By a poor human struggle? By self-ablution? By self-mutilation? Is sin to be taken away only by taking away the *sinner?* What originality would there be in so obvious and coarse a method? The question is, How to save the man and destroy the sin? and the answer to an inquiry so vital cannot but be waited for with anxious impatience! In the midst of speculative debate upon the point, the Bible comes forward with this startling answer—*God Himself will die, the just for the unjust!* If this be not the supreme blasphemy, it is the very gospel of God! One or other it certainly is. It is not an answer that can be spoken of with indifference. As a human suggestion it is utter madness. It is salvation that is contemplated, in the terms of the inquiry; but how can salvation come by death? Observe, this immediate argument does not touch the theology of the proposition; it is wholly concerned with the mere facts which lie upon the very surface of the inquiry, the most tragical of which is

the proposition that the Just should die for the unjust, and that by the shedding of blood should come the remission of sins. It is enough, in this connection, that we merely point it out, with the humble confession, indeed, that if it be not the most awful of all irony, and therefore the most sinful of all sins, it is the most affecting doctrine that ever appealed to the human heart! There it is, however, and the student must deal with it. If he gives it the go-by, he instantly disqualifies himself for this high investigation; he flees from difficulty, and becomes a mere trifler in controversy. If he takes it up seriously, he may possibly find that it gives articulateness to emotions that have long troubled his own heart with a kind of pleasurable pain,—the pain of suffering and death, that he might make a way for the pardon and restoration of his own sinning child. The child may never have measured his own sin until he has seen the agony of his father's wounded love. But here we are touching points beyond our argument. This, suffice it now to say, is a mystery not to be illuminated by words,—any heart that has suffered much through the sinfulness of others will catch some far-off hint of its meaning : for the rest, there is no interpretation possible to us.

5. The Bible is marked by *a marvellous combination of sublimity and condescension alike as to subject and to method of treatment.* There are heights from which descent would seem to be impossible, and there are familiarities which are apparently too minute and common to permit of return to the

highest dignity. Yet the return, in both directions, is made with an ease which even in a literary point of view is undoubtedly wonderful, as if the heights and the depths were in reality but one plane to the Invisible and Ruling Spirit. If astronomic motion smooths the mountainous and rugged surface of earth, what if spiritual velocity make one line of things which to us are high and low, sublime and approachable? What a book is the Bible in the mere matter of variety of contents! Everything seems to be in it; poem, narrative, music, friendship, personal news, national intelligence, judgment, battle, prayer, song, anathema, and benediction. The bush is common enough, but what of the fire which makes the shepherd turn aside? The bread is such as has been used at supper, yet presently it will become the body of Christ! Paul is almost in heaven, yet in the very height of his anticipations he asks for his parchments and his cloak, and he knows exactly where both were left. Whole pages are taken up with obscure names, and more is told of a genealogy than of the day of judgment. Stories are half-told, and the night falls before we can tell where the victory lay. Where is there anything to correspond with this? Not in any book certainly,—but in actual life there is the self-same thing over again without the loss of one line. If the sun could print for us what he sees on any day in the year, he would print a second edition of the Bible. We should have it all over again, including perhaps something even of creation itself,—with its light, its ascending and descending waters, its trees bringing forth each after its kind, its sunny day, its starry night; but the humanity would be the same, still more vividly;—family life, love, fear, envy, covetousness, magnanimity; chosen people and alien lands; temples warm with the fire of the Lord, and houses of vain and corrupt idolatry; the noise of war and the song of peace; shepherds keeping their flocks, and soldiers listening for the foe; David in the wilderness and Jonah on the sea; weird dreams, spectral hands on the wall, baffled magicians, and truth-telling prophets; psalms for which no music is good enough, and proverbs that glisten with wit—all these, and more, we should have on every or any day in the year, if the sun could but print as well as shine! This is just the Bible. It is a page torn out of the great volume of human life; only, torn by the hand of God, and annotated by His Spirit. What is the daily newspaper but a revised translation of the Bible, often, indeed, with God left out in the spelling, though He cannot be left out in reality. Take to-morrow's paper in one hand and the Bible in the other, and see if the paper be not full of repetitions, and if there be not something like an echo in all its utterances.

Other indications might be made, but these will do in the meantime, as indicating at least a basis of judgment. Here is a book which is marked by a wonderful reserve of power; which grapples with the greatest subjects which can engage the attention of mankind; which so grapples with them as to demand (under sanctions too) the attention of all men through all time; which offers the most startling proposition for the removal of sin; and which is marked by a marvellous combination of sublimity and condescension, alike as to subject and to method of treatment. Is such a book, judging by these characteristics, likely to sustain any claim to be an inspired and authoritative revelation of the will of God? We only ask for a *prima facie* case. If such a case be granted, probably a careful and honest perusal of the Bible will follow, and this will be something gained.

V.

INSPIRATION OF CHRIST'S BIOGRAPHY.

THE argument which has been thus pursued admits of still further extra-theological treatment; for example, here is a fourfold account of our Lord's life and ministry—confessedly a life and ministry of extraordinary eventfulness and individuality,—is that account consistent with itself; is the progress of the narrative merely a high monotony, very successfully maintained, or is there in it an ascending motion, carrying each point to higher significance, and covering the whole with accumulating glory? If we can find such harmony between the parts, and elucidate the progress of such a motion, we shall leave it to the reader to say whether such a result is merely a clever literary feat, or is an instance of what is meant by the inspiration of the Holy Ghost. In pursuing this inquiry we shall write critically rather than theologically, honestly endeavouring to collate the facts, and leaving the reader to determine his own theology. We put no inquiry just now as to the historic credibility of the New Testament writers; we do not discuss any questions in grammar or exegesis; we know nothing of commentators or schools of interpretation; our one business is to inquire whether the fourfold account of the life of Jesus

Christ is consistent with itself, and whether there is anything so peculiar in the consistency as to suggest that the evangelists wrote their gospels under the inspiration of the Holy Ghost.

The unique and perilous line of judgment is determined by the claim (at least) of *miraculous conception.* Not one point of departure from that claim can on any account be allowed. We must watch the evangelists with the keenest vigilance lest they slip from that elevation, so dangerous if not true, and become commonplace narrators of a sensational story. Miraculous conception is undoubtedly claimed for our Lord by His biographers. How, then, can *such* a beginning have a corresponding progress and an appropriate culmination? Let us see.

Under the ancient economy, God had elected His ministers in a manner which was directly inverted in the birth of our Lord. In the ministers of the Old Testament God had sought to call up the human to the Divine; but in the Minister of the New Testament God brought down the divine to the human. Viewing the Old Testament dispensation as an elaborate attempt to train a man who should so far overcome all natural and incidental difficulties as to exert upon society the influence of a life absolutely perfect in its purity and aspirations, we are brought to the conclusion that the attempt, though conducted by the mysterious ministry of the Holy Ghost, was obviously unsuccessful: in Abraham, Jacob, Moses, and David, it is not difficult to find the blemish which proves this, and in proving it demonstrates the impossibility of training, under ordinary human conditions, an ideally perfect ministry. In reading the Old Testament we cannot escape a sense of gloomy and humiliating disappointment with the quality of its foremost men. They have excellences, and yet are not excellent; they have characteristics rather than character; at all events their character is more remarkable for its sides and aspects than for its unity and indivisible massiveness;—only momentarily do they get away from the herd of common men, and afterwards they are the weaker for their transient elevation. The prophet and the minstrel often descend from their ecstacy, and resume the ordinary associations of life; the warrior never quite advances to victory; the sufferer always falls a little short of the perfection of patience; and the godliest saint seems to miss divinity by a hair's breadth. Under these circumstances, the promise of a *New* Testament does not altogether allay the anxiety of hope so long deferred, and so vexed and mortified. Let imagination pause awhile at the last of the prophets, and attempt the task of outlining a Testament that shall be *New*; New, and yet related to the Old; that shall be faithful to the great purpose of the former dispensation, yet bring to bear upon it an order of instrumentality that shall neither make a machine of man, nor convict God of capricious changeableness in His method of working. A great task will thus fall to the lot of imagination; let us see as clearly as we can what it is:—Imagination has before it, in the Old Testament, a written account of the creation of men, the giving of law, the establishment of family life, the appointment of religious ritual, and the history of mankind for thousands of years;—on the other hand the world is tormented and disquieted exceedingly, every method of alleviation seems to have been exhausted, and every new proposition is treated with angry or sorrowful distrust. Under these circumstances, it is required of imagination to suggest a Testament that shall be *New*. Suppose that after the most careful reading of the ancient scriptures Imagination should decline the task as intellectually hopeless—protesting that everything possible to its own conception has already been attempted and exhausted—Imagination may on that very account be allowed to encounter with the severest criticism any suggestion that may be offered as a solution of the difficulty. Now (whatever may be thought of the theology of the case) it must be admitted that the writers of the New Testament do instantly address themselves to the one point which the Old Testament often promised but never reached. With most startling abruptness they invert the ancient method, so that instead of man being made by God, God Himself becomes man—a virgin is found to be with child of the Holy Ghost—and for "thus *saith* the Lord" we have "thus *is* the Lord"! True or not true is not the immediate question. As a mere matter of fact here is progress : the first page of the New Testament presents a more wonderful disclosure than all the pages of the Old, and by so much excites a hope that the answer so long looked for may at last be about to come. A miraculous birth must not be followed by a commonplace life—the discrepancy would be intolerable—yet there must be in that life, if its mission be to recover and sanctify the world, such simplicity and approachableness as shall qualify it for admission into society as ordinarily constituted ; it must proceed to its loftiest acts with the stoop of inimitable condescension, and do its lowliest work with original and ineffable dignity. With a test so unique the least flaw in homogeneousness must be instantly detected.

Starting upon the basis of the incarnation—understanding by that term the miraculous conception—the student will put in two conditions, the fulfilment of which he must regard as absolutely indispensable to the completeness of Jesus Christ's claim. Let us mark these two conditions very distinctly :—

1. The student must demand in an agent of professedly divine descent, such redundance of power as will carry him through all his engagements with the most perfect ease. He must never go up to his work as if it lay above him, but continually *descend* upon it as if his most marvellous achievements were rather a relaxation than an effort of his strength. If in any case there be a *strain*

upon the power, the laboriousness of the attempt must tell against his claim; and if in any case there be the slightest possible *failure* of power, the aspirant must be convicted of the most shameful wickedness. In the work of one who has been begotten by the Holy Ghost, and who therefore claims to be " God with us," we must never meet with *almost* a miracle,—a miscarriage of power,— we must have omnipotence, and must condemn anything short of the almightiness of God, as an unpardonable sin. In what direction, then, does the evidence point? There are four witnesses: in what degree do they approach unanimity? There are blind, deaf, lame, leprous, and lunatic sufferers claiming Jesus Christ's attention; He is brought to the sick, the dying, and the dead; He is asked to appease hunger, to expel devils, to silence tempests; and the student demands that all these things be done—not *merely* done, as if by a tremendous strain—but done with infinite ease, with inexhaustible wealth and exuberance of power. The evangelists say that Jesus Christ did so. Not an instance is recorded in which Jesus Christ's power to work miracles showed the faintest sign of exhaustion. If there is such an instance, let it be pointed out. The disciples failed and confessed the failure, and even where they succeeded they disowned applause by ascribing the result to their Master. The student must insist that the ease which marks the processes reported in the first chapter of Genesis, mark also the whole course

Inspiration of Christ's Biography. 49

of the ministry of Jesus Christ if He be the incarnate form of the Creator. He must be more than *powerful*,— He must be POWER; the mere attribute of strength must be swallowed up in His essential almightiness. The universe in all its compass and wonderfulness must lie in the hollow of His hand, and be as perfectly under His control as it is dependent on His sufficiency; He must not avail Himself of any calculus of probability; the law of distance, weight, force, adaptation, must be in Him as the *lawgiver;* His word must carry with it creation and destruction; He must *fill all things*. An exercise of power which is merely occasional, however startling and however beneficent, would rather excite suspicion than work conviction. Great efforts are often unintended signs of weakness, securing momentary applause for the discipline which they imply, but also eliciting pity for the exhaustion which they leave behind. A life of great efforts may very possibly be a life of great failures. The difficulty of the most honest and patient discipline is to keep a steady hold of its highest points, and so to become permanently equal to still higher tasks and aspirations. The most resolute disciplinarian can instantly point out the line of his ability; within that line he is mighty, but beyond it he is powerless. In Jesus Christ something higher than mere discipline must be found. His power must be native, instant, immeasurable. He must, too, stand clearly out from all surroundings, not having even so much as where

E

to lay His head,—He must have nothing but pure, naked life, and with that He must rule all things as with the almightiness of God. The source of His power must not only be secret, it must necessarily confound every attempt to discover it, and its effects must be so thorough and so numerous as to force astonishment to the point of distraction, and to drive men either to spiritual homage or intellectual despair. Surely the attitude of the student as thus described is sufficiently vigilant and sufficiently obstinate. What, then, is the concurrent evidence of the four evangelists? A few quotations will make it clear: "The people were astonished and said, Whence hath this man this wisdom and these mighty works?" "Whence hath this man all these things?" "No man can do those miracles that Thou doest except God be with him." "They were beyond measure astonished, saying, He hath done all things well; He maketh both the deaf to hear and the dumb to speak." "They were sore amazed in themselves beyond measure, and wondered." "The multitudes marvelled, saying, It was never so seen in Israel." Now the student may decline at this stage of his inquiry to discuss the strictly theological import of these passages, as his one business is to determine how far such expressions harmonise with the alleged descent of the Worker who elicited them. Are they the common expressions of vulgar amazement, or do they carry with them the wonder and pathos of the heart? Are they collated with cunning artistic skill, or is there behind them a secret which can be best accounted for by the ministry of the Holy Ghost? What can have been the richness of the power, which led one poor suffering woman to utter the greatest saying about it that probably was ever uttered,—" If I may but touch the hem of His garment I shall be made whole"! The critical inquirer will put peculiar value upon this testimony because it condenses into one pathetic sentence a great body of public opinion. If it is merely a stroke of dramatic genius it is a stroke of consummate power; if it is historically true it is conclusive evidence that Jesus Christ had produced in the public mind of His day an impression that His power was at once beneficent and boundless. There is, too, in connection with this incident a feature which the inquirer will appreciate as showing that the power, though boundless, was not lawlessly expended; instantly that the woman was healed, Jesus Christ knew that virtue had gone out of Him, and demanded to know who had touched Him. Was the power of His omniscience equal to the scope of His omnipotence? Was this carefulness of a merely infinitesimal particle of His power at all in keeping with that minute economy which insisted that the fragments be gathered up that nothing should be lost? The honest and patient inquirer will not leave these inquiries without a thorough sifting.

2. In the second place the student must demand that in no case shall the exercise of Jesus Christ's

ability, how useful or splendid soever the result, be accompanied by any sign of astonishment on the part of the worker. Whilst astonishing the world, He alone must be free from astonishment. All unexpected successes, like all great efforts, betray the weakness of the workers as well as illustrate their strength, so much so that every discovery in civilisation is quite as certainly a lamp hung over human ignorance as it is a contribution to the brilliance of human wisdom. The student will proceed upon the principle that as it is impossible that omnipotence can put itself into doubtful competition with a difficulty, so God can never be surprised at the result of His own work. Surprise comes of ignorance, and elation of weakness. Yet, looking at the written life of Jesus Christ, the absence of astonishment is most marked. Not one trace of vain self-satisfaction is to be found in any part of the fourfold narrative. Amazement is not forbidden to common workers,—it may, indeed, be advantageous to them, as well as to those in whose interests they work; for wonder should stimulate inquiry, and every unexpected glimpse of light be regarded as an invitation to profounder duty. There is no monotony in the highest and serenest intellectual life, for even when youthful passion subsides it is only to be succeeded if by a more placid yet by a more exquisite enjoyment; the young worker may be unable to suppress his Eureka, but the silence of the maturer thinker is not to be mistaken for insensibility. Can men receive revelations of the depth and beauty of truth without emotion?

Or can they put into common words the divine addresses which they have heard in the secrecy of their own souls, without being startled by every tone which even imperfectly reproduces the mystic music which divides the realm of utterance from the realm of silence? Articulation (we must again insist) is the difficulty of the highest thought. What if articulation should so far reach the point of success as to betray surprise and joy on the part of the startled speaker? Nothing will be more natural or more rationally explicable. He is accounted the strong man who can suppress his emotions while prosecuting his work, and so highly is this self-suppression valued, that not seldom is the dignity of noble self-control counterfeited by the unhealthy and demoralising conceit of indifference in the presence of the most exciting events. Let it be assumed, however, as proved by the best human culture, that strength brings quietness, and that conscious power holds surprise in check, we have to account for the fact that a man who enjoyed no such culture, healed the lame, the blind, the deaf, the leprous, and all manner of diseased people; that He quieted the sea, dispossessed devils, and raised the dead, and yet never betrayed any symptom of surprise, was never startled by unexpected results, or excited by successes which filled all orders of society with the most bewildering amazement. The worker was never unbalanced: the worker was always greater than His work: He worked as though power was the least of His characteristics, and was put forward only as an introduction to an infinitely higher blessing. The student will find that his demand for the entire absence of surprise is thoroughly satisfied by the fourfold biography of Jesus Christ; and in noting the variety and completeness of the evidence, he will not overlook an incidental but most vivid illustration of Christ's estimate of surprise in others. On one occasion the disciples told Him with wondering joy that even the devils were subject to them through His name, and He answered that they were not to rejoice supremely in such events, but rather to rejoice that their names were written in heaven,—personal rightness being better than functional success. Another aspect of the same teaching is shown in an instance of surprise at their failure; they had tried to expel a devil and had not succeeded; their failure occasioned them surprise as well as humiliation, whereupon Jesus Christ expelled the tormentor, and told His astonished disciples privately the spiritual conditions by which alone success was possible in such cases. So that He had actually to deal with the operation of surprise within the circle of His nearest friendships, and to save His disciples from the effects of elation and disappointment by drawing them into deeper appreciation of purely spiritual privilege and discipline.

Next—how to humanise *such* a life—how to make it approachable—how to adapt it to ordinary society! Is this done by the evangelists, and if done is it so accomplished as to be but a literary feat or the work of a supernatural and inspiring agent? Jesus Christ was the Son of Mary as well as the Son of

God, and therefore His course must supply some conditions in many respects almost irreconcilable with the claim of divinity,—in one word, how to be God and man at the same time! If as God He has entered into the flesh that He may be visibly nearer men, and more sensibly accessible to them, He must so attemper or conceal His divinity as not to alarm them by unearthliness, and yet so gloriously display it as to secure their confidence and homage. His life must answer the question, Can God in very deed dwell with men upon the earth? To be God and man so distinctly that each can be felt, and yet so unitedly that no division line can be seen, is the intricate part which He has to play. This is surely a great problem in art, giving scope enough for failure : one slip will dispossess Him of His crown,— one false accent will prove Him the most daring of empirics. He must be *with* men, yet not *of* them : on the earth, yet in heaven : familiar with men, yet separate from sinners : he must enlighten the world, yet be as a sun which no hand can touch ;—this is His task—how to simplify the infinite—how to stoop from heaven !

In putting the existence of these conditions to the test, it must be noticed that Jesus Christ lived much in public, and so gave opportunity enough for general criticism. There is no evidence in the fourfold narrative that He was ever indisposed on the ground of fear to meet any section of society : He conversed with equal freedom with doctors and peasants, and His social life was even too liberal for the narrow notions of conventional purists. His was not a monastic life; He went to be guest with men known to be sinners; He sat at the tables of men whose hospitality was intended as a temptation; He went to the marriage feast and the house of mourning; He loved Martha and her sister and Lazarus; He took little children in His arms and blessed them; He spoke hopefully to women who had lost the standing of sisterhood. In His manner of doing all this was there any originality of movement, any savour of heavenliness, any grandeur of simplicity? The critical student will look everywhere for the divine signature: the minutest things must bear the sacred initials, and the greatest must be glorified by the incommunicable Name. When Jehovah descended into the bush He filled it with undestroying fire,—when, in our flesh, He walks along the common highways of life will He scorch us with intolerable heat? In ordinary life there is seldom any difficulty in distinguishing the quality of the actor, even in the simplest actions; a tone will tell the education of the speaker, a courtesy will discover his status. Nor can the quality of the actor be altogether concealed by external accidents: under the richest surface it is not difficult to see the native meanness of some souls, whilst through the poorest raiment there may shine transfiguring light. Little natures reserve themselves for great occasions: majestic natures make all occasions great. There are codified lives that can move only as the book permits, and there are controlling lives that hold prescription in contempt. A remembrance of this

Inspiration of Christ's Biography. 57

fact must be carried into our examination of Jesus Christ's written life, and to Him must be given the advantage which would be justly conceded even to an unknown name.

When Jesus Christ sat down to meat with the leading men of the times, did He ever omit to turn the conversation towards heaven? When an ardent admirer exclaimed, " Blessed is the womb that bare Thee, and the paps which Thou hast sucked," did He not instantly answer, " Yea, rather, blessed are they that hear the word of God and keep it"? When called upon to define neighbourliness, did He fear to exalt the despised Samaritan above the priest and the Levite? When the disciples would have turned away the aspiring mothers who brought their children to be blessed, did He not receive the little ones with condescending grace, and startle the self-consciousness and self-idolatry of many by saying, " Of such is the kingdom of heaven"? Did He fear to put a higher value on the mites of the widow than on the gold of the rich? These inquiries must be answered, and the reasons of the answers must be searched into with inexorable resoluteness.

Not only was Jesus Christ much in public, He was also much in secret. He withdrew to solitary places, and was accustomed to be alone in prayer. These withdrawments must have some meaning; they throw an air of solemnity over the narrative, and almost constrain criticism into worship. What if in some instances they imply weakness, and even exhaustion, on the part of the worker? This is precisely what was wanted to complete the argument upon the all-sufficiency and redundance of Jesus Christ's power, for nowhere along the line of that power have we come to any assurance of Jesus Christ's *manhood;* it steadily ascended rather towards the terribleness of omnipotence! What was wanted was a pause, a break of weakness, perhaps a cry of exhaustion. An unwearying flesh could hardly have prepared us for a compassionate divinity; it required the imperfection of infirmity to complete (for human purposes) the perfection of strength : so great is the mystery of godliness! Yet the inquirer will watch tremblingly lest there be any decay of power on the side that is supposed to be divine : he will read that Jesus was weary with His journey, and yet in the moment of His weakness He offered to give the water which springeth up into everlasting life; he will find that though Jesus felt the cravings of hunger, yet there was power enough in His word to wither the fruitless fig-tree; he will find Jesus Christ asleep on account of weariness induced by long service, and in a moment he will hear this same Jesus commanding the winds and the waves to be still; he will find that Jesus wept, and while the tears were yet in His eyes He called Lazarus from the grave. All these things are plainly written in the evangelical narrative, and it is, therefore, for the student to say how far such perilous juxtapositions of weakness and power, tears and almightiness, were bold literary conceptions on the part of the writers, and how far they have any claim to have been dictated by an inspiring Spirit. The critic must say whether in this dual manifestation there is the peculiar kind of consistency which is required to support the theory that Jesus Christ was begotten of the Holy Ghost; and he must assign some value to the fact that in no instance did Jesus Christ employ what may be called the purely divine side of His power to save Himself from the infirmities incident to ordinary human life : He wrought no private miracle for merely selfish protection, but was in all points tempted as other men ; in short He never made any deceptive use of His omnipotence ; He was not a man by mere pretence, professedly weak and suffering, yet secretly availing Himself of sources inaccessible to His deluded disciples. The consideration of this circumstance is the more important because all the signs of destitution which marked the life of Jesus Christ were precisely such as common reason would pronounce incompatible with the claim of a divine personality and ministry; they provoked contempt, they enfeebled and actually contradicted the very aims which Jesus Christ was so desirous to subserve. How, then, to find consistency in such apparent inconsistency? The student will pause to ask whether it is not through seeming contradictions that the verity of truth is most strongly established ? Falsehood descends from verity to contradiction ; truth ascends from contradiction to verity : the child smiles at the self-contradictory idea that motion can be so rapid as to become rest,—the man knows that but for this fact the universe would stagger and perish. What if Jesus Christ has shown that to be most a man it was necessary to become hardly a man at all,—that is, to go down to the lowest possible point, and to be without form or comeliness or reputation?

Passing from the works of Jesus Christ the student has next to consider whether the scope and tone of His teaching (regarded as a spiritual revelation and an ethical testimony) are in keeping with the theory of His miraculous conception. It must be insisted that Jesus Christ's teaching shall prove itself to have properties which contradistinguish it even from the inspired teaching of Moses, the psalmists, and the prophets. But in insisting upon this contradistinction is the student aware how great a question he is raising? Nothing less than the inquiry—How can inspiration exceed itself? This question is met by the bold answer that in coming to Jesus Christ we have passed from Inspiration to the Inspirer,—a teacher whose doctrine is rather a living Presence than a written testimony. The student must bear in mind that this supposed Son of God cannot be allowed to contradict Moses, the psalmists, and the prophets; He must work strictly in their line, and undertake to carry their work forward to the point of culmination: He cannot be permitted to begin by ignoring the moral history of the world; He must accept it, and prove His authority not by disputation but by fulfilment. To deny or underrate the claim of Moses and the prophets would be to bring divine inspiration into discredit; on the other hand, to give them a higher signification, and actually to displace them as the fruit displaces the blossom, is the most difficult, as it is the most ambitious, work which any man can propose to accomplish. Candour, then, requires instant recognition of the fact that in the fourfold narrative of His life Jesus Christ is distinctly represented as addressing Himself to His apparently impossible task. Here, at all events, is dauntless courage. Of course mere intrepidity considered strictly in itself may amount to nothing, yet in such a case as is now being examined the *absence* of it would be fatal to any claim of divinity, for God cannot hesitate, omnipotence cannot falter. That Jesus Christ frankly accepted the history of the divine government of men, as expounded or administered by inspired agents, is clear from His own words,—" Think not that I am come to destroy the law or the prophets; I am not come to destroy, but to fulfil." At this point the intrepidity of Christ assumes peculiar value, because He defines its function, and that function is sublime alike in its difficulty and purpose. He admits nothing of failure in preceding dispensations : He does not depreciate the work of others that He may magnify His own ; He undertakes to deal with the intentional incompleteness of introductory economies and to complete the circumference of revelation. In this, He proceeds upon the theory that God's government is indivisible, always consistent with itself, constantly evolving homogeneous and progressive truths. If it be justly held that teachers are reliable in proportion to the compass and grasp of their minds, some confidence must be due to Jesus Christ on the ground that He —a peasant unlettered and poor—is represented in the narrative of His ministry as dealing with doctrines which relate to nothing less solemn and comprehensive than the growth and destiny of human nature. Instead of denying the beginning, He founded a distinct claim upon it,—" Had ye believed Moses ye would have believed Me, for he wrote of Me; but if ye believe not his writings, how shall ye believe My words?" A great plea for the oneness and simplicity of God's government!

As in the case of the works, so in the case of the words, there are two conditions which must be fulfilled: (1) An unequivocal claim on the part of Jesus Christ to be the Inspirer; and (2) A corresponding excitement on the part of those to whom the claim was addressed. Let us attend to each of these conditions. With regard to the first we cannot but be struck with the persistent identification of His own personality with the doctrine which He taught; He did not merely say, I *teach* the truth, He said I *am* the truth,—not merely I *show* the life, but I *am* the life; I am not merely inspired, I *am* the Inspirer Himself. The inspired man is the exceptional man; of him it may be said not so much he *knows*, as he *is*, for inspiration increases as well as sanctifies the volume of a man's being. Most of us stop at education, being unable to reach the higher point, the point of inspiration; we have property, but not life; we are an accumulation of details; we *know* much, but *are* nothing. In the case of Jesus Christ, we find Him constantly work from His own personality, thus:—" The words that I speak unto you, they are spirit and they are life; I am the bread of life, he that cometh to Me shall never hunger, and he that believeth on Me shall never thirst; he that believeth on Me hath everlasting life; I am the living bread which came down from heaven; I am the vine, ye are the branches; without Me ye can do nothing; I am the way, the truth, and the life; no man cometh unto the Father but by Me; I am the good Shepherd; I give unto My sheep eternal life; he that seeth Me seeth Him that sent Me; he that hath seen Me hath seen the Father; I and My Father are one." Here is certainly a new type of man. To have conceived the notion that truth was capable of personal embodiment, and that life was the highest expression of law, was a great advance upon all former thinking; and to set *Himself* forth as that embodiment and that law was an assumption so novel and so startling as only to be justified by the highest evidence. Is there, then, any accord between such an *assumption* and such a *birth ?* Is it possible that never man *spake* like this man, because never man was *born* like this man? Look at the peculiarities of His speaking before answering this question. His speaking was extemporaneous as well as considered and deliberate: He gave immediate answers to all kinds of questions suddenly and carefully put; attempts were made to take Him unawares, to entangle Him in His speech, and to lure Him towards dangerous ground, yet He confounded the wise and took the crafty in their own craftiness. He never asked for time; he never complained of inequality; He was never betrayed into unguarded expressions which were recalled to be amended,—all this is upon the record: how came it to be there—by dramatic genius or by divine inspiration? Say that in Christ dwelt all the fulness of the Godhead bodily, and these peculiarities of speech are at once made plain; deny it, and there remains the mystery that He did in the most explicit terms claim to be the Inspirer and Lord of the church.

What of the second condition, that is to say a corresponding excitement on the part of those who heard Jesus Christ put forth the claim? In answering this question the inquirer will bear in mind that the people who heard Jesus Christ had enjoyed the advantage of long training, ancestral and personal, in divine things, and were by so much specially qualified to form an opinion upon religious teaching: "Unto them were committed the oracles of God, . . . to them pertained the adoption, and the glory, and the covenants, and the giving of the law, and the service of God, and the promises;" to them had been addressed the question, "What nation is there so great that hath statutes and judgments, so righteous as all this law?" Upon such a people it would be difficult, with merely commonplace sentiment and utterance, to make a deep impression. According to the narrative (four-fold, be it remembered) Jesus Christ roused their deepest emotions:—" The people were astonished at His doctrine, for He taught them as one having authority: they were all amazed, insomuch that they questioned among themselves, saying, What thing is this? what new doctrine is this? and all bare Him witness, and wondered at the gracious words which proceeded out of His mouth: they were astonished, and said, Whence hath this man this wisdom and these mighty works? They were astonished at His doctrine, for His word was with power." On the other hand He provoked contemptuous criticism: He came from a proscribed place; He adopted the most lowly surroundings; He drew upon Himself the extremest hatred of so-called righteous men: in His case the law of analogy and sequence was upset; the ascertainable elements of His personality did not account for the sum total of His Being,—so there He stood, at once a plague and a blessing, a stranger and a friend, a miracle and a worker of a miracle, a monster or a God! The student has to consider whether such results are mutually accordant, whether the Inspirer could have hesitated to make a distinctive standing ground for Himself, whether the Inspirer could possibly have taken any but the foremost position, and whether the rejection of the Inspirer is not precisely the offence which would bring to a crisis the sin and madness of the world.

Here a difficulty may arise. A man who claims to have been begotten by the Holy Ghost may, from that very circumstance, be expected to be so transcendental in his teaching as to disqualify himself for being a factor in the practical morals of the common-place and everyday world; his standpoint will be so distant and so unappreciable that even the strongest reasoners will be unable to follow him; his teaching will be so apocalyptic and celestial as quite to miss the earthward and disciplinary side of human life. In one word, Will not such a man be too great for the occasion?

In looking at this difficulty, the student will remind himself how nearly impossible it has been for some of the highest mortal minds to simplify themselves so as to be understood even by average thinkers: those minds have almost originated planes of their own, and the universal language of a nation has been minted into new values by the unique uses to which such minds have turned it. This, however, will but remotely touch the difficulty in hand, because Jesus Christ's pretensions exclude Him from the class of so-called original thinkers: such is the professedly *benevolent* purpose of His mission, that we must insist that the light which is shed out of the heavens of His divinity be so attempered as neither to dazzle nor scorch this everyday life of infirm and erring mortals. In a word, there must be the same approachableness on the side of His wisdom, as was happily discovered on the side of His power. Can the fact of such approachableness be established?

There are two sources of proof: there is first of all the direct moral teaching of Jesus Christ,—notably the sermon on the mount, abounding in laws and maxims which the most ordinary perception can comprehend; and secondly, there is the most considerate reticence on the part of Jesus Christ, shown in such passages as—" He spake the word unto them as they were able to hear it,—I have many things to say unto you, but ye cannot bear them now." Was it the least of His mercies that He carried *the burden of truth* for His church? His followers were eventually to bear it for themselves, yet (according to the promise) it was to be so gradually and effectually wrought into their very being by the Holy Ghost that, instead of being a burden, it was to be their peace and joy. Thus we come upon a power boundless and terrible, yet controlled and repressed; a power, in fact, that rises to the perfection of gentleness; and then we come upon a doctrine of like kind, stretching beyond the ken of all human sagacity and genius, yet descending into common daily life, and calling all men to a morality ineffable as the purity of God. In doing and teaching all this, there is on the part of Jesus Christ a most sweet harmony of power and wisdom and love. What He *could* have done! What He *could* have said! Yet as God, all-mighty and all-good, adapted the light to the eye and the eye to the light, so as to bless men with the gifts of day and summer, so this worker of miracles and setter forth of strange doctrines tempered His majesty by an unspeakable condescension.

As the narrative of Jesus Christ's life moves towards its more tragic scenes, the reader who believes in the miraculous conception feels at a loss to anticipate an exit which will be in keeping with so remarkable a beginning. For a time the line of consistency if not broken is most darkly obscured. The mighty Man is bound as a prisoner; the Inspirer is dumb; He who never paused for an answer allows His life to be sworn away by false witnesses! Here the line of consistency appears to be at end, and Christianity, in the person of its Founder, perishes in an ignominious anticlimax. This is a moment—this moment of the Cross—of almost intolerable excitement to the reader. In his distress, he may forget the great law of life and all its labour—"Thou fool, that which thou sowest is not quickened except it die." Jesus Christ died and rose again; but having risen again, how is He to leave the world in a manner befitting the peculiarity of His coming into it? To this question there is a wonderful answer—so quiet, so complete—*He ascended!* Not in a chariot of fire, as if He had been sent for; He went up of His own will and by His own power; the consenting heavens received Him out of sight, without a sound to break the awful stillness. He who came as never man came, went as never man went. He *ascended!*

This is the argument. The question for the reader is—How can such a narrative be accounted for? How did so minute and subtle a unity come to be? Before answering it he will be reminded that as all writers of fiction endeavour to secure artistic completeness, so the writers of the gospels may have succeeded in inventing a coherent romance. To this suggestion there is a decisive answer:—

First: There are four authors,—not one merely, who had but his own taste to consult and satisfy.

Second: No dramatist ever attempted to work with such extraordinary conditions as are found in the life of Jesus Christ.

Third: The Christian narrative is singularly defective in the very kind of unity which mere artists regard as essential to completeness,—so defective that some critics have not hesitated to say that they have discovered in it several discrepancies. In the construction of the gospels there is no sign of artistic effort; the unity is spiritual and latent, not literal and demonstrative.

Fourth: The *moral* purpose sought to be accomplished by the gospels makes it impossible that they can be mere inventions of dramatic genius. That moral purpose is to save men, to bring them to God, and to give them peace; the inconsistency of such a purpose with the representation of a dramatic personage as a living Saviour is so gross as to be, not only an offence in letters, but a crime in morality. On this theory we are asked to believe that lies are a proper medium for the transmission of truth, and that truth itself is so unimportant that it may be modified, intermixed with error, concealed or perverted, without the slightest disadvantage either to itself or to mankind. This theory is the more monstrous and incredible when viewed in the light of the fact that certain portions of the book which present this subtle and impressive unity, distinctly claim to be merely parabolical and figurative; in doing so, they separate themselves from other portions which are thus by implication clothed with a different quality and degree of authority. We must insist that where one portion is distinctly marked as parabolical, the implication is that the portions not so marked are to be taken as history is taken in contradistinction to fiction.

With this strong protest against the merely artistic or fictional theory, we must leave the reader to answer the inquiry,—How can such a narrative as is found in the fourfold life of Jesus Christ be accounted for?

The reasoning of the last three chapters has proceeded upon the principle that Inspiration should be its own witness; that is to say, there should be something about an inspired book which there is about no other, and that particular something should not be (1) mere fineness of words, for that is possible (and all the more probable) where the

Inspiration of Christ's Biography. 71

thought is common-place and feeble; nor (2) mere solemnity of formal claim, which would in all likelihood be the first thing provided for by an ordinarily prudent impostor; nor must it be (3) the unapproachableness which forbids the scrutiny of reason, and precludes the possibility of forming a personal and independent opinion. It must be an *indescribable* something, which is in the very life and texture of the revelation itself, which is all the more definite because of its indefiniteness, and all the more authoritative because of its want of that special kind of assumption which marks human legislature and judgment. Undoubtedly an inspired book will have much in common with ordinary life and thought, simply because life and thought are themselves the work of the same Spirit. It must never be forgotten that man himself is an inspiration, seeing that God "breathed into him the breath of life," and especially remembering that it is in the Bible itself that man is thus described—" There is a spirit in man, and the inspiration of the Almighty giveth him understanding:" in speaking, therefore, of an inspired book, it must not be forgotten that it is addressed to a being who has himself received some degree of the inspiration of which the book is probably the most distinct and copious expression, and for this very reason there may be (perhaps must be) much in the book which man will think he could have found out for himself, something also which he may suppose himself capable of rivalling, yet something just above him, tempting his ambition and tantalising his efforts,—so near yet so far,—a sheet, plainly enough, and full of common looking things, yet the four corners are fastened in heaven! Is this the method of inspiration which commends itself to the human judgment? Is it not in its very nature most human, yet something more? Does it not stand in relation to all other methods as Nature stands to Art? In some instances, especially in the distance, Art does seem to rival Nature; she makes beautiful figures and delicate flowers, and has attained marvellous skill in the treatment of colour; yet may it not be said most truthfully— Among those that have appeared in sculpture there hath not been a greater than the master-piece of Angelo, nevertheless the poorest and meanest child in the kingdom of *life* infinitely transcends his proudest monument. It is, if this argument is sound, the same with inspiration. Even as it is found in the Bible, coming through all human imperfection and dependent in some degree on the weary and erring fingers of many scribes, it asserts itself with a vitality and a dignity which cannot be mistaken. Inspiration must *inspire*, or its claim is arbitrary and untenable. On this ground the foregoing argument has inexorably proceeded, and there we are content to rest it; still, it is only just to the case that the Bible should be allowed to give what may be called its own notion of inspiration : here and there in its pages may be found some account of how it came to be inspired, and some idea of what the term "inspiration" means. Let it be observed it is *only* here and there that such indications are to be found, and let the reader reflect whether the very casualty of the references is not an argument in favour of the Bible. Which is the man of true quality,—He who labels himself with genealogical tables and lives on the reputation of his fathers, or he in whose conversation and behaviour there are references and characteristics positively unaccountable except on the hypothesis that his descent is pure and illustrious. Let us hear what the Bible says about its own inspiration :—

"*God in divers manners spake in time past unto the fathers by the prophets.*" Does not this read rather as an incidental reference than as a formal assertion of superiority? It certainly does so when taken with the context, thus—" God, who at sundry times and in divers manners spake in time past unto the fathers by the prophets, hath in these last days spoken unto us by His Son." Is this a probable method of revelation; is it likely that a revelation from heaven would be broken up in time and method? It strikes us not only as pre-eminently probable, but as *necessary* if it was to address the whole world. The diversity of manner must not be overlooked as bearing upon the universality of the revelation; here is repetition without sameness, identity without monotony. Not only were the "fathers" themselves variously constituted, there was variety in the "manners" which God Himself adopted. Is it in harmony with His known administration in nature and providence to be varied in His methods, or did He hide this phase of His power until He came to indite the Bible? The argument is not that men are differently constituted, and that therefore inspiration would have different effects upon them; it is that the variety of manner was chosen by the Almighty Himself, and that the Bible would have been just as varied as it is even though it had been written throughout by the same human hand. Then as to the method of development, is that at all natural or likely? Is it probable that the Almighty would proceed by an ascending or descending scale? We are told that He began by sending the prophets, and that afterwards He sent His Son. Is it *likely* that He would do so, or is it not? Would He first have sent His Son and subsequently have sent the prophets? Look at His plan in nature, in physical growth, in intellectual expansion, and in the light of undisputed instances determine the probabilities of a hypothetical case.

Another account is this—"*Holy men of God spake as they were moved by the Holy Ghost.*" Is this laboured or far-fetched? Observe the variety of the particulars in this one brief sentence: "Holy," then the *character* was in keeping with the work; "Men," then the Bible is the product of various witnesses, and thus the points of confirmation or disproof are numerous; "As they were moved," then they had no control over their inspiration; it might come upon them without notice, it might use them as instruments for the occasion, and then leave them as common men. We know that their speech was fervent, broken, impassioned, urgent, and emphatic as the hammer of the Lord. But is such speech at all in harmony with the "movement" by the Holy Ghost which is claimed for them? Is there ardour enough to suggest the Spirit of burning? Is there coherence enough to suggest the Spirit of judgment? Of course human curiosity wishes to know *how* the holy men were moved; but this is not the only point on which human curiosity must remain unsatisfied,—"the wind bloweth where it listeth, thou hearest the sound thereof, but canst not tell whence it cometh or whither it goeth, so is every one that is born of the Spirit," whether by way of inspiration, regeneration, or sanctification. The prophets themselves probably knew as little of the mystery of this "movement" as we ourselves do, for what can the instrument know of the music which is breathed through it, or how can the brain tell how the dream passed through it without asking consent or favour? Until men can explain their own intellectual excitements, they need not make an insuperable difficulty of the inspiration of the "holy men of God." Every man is his own mystery.

Again: "*All scripture is given by inspiration of God, and is profitable for doctrine, for reproof, for correction, for instruction in righteousness, that the man of God may be perfect, throughly furnished unto all good works.*" So inspiration, like every other great gift of God, is for man's sake. Consider how this argument might have been turned. thus—" All scripture is given by inspiration of God, therefore all inquiry is foreclosed, every exercise of reason is forbidden, private judgment is disallowed, the whole book must be accepted with blind unquestioning faith, and kept at a distance like an idol in a sacred house." Instead of this, the doctrine is that inspiration was granted solely in the interests of man. There is nothing said about the abstract glory of God, the majesty of the Creator, or the sublimity of the invisible kingdom; the whole idea turns upon the culture, the correction, and the edification of man, and therefore, instead of being clouded into a theological mystery, it becomes a gracious human benefaction. Happily we can compare this representation of its purpose with other statements which bear upon the divine government: if it harmonise, well; if not, something will be taken from its value. Is it in harmony with the gift of Jesus Christ? The purpose of that gift was distinctly the salvation of man. Is it in keeping with the departure of Jesus Christ out of this world? That departure is thus explained: "It is expedient *for you* that I go away." Is it in harmony with the general intention of the gifts of God? That intention is thus declared: all things *are yours*, and again, all things are for *your sakes*. Within this scheme how naturally does inspiration come,—Scripture is inspired that *you* may be instructed and perfected!

Inspiration of Christ's Biography.

This, then, is the testimony of the Bible respecting its own inspiration. Whether that inspiration is the formidable and inexplicable difficulty which it has been supposed to be, the reader must be left to decide for himself.

VI.

THE HOLY SPIRIT AS THE INTERPRETER OF SCRIPTURE.

PERHAPS there is no function assigned to the Holy Spirit more important for us to understand than that by which He assures to the church a profound and correct interpretation of Scripture. According to the teaching of the apostle Peter (than whom no man was more experimentally qualified to speak on the subject, seeing that he had often been rebuked for his impetuous treatment of divine utterances), " no prophecy of the scripture is of any private interpretation ; " and the reason which he gives for this is philosophically satisfactory, viz., as the prophecy did not come by the will of man it cannot be fully comprehended and explained by the intellectual power of man. In this case man was an instrument in receiving and pronouncing the word, and he must be an instrument also in the study and mastery of its meaning. As holy men of God were moved by the Holy Ghost to speak, so they must be moved by the Holy Ghost to feel and understand, the divine oracle Yet above all other books the Bible calls for exposition ; its very form sets at naught the laws of literary structure, whilst all its problems and questionings have about them the solemn yet fascinating weirdness of an unknown origin and purpose. Its

The Holy Spirit as the Interpreter of Scripture. 79

preface is simply—"In the beginning God," and its epilogue is a curse on the man who takes away aught of its sacred store. Between these extremes, so appropriate yet so startling, is found the apostolic caution not to enclose for selfish uses any portion of the freehold meant for the whole world. The very fact that a protest is entered against the narrowness and insufficiency of "private interpretation" should beget a deeper confidence in the divinity and consequent pureness of the revelation. On the other hand what becomes of the right of private judgment? Can it be maintained without extorting from the holy word mistaken sanctions of personal crotchets or sectarian hobbies? Are unholy men to be turned promiscuously into the Book, and told to get out of it such advantages as they may suppose themselves to find? Is it so, or otherwise? This is a delicate inquiry, demanding treatment that shall in its human aspect be austerely reverent.

It is evident that the inevitable and most serious perils attending "private interpretation" constitute an unanswerable argument against it, as its exercise is commonly understood. Yes; the perils are inevitable as well as most serious, for in the first instance attention must of course be fixed on the letter, and the letter brings up instantly some of the most vexatious difficulties arising out of secondary interpretation, that is secondary in point of value and importance. There is, if one may so put it, a battle of grammars as well as a battle of doctrines, and by the very nature of the case it is but a small minority of mankind that can take an enlightened and helpful part in such a controversy. Think of the intellectual training that is needful, the self-control, the patience, the thorough acquaintance with comparative philology, and the inexplicable sympathy which *feels* the meaning it cannot *see*. But turn untrained and spiritually incompetent men into a literature of which in its original form they are wholly ignorant, and who does not see that the results must be at once critically absurd and spiritually calamitous? Unfortunately the only man who does not see this is the man whose pride is wounded by the suggestion that there is some difference between a literal form and a spiritual meaning, and the consequence of his humiliation is that he repeats his errors with the greater emphasis, and proclaims that his most sacred rights are threatened or denied. Then there is the certain danger of fixing attention upon isolated passages, and so setting up denominations and schools upon texts, which being torn from the vital body of evidence, are perverted and exaggerated to the point of impiety,—the worst sort of impiety, too, namely the sort which sets aside common sense and literary rectitude under the pretence of superior sanctity and more humble faith. Is there a single monstrosity in the religious world that does not defend itself by some stray line of scripture, which if compared with other testimony, and read in the light of Jesus Christ's method of quotation—" it is written *again*"—would assume another meaning, and probably tend in an opposite direction? Can we wonder that such partial interpretation is forbidden

The Holy Spirit as the Interpreter of Scripture. 81

in Scripture itself, and that the Bible prays to be protected from the ravages of bigoted and ignorant men? That the Bible exposes itself to such ravages is obviously in its favour, as suggesting that it is not cunningly fabricated and defended as a work of literary art, but that it comes upon the world as a living and generous revelation of spiritual truth addressed to the attention of the whole human family throughout all the ages of its progress, and *so* addressed (for there is a question of manner as well as of matter) as to challenge the most careful and unselfish thoughtfulness on the part of those who receive it. Given a God to find out what degree and quality of revelation He will grant, and no human mind would ever indicate such a book, as to structure and method, as the Bible. What dramatic action, rapidity of movement, brokenness of style, and apparent incoherence of plan! What little things are exaggerated, what obscure names are preserved, what trivial incidents are magnified! Stones enough, but where is the altar? Life in profusion, but how does it individualise itself into friendship, sympathy, and benediction? In proportion to the *life* that is infused into any work would seem to be its exposure to variety and keenness of criticism. Insipid books soon find the way into oblivion, but books that have life compel the world to read them even though the reading lead to anger and hostility. A painted portrait offers more points of attack than a photograph though the subject be the same; necessarily so; there is more life in the one than in the other; the sun is said to be a faithful

G

painter, but that is not an unquestionable statement, —the sun cannot get at the soul; only soul can paint soul, only life can delineate life, man can see his *shadow* anywhere, but where can he see *himself?* As the portrait will excite more criticism than the photograph, so the living man will, by a glance or an attitude, a tone or a smile, elicit a thousand remarks which the most brilliant painting could never have suggested. So much for the subtle illimitableness of life! Is it just to determine the character of a man by a single feature of his personality,—a feature detached and viewed apart? We should then have one estimate founded upon his stature, another upon his voice, a third upon his mien, a fourth upon his face, and so on according to the fancy of each observer, and yet we should, amidst all this variety, have little or no idea of the man himself: we should still require an estimate which recognised the relation of the parts to the whole and distinguished the incidental from the vital and inseparable. So in the work of Biblical interpretation,—there must be an eye that can take in the whole landscape and a judgment which can allow for distance, light, and colour.

How, then, to realise these conditions and to bring them to bear? And especially how to do so as not to deprive any man of his Bible by shaming him into the consciousness of utter inability to read what he has hitherto prized as the plainest and wisest of books. He will not, as he ought not, give up the Bible easily; and probably he will insist on the right of private judgment, and in a moment of jealous anger may claim equality of power with his teacher or friend. But such vehemence will be misspent if directed against the present argument, inasmuch as it has no felonious intent upon any man's Bible or upon the rights of any man's conscience. The question is, How to make the most of the Bible; how to get at its proper spiritual meaning; and how to express its revelations in the daily behaviour of life? Is every man qualified to interpret and decide the purpose of the Scriptures? From the point of view of this argument, interpretation is the result of spiritual preparedness, and spiritual preparedness is the work of the Holy Ghost. A reader going to the Bible in a self-sufficient and self-dependent spirit will narrow and dishonour it by private interpretation, and probably bring from its perusal nothing higher than a crotchet; but going to it in another spirit he may see it and know it as a revelation from heaven.

What, then, is that other spirit? It is so specifically defined by an apostle as to prevent all doubt of its meaning; it is "the spirit of power, and of love, and of a sound mind," and this spirit is the direct gift of God! He who is thus qualified can make no vital mistakes in the interpretation of Scripture; whilst he who has every other qualification but this will never apprehend the genius and purpose of the Bible. So, instead of taking the book from its humblest reader, this argument would make it doubly his, and enrich him with the most comforting promises throughout its perusal. This qualification will give a man so just an estimate of his own powers as will save him from meddling with things which are too high for him, and will move him with so enlightened and gracious a charity as will guard him from the self-exaggeration which expresses itself in illiberal censure or contemptuous distrust. Under the influence of a "sound mind" he will remember that there are some things in the Bible which are not meant to be determinately interpreted, and thus he will escape the vexation which follows abortive efforts to explain and understand every mystery; "the spirit of love" will dictate large and generous interpretations of difficulties; and "the spirit of power" will liberate him from the bondage and hardness of the mere letter. It may be worth while to vary the wording of so important a doctrine, if haply we may set it in a clearer light. Given, then, a man who approaches the Bible in a "spirit of power, of love, and of a sound mind," and the following results will certainly attend his reading : first of all, he will carefully distinguish between what is particular and what is universal, because his whole manhood will be enlarged and elevated according to the grandeur of the occasion ; in the next place, he will be dispossessed of every desire to propagate theories of his own, and so to strain and debase the Bible into an *ex parte* witness ; and in the third place, he will be so completely under the dominion of "the spirit of love" as to be saved from the persistent and impious self-conceit which is the very mainspring of ungenerous and demoralising zealotry. He will go to the Bible in quest of *God;* he will go to it in a spirit of self-control; he will read it that he may find a *Gospel*, not that he may confirm a creed. The right of private judgment will thus be held in the interests of humanity, and the private reader will, in the best sense, become a public interpreter. Under these conditions let every man have the Bible for his own use, for he cannot forget that it is the book of God and the charter of the world.

Undoubtedly each reader will have his favourite passages,—texts to which he will turn in danger or sorrow with special expectation, and promises which will seem to have been expressly written for his personal use. This is natural and unavoidable; it is even useful and edifying, as showing the illimitableness, the variety, the infinite adaptation and sufficiency of biblical doctrine and counsel. It is thus that each reader reprints the Bible, and that each life repronounces, with individual emphasis and unction, the righteous commandment and the tender promise. Still, this legitimate privacy of enjoyment and sense of invincible security is happily compatible with all that is claimed on behalf of the universality of the Bible. It should be borne in mind that the divine promise of satisfaction in all spiritual inquiries is independent of accidental, technical, or arbitrary conditions, and is made to rest solely upon the spiritual temper and purpose of the inquirer. In this respect the Bible is wholly unlike all other books. Letters can be interpreted by letters; but here is a book in the reading of which literary instruments can give but secondary and imperfect help;—a book which says—You must read me through your hearts if you would see all the fulness of any meaning. A few proofs will show the scope and quality of the whole evidence. "To this man will I look, even to him that is poor and of a contrite spirit, and that trembleth at My word." "Thus saith the high and lofty One that inhabiteth eternity, whose name is Holy; I dwell in the high and holy place, with him also that is of a contrite and humble spirit, to revive the spirit of the humble, and to revive the heart of the contrite ones." "Blessed are the poor in spirit, for theirs is the kingdom of heaven." Such conditions are in happy consonance with the genius of any revelation meant for the use of the whole world; everything that is merely national, temporary, casual, or adventitious is ignored, and a great human condition, independent of place and time, is asked for by the merciful and condescending God,—"the sacrifices of God are a broken spirit; a broken and a contrite heart, O God, Thou wilt not despise,"—the things of the spiritual kingdom are hidden from the wise and prudent, and are revealed unto babes; so it seemed good in the *Father's* eyes.

We shall never be able to dispense with literal criticism in reading and interpreting the holy oracles, simply because they are made known to us through a literal medium; but probably we have yet to receive the profoundest commentary upon those oracles, because we have yet to attain the spiritual

The Holy Spirit as the Interpreter of Scripture. 87

purity and sensitiveness necessary to their fullest apprehension. What is true of the written commentary is true also of the oral exposition. Preaching will undergo modifications which some of the elders would have deemed startling, and perhaps more than startling. It will have to throw off everything narrow and technical, and to speak the universal love in the universal language. It is not unkind to say that the pulpit, here and there at least, is marked by a smart trickery infinitely out of place, and truly pitiable, in this matter of biblical interpretation. Probably the inspired writers would be shocked could they know how their utterances are broken up into what are called "texts," and what hothouse forcing there is in making a little text grow in one hour into a long discourse. No doubt a good deal could be said about the botany of a single blade of grass, but the flock is starving whilst the green pastures are interdicted by the fluent but most unshepherdly botanist. Text-beating is most irreligious work, and woefully thriftless as to pastoral service. Clever, no doubt,—showing skill in word-twisting and literary legerdemain, thus making vulgar people wonder how the preacher can find so much in a vessel so small,—but no more. An impious cleverness, leading away from interpretations profound, beneficent, wise, such as restore the soul and magnify the excellence of truth, into critical nibbling, and into rhetorical clamour where one cannot hear the little sense on account of the great noise. Spiritual interpretation is directed differently. It is not so much textual as *biblical*,—that is, pervaded by the very life and purpose of truth, and in harmony with the whole plan of the universe. Great expositors will be less anxious that their hearers should listen to a discourse upon a particular sentence, than that they should comprehend the meaning of a whole epistle. Who thinks of giving out the epistle to the Galatians as his text, or the Acts of the Apostles, or the gospel by John? Would this be inconvenient? Probably so; yet (and this is the point of the suggestion) it is possible to go through the parts *in the spirit of the whole*, as it is lamentably actual that the whole is often slurred as if it were a chaos of unrelated *parts*. Will it be arbitrary to insist that the part can be thoroughly understood only in the light of the whole? To hesitate to say so, is to save the feeling of preachers who, through no irreverence or idleness, may have spent the most of a public lifetime in seriously dishonouring the Bible in the very act of preaching from many of its texts.

It may be asked, How far is an expositor of the Scriptures at liberty to depend upon the inspiration of the Holy Spirit in the public interpretation of the word? No categorical answer ought to be given to an inquiry like this, in which there is probably more implied than is expressed; still, the inquiry is of the first importance as bearing upon ministerial responsibility and Christian edification. We must recognise the difference between

Interpretation and Utterance. Interpretation may come slowly; in some cases it may be the reward of patient diligence, in others it may come suddenly and startlingly. Interpretations are often given in the course of silent, devout, expectant reading, and, from our point of view, this would seem to be the natural application of the divine method; yet the Holy One of Israel must not be limited, nor His pleasure be questioned or thwarted by the obstinacy of man. To go into the pulpit and stand there avowedly waiting for inspiration to understand the word would seem to be but one remove (if indeed it be so much) from the most impious affectation; *that*, surely, would be to limit the Holy One of Israel under pretence of magnifying His power. A written revelation implies by the very terms that it may be considered and pondered in quietness; it is already in existence; it is within reach; it is by its very nature an appeal to devout regard; why wait for public circumstances under which to inquire into its import? If, on the other hand, the question relate to Utterance rather than to interpretation, the reply may be fairly modified. Life itself is not the same thing alike under private and public conditions; it admits of expansion, of electrical sympathy, of subtle combination with the living elements and influences around it, and under high excitement it will surprise itself by the variety and intensity of its emotions. All this may come without any suggestion of what is known as divine inspiration; it is rather *human* inspiration, man quickening man as iron sharpeneth iron. It may, however, have its counterpart and complement in the direct action of the Holy Ghost upon the intellectual and spiritual faculties; and where that action supervenes there will almost certainly be enlarged power of sympathy and expression. It cannot, other things being equal, be an offence to the Holy Spirit to ask Him for extemporaneous utterance that shall reach the hearts of the congregation,—a very different thing, be it observed, from literary expression, sentences meant for a book, paragraphs measured and numbered for printing. There is an utterance which belongs to the speaker and not to the writer, an urgent, rapid, percussive, and living utterance, that cannot be printed. In the very hour of duty such utterance shall be given by the Holy Ghost to the faithful and honest servant. But ought not a minister to prepare his sermon? There we come upon a difficulty,—the difficulty of *sermonising*, writing and speaking by the hourglass, and running the risk of artificialising the divinest life. Preaching so soon becomes an art, a craft, a profession. A sermon is so measurable, so cold, so little, as commonly understood, only a mouthful, a hollow word perhaps, an uncertain sound may be. Yet what should it be? A stream of life, love, light,— the very blood of the heart, the very divinity of life. To talk of "preparing" it, is to run a great risk of talking insanity, and yet, as generally thought of, what can be easier than to "prepare" a sermon!

Will it be unduly bold on the part of a writer to give counsel to—what ought to be the greatest of all men—the Christian preacher? The advice would be, not that he should prepare his *sermon*, but that he should prepare *himself*. His exegesis he has of course prepared in secret; he has meditated upon it in the night-watches, and prevented the day by an eager desire to know it still more perfectly; he knows what things new and old he has in the treasury, and as for his searching of the Scriptures, he has dug in them as for choice silver and stones of great price. So far the preparation has been honest, full, even jealous less aught should have failed in the minuteness of detail; but as to verbal expression, what if he should have left it to the inspiration of the moment? Were it a question of mere phraseology there is no reason why he might not have prepared it in secret; but it is phraseology with a difference: it is phraseology *plus*, and what that *plus* is no man can determine exhaustively. Perhaps it is most fitly expressed by the word *life*,—that word being a compound of such terms as sympathy, *rapport*, adaptation, responsiveness. When the preacher knows his subject, and clearly apprehends the line upon which his thought is to proceed, it may show a trustful and humble spirit on his part to depend upon the Holy Ghost for the gift of suitable and efficient utterance. But may he not write, so to speak, to the dictation of the Holy Ghost? He would be a bold man who would answer such an inquiry in the negative; yet he might be reverent and wise in hesitating (considering the peculiar vocation of the pulpit) to answer it in the affirmative. "But may the preacher not stumble, blunder, or utterly fail? May he not be disquieted and indeed disabled by the fear of man? How deplorable that it should be so!" Such a suggestion is certainly not without foundation in natural reason, yet the "deplorableness" which is deprecated is not without mitigation when viewed in a proper light. It is out of weakness that good men are made strong; it is by their falling that they learn lessons which are denied to the proud and the strong; it is by the very earthenness of the vessel that the excellence of the power is often vindicated and magnified,—so these human stammerings and down-breaks may not be so deplorable as was supposed. "But to fail in the pulpit —to come to a standstill!" Painful no doubt, but not at all necessary as a consequence of depending upon the Holy Ghost. It is human fear, not human piety, that suggests the collapse and shame. But what is *failure?* What is *success?* There may be a misapprehension and a misapplication of terms in such a discussion. "A preacher has read his discourse with unbroken fluency: that is success;" so it may be said, but the opinion may be unsound notwithstanding its positiveness. The fluent reader may have failed. He may not have lingually stumbled, and yet he may have spiritually broken down, and grieved the Spirit of God. His breakdown was not towards earth but towards heaven, to man he was a hero much applauded and flattered; to God and the angels what if he was a coward and a hireling much pitied and wept over! "Failure" is a word often wantonly used in the church, greatly to the grief of honest workers and godly souls. But supposing what is usually called "failure," under the conditions demanded by this argument, who is it that has failed? Man? God? Having strict regard to the conditions insisted upon in this contention, it was certainly not *man* that failed, and therefore we must leave the blasphemy of the alternative answer to those who can utter it. One thing only we must ask to be borne in mind, namely that there is a success which is failure, there is a failure which is success. Given the kind and degree of dependence upon the Spirit of God indicated above, and probably there may be great changes in the form or mode of public ministration. Sermons may be less artistic, language may be less ornate or polished, appeals may be more abrupt and penetrating, methodical propriety may be disorganized, the pulpit may cease to be a refrigerator: great changes of many sorts may take place,— amongst the rest the Lord Himself may come to His holy temple as in these latter days He seldom comes, and the eloquent orator may be silent before Him. In the olden time the word came very brokenly, but did it not come with wonderful power? Did not the "babbler" arrest the attention of the world and force new themes upon its reluctant consideration? We shall be told that times have changed, and that the education and intelligence of the age must be addressed. Herein, then, the *distinctiveness* of the preacher is in danger of being lost, and instead of standing alone, in a noble and awful solitude as to method and claim, he may become but one of a crowd,—he may become weak as other men. The philosophical lecturer, the academician, the travelling elocutionist, the Christian preacher, each has his manuscript and each his private art. Where is the ancient distinctiveness? Where the voice of the Lord, the background of eternity, the momentum of infinitude, all the old signals of a direct representation of the Invisible and Everlasting? Preaching should never lose its *distinctiveness;* it should stand apart; all coalitions it should avoid as unholy and unequal. When it tampers with the mean idolatries of the common arts, it goes astray from the Cross, and sells its power to the enemy; it does not adapt itself to the age, it allows the age to take its crown and to despoil its power. But what if others imitate the preacher, and rival him in his peculiar vocation? Let them try. Their imitation will be the highest compliment; but beyond imitation they can never go. The servant of the Lord will for ever hold a secret entirely his own; his method may easily be borrowed, but his fire is hidden where thieves cannot break through and steal.

As for this Interpreter of the book and Inspirer of the ministry, He is to be had for asking. "If ye then, being evil, know how to give good gifts unto your children; how much more shall your heavenly Father give the Holy Spirit unto them that ask Him?" The very sublimity of simplicity! "Ye have not because ye ask not, or because ye ask amiss." Who can tell the result were every man resolutely, with all love and zeal, to pray for a double portion of the Spirit of God?

VII.

THE MINISTRY OF THE COMFORTER.

THE teaching of Jesus Christ respecting the ministry of the Holy Ghost is so peculiar as to raise the inquiry, Where was the Holy Ghost during the earthly ministry of the Son of man? Throughout the Old Testament there are the clearest testimonies as to His personal service in the ancient church, and yet Jesus Christ speaks of the descent of the Spirit as a new and special gift: for example—" I will pray the Father, and He shall give you another Comforter;" "the Comforter which is the Holy Ghost, whom the Father will send in My name;" " If I go not away, the Comforter will not come unto you." All this is strange, almost startling indeed, after reading the Old Testament. Where was the Spirit that had moved on the face of the waters, that had garnished the heavens, that had striven with antediluvian man, that had been poured out upon Israel? Was His ministry suspended? It may be suggested that the *fulness* of the Spirit had not been realised in the ancient church, which is undoubtedly true; yet though true it is insufficient to account for the treatment of His descent as a new visitation and benediction of God. The answer would seem rather to be, that the Holy Ghost was *in* Jesus Christ Himself, and could not be given to the church as a distinctively *Christian* gift until the first period of the incarnation had been consummated in the Ascension of the Son of man, —"If I go not away, the Comforter will not come unto you; but if I depart I will send Him unto you." Jesus Christ was *Himself* the New Testament: whatever happened aforetime was but preparative and typical: from His coming the world was to date its regeneration and the church was to reckon its birth. "In Him dwelt all the fulness of the godhead bodily;" and when the influence of that godhead was poured out upon the church, it came as if from the very heart of Christ, and was impregnated with all the elements which made up the mystery and beneficence of the Incarnation.

Jesus Christ gives a specific definition of the work of the Holy Ghost. That His work admitted of definition is itself a significant circumstance; and that the Son of Mary should have presumed to define it is a marvellous instance of His spiritual dominion, if it be not a covert yet daring blasphemy. At this point Jesus Christ seems to pass from the theatre within which He had dazzled the eyes of curiosity by the number and splendour of His miracles, and to enter into the holy of holies, the secret place of the Most High, and to seat Himself there as the donor of spiritual riches. It is a withdrawment (even if considered merely as a conception) which invests the Man with peculiar awe. He says He will do mightier works than ever; He will touch the life, the will, the love, of the world; He will ascend above principalities and powers, and subject all hosts and forces to spiritual control, invisible and almighty. Daring, truly, was this Son of Mary! The very idea of putting the spiritual above the material, and consequently of preferring a thought to a miracle, is the sublimity which seems narrowly to escape the charge of insanity. Let us now see with what simplicity and decisiveness Jesus Christ defines and limits the functions of the Holy Ghost :—

1. He shall not speak of Himself.
2. He shall glorify Me.
3. He will guide you into all truth.
4. He will show you things to come.

Besides the work of comfort within the church, He has a great work of *conviction* to do in the world at large : " When He is come, He will reprove the world of sin, and of righteousness, and of judgment." It will be convenient to study primarily the function of comfort which is assigned to the Holy Ghost, and then to discuss the ministry of conviction which He is to conduct in the hearts of all men.

1. "*He shall not speak of Himself.*" Why not? Because He would be speaking an unknown tongue. We cannot understand the purely spiritual. Whatever we know of it must come through mediums which lie nearer our own nature. The ministry of the Holy Ghost, therefore, is limited only because we ourselves are limited. The whole ministry of

God is an accommodation to human weakness. When He would teach *truth* He must needs set it in the form of *fact:* when He would show Himself, it must be through the tabernacle of our own flesh; when He would reveal heaven, He must illustrate His meaning by the fragments of light and beauty which are scattered on the higher side of our own inferior world. Everywhere, could we but see it, He has set up a ladder by which we may reach the skies. God would have talked to us without any intervention, but we could not have known the meaning of utterances which were not bounded and illustrated by things lower than ourselves; therefore hath He set His tabernacle in the sun, and made manifest His invisible kingdom and power by the wonderful works of His hands. We must begin with His hand, or we cannot know His heart. The doubting disciple said of Jesus Christ, that only the print of the nails and the wound of the spear could convince him of the identity of the Lord: and at best are we not all, by the pitifulness of the great mercy of God, allowed to begin with the divine hand instead of going at once into the sanctuary of the divine heart? The Holy Ghost does not speak of Himself, because there must be a common ground upon which He can invite the attention of mankind. Where or what is that common ground?

2. "*He shall glorify Me.*" The common ground is the work of the man Christ Jesus. What is meant by glorifying Christ Jesus? We know what

is meant by the sun glorifying the earth. Let us familiarise ourselves with that process, as it most completely represents the spiritual idea now under consideration. The sun does not *create* the landscape. The mountain and the sea are just as high and as wide in the grey cold dawn as at noonday. The sun adds nothing to the acreage of the meadows or the stature of the rocks. Yet how wonderful is the work of the sun! Look upon the earth in the pale dawn, and watch the ministry of the sun from hour to hour. How the light strikes the hill, burnishes the sea, flushes the trembling dew, and makes the blossoming bush burn as if with the presence of God! Everything was there before, yet how transfigured by the ministry of light! The commonest things are made almost beautiful by that benign service, and as for the higher forms of culture it would seem as if one more flash of sunshine would make them as the angels of God. In this respect, what light is to the earth, the Holy Ghost is to Jesus Christ. The Saviour is glorified by the Spirit. The work of the Spirit is revelation, not creation. He does not make Christ, He explains Him. The sun in doing all his wonderful work does not speak of himself; he will not, indeed, allow us to look at him. If we turn our eyes upon him the rebuke is prompt and intolerable: the language of that rebuke is—Look at the earth, not at me; see the opportunity for service and culture which is given you; do not intrude upon my tabernacle, but work within your own sphere while it is called day. The Holy Ghost, in like manner, does not speak of Himself. He will not answer all our inquiries respecting His personality. We cannot venture with impunity beyond a well-defined line. To the very last men will inquire, What is the Holy Ghost? showing that all attempts at exhaustive definition have ended in failure and disappointment. Yet whilst He Himself is the eternal secret, His work is open and glorious. His text is Christ. From that theme He never strays. To the individual consciousness He reveals the mystery of the beauty of Christ. The Christian student sees a Christ which he did not see twenty years ago,—the same, yet not the same; larger, grander, tenderer, every day; a new music in His speech, an ampler sufficiency in His grace; a deeper humiliation in His cradle; a keener agony in His cross. This increasing revelation is the work of the Holy Ghost, and is the fulfilment of Jesus Christ's own promise. That the Son of Mary should have claimed the Holy Ghost as His interpreter! Observe this as an incidental contribution towards the completeness and harmony of the mystery that is embodied in Christ Jesus. Regarded in this light it is very wonderful. The beginning and the end are the same,—equal in mystery, in condescension, in solemn grandeur. Thus: "That which is conceived in her is of the Holy Ghost,"—this is the *beginning;* "He shall not speak of Himself, He shall glorify Me;"—this is the *end:* are the tones discordant? The *incarnation* of the Son of God was the work of the Holy Ghost; how natural that the *explanation* of the Son of God should be the work of the same minister! As He was before the visible Christ, so He was to be after Him, and thus the whole mystery never passed from His own control.

The life of the Son of man, as written in the gospels, *needs* to be glorified! He was despised and rejected of men, a man of sorrows and acquainted with grief: He had not where to lay His head: He gave His back to the smiters, and His cheeks to them that plucked off the hair: He made Himself of no reputation; He humbled Himself and became obedient unto death, even the death of the cross: He was rich, yet for our sakes He became poor: upon all this chasm, so deep, so grim, we need a light above the brightness of the sun. When that light comes, the root out of a dry ground will be as the flower of Jesse and the plant of renown, and the face marred more than any man's will be fairest among ten thousand and altogether lovely. Such is the wizardry of light!

This claim to be glorified by the Holy Ghost is without precedent in human history. That is a fact which ought to have some value attached to it. It is the kind of claim which could be tested promptly and thoroughly by the consciousness of Christianised mankind, and presumptively, on that very account, the kind of claim which an impostor would have avoided. Besides, for such a man, or for any man indeed, to have had such an idea is most marvellous. Had He merely committed His case to the care of time and the judgment of posterity, He would have taken the course of ordinary sagacity; but instead of the general appeal which is commonly made to the arbitrament of God and good men, He expressly stated that the Holy Ghost would glorify His person and complete His mediation on the earth. The work of the Holy Ghost was to be infinitely more than a work of mere explanation: it was to move forward to the very point of glory, even the glory which the Son of Man had with His Father before the world began. This statement came from the lips of Jesus Christ Himself, and therefore it leaves Him a blasphemer without excuse if He was merely a virtuous and courageous teacher. On the other hand, taking our Lord's word as true, there is now going forward in human thinking a spiritual process which is identified with no other name than His own, and which will culminate in splendour ineffable and eternal. The prayer of our Lord to be "glorified" is peculiarly affecting: "I have glorified Thee . . . now, O Father, glorify Thou Me;"—"glorify Thy Son," as if the full bitterness of His humiliation had been realised, and He could defer the resumption of His glory no longer. He distinctly speaks of it as a resumption and not as an unknown experience:—"Glorify Me with Thine own self with the glory which I had with Thee before the world was." A fierce hunger seized His heart, a home-yearning of which every child knows something.

Having spoken of the ministry of the Holy Ghost in relation to Himself, our Lord proceeds to speak of it in relation to His disciples :—

3. "*He will guide you into all truth.*" Not, "He will add to the number of miracles which you have seen at My hands," but "He will guide you into all truth :" "I am the Truth ; He will glorify Me ; He will show you all My riches." Our Lord Himself did not guide His disciples into all truth, nor have men even yet been so far guided ; they are travelling the upward road, but the summits are still beyond. Truth is an infinite quantity. At first it may seem to be compassable, but it recedes as it is approached ; yet it throws the warm rays of promise upon every honest and loving pilgrim to its shrine. The highest grace of manhood is the truth-loving spirit : it purifies like fire ; it throws a strange and holy majesty upon life, yet makes men tender and charitable. Our Lord's expression is comprehensive,—"into all truth ;" not only into truth that is distinctively theological, but into all truth, scientific, political, social, religious. Is truth not larger than the formal church ? Is not the physicist under the tuition of the Spirit as well as the theologian ? Our Lord does not divide men into hostile tribes ; He does not open one department of truth and refuse the key of others. His is a universal speech,—He speaks of "truth" as indivisible and complete, and of the Spirit as the one Guide. It is not to be supposed that any *one man* is to be

guided into all truth. Some possessions are put into the custody of the whole race. Paul did not claim to have known truth in its entirety; nor did Peter; nor did James. No single star holds all the light. No single flower is endowed with all the beauty. What man is there who knows all things? It is proverbial that the wisest men are the humblest, and that those who have seen the fullest disclosures of truth are assured that the supreme glory is yet concealed. Has not every honest student some portion of truth that is in a sense his own? Does not every eye see at least a tint which no other vision has seen so clearly as itself? It is important to consider these questionings well, because they point towards the mutual trust and the mutual honour without which society would be disorganized and debased. Men make up *Man*, churches make up the *Church*, truths make up *Truth*, and it is only by a complete combination of the parts that the majesty and lustre of the whole can be secured.

It should be observed that in this connection the Holy Ghost is designated by our Lord as "the Spirit of truth" (τὸ Πνεῦμα τῆς ἀληθείας), and *as such* He is to "guide into all truth" (πᾶσαν τὴν ἀλήθειαν) those who are under His tuition. Observe the quantity—"ALL TRUTH:" observe the method—"He will guide." The quantity is unlimited; the method assumes consent and co-operation on the part of man. A reference to Old Testament history will throw some light upon the scope of the Spirit's ministry, and show how grave is the error which limits it to thinking and service which are supposed to be purely theological. It may indeed (and we believe it will) show that "theology" is actually the all-inclusive term, holding within its meaning all the highest aspects and suggestions both of speculative and practical science. The theologian is entitled to claim astronomy, geology, botany, agriculture, and chemistry, as sections of theology. If he trifle with this claim he will not only surrender his best weapon as a controversialist, but mistake brethren and friends for rivals and enemies.

Can anything be farther from theology, as popularly understood, than stone-cutting or wood-carving? Can any two spheres be much more widely sundered than those of the preacher of the gospel and the artificer in iron and brass? Apparently not. But the biblical testimony sets the inquiry at rest: "I have called Bezaleel, and I have filled him with the Spirit of God, in wisdom, and in understanding, and in knowledge, and in all manner of workmanship, to devise cunning works, to work in gold, and in silver, and in brass, and in cutting of stones, to set them, and in carving of timber, to work in all manner of workmanship" (Exod. xxxi. 2–5). Bezaleel was an inspired theologian. More than this, and apparently still farther away from the theological line :—"I have created the smith that bloweth the coals in the fire, and that bringeth forth an instrument for his work." Then, intermediately at least, may stand the agriculturist, of whose treatment of the earth is said :—" This also cometh forth from the Lord of hosts, who is wonderful in counsel and excellent in working." The rulers and soldiers of Israel were qualified for their work by the Spirit of the Lord. "The Spirit of the Lord came upon Othniel, and he judged Israel and went out to war." The ministration of the Spirit is various: by it Moses was made wise, Bezaleel was made skilful, and Samson was made strong. "All these worketh that one and the selfsame Spirit, dividing to every man severally as He will" (1 Cor. xii. 11). Wonderful is this inclusiveness of the Spirit's work. " Hic Spiritus Sanctus omnium viventum anima, ita largitate sua se omnibus abundanter infundit, ut habeant omnia rationabilia et irrationabilia secundum genus suum ex eo quod sunt et quod in suo ordine suæ naturæ competentia agunt." A thorough persuasion of this inclusiveness will put an end to the needless hostility between what is distinctively known as science on the one hand and theology on the other. All things are theological primarily and ultimately, though certain intermediate points in their processes and relationships may seem to be without the higher light. There is a common teacher—"the Spirit of truth;" there is a common end—"all truth;" there should be a common bond —mutual trust.

But what if the fact of the Spirit's ministry be denied on the one hand? Denial proves nothing against the case as it is now put. God works even where He is unknown. There are truths which lie below our very consciousness. Men have denied not only the work of God, but the very existence of God, yet their denial has not destroyed the divine supremacy. "He maketh His sun to rise on the evil and on the good, and sendeth rain on the just and on the unjust,"—and this not only in a material but in a spiritual sense; He has servants who have signed no covenant, and messengers who do His errands in their own name. Nor does He blight them for their ingratitude, or put them to open shame,—"He is kind unto the unthankful and the evil," and not willing that any should perish. The worshippers of Intellect may not know that they are worshippers of God under another name. Our spirit may not be equal to our work: we may profane the name of God in the very act of building a cathedral for His praise. We may, then, venture to speak a word of caution to the men who deny the ministry of the Holy Ghost, and in doing so to suggest whether after all there may not be mysteries in their life which they have not altogether explored and comprehended. They will not ruthlessly resist the hand that would bring them into the inner sanctuary on whose outer walls they have wrought so much exquisite and invaluable decoration.

Upon the church itself this promise of guidance into all truth should exert a healthful influence, especially in the direction of enlarging and refining its charity. The danger is that the church should be content with a limited range of dogma and purpose when it is invited to the mastery and enjoyment of a kingdom that cannot be measured. The church should not be anxious about uniformity of stature and countenance, when God has made it so evident that He Himself delights in variety and contrast. Men of the most inquisitive and even sceptical mind should be encouraged by the church to lead the van of inquiry, and subject every doctrine and every spirit to a cross-examination which to minds of an opposite type may become wearisome and even vexatious. The church should extend to its adventurous sons who go out to shores far away and to lands unmapped and unclaimed, the most ardent and loving recognition. Even when they return with hopes unfulfilled and with banners torn by angry winds, proving the abortiveness of their chivalry or the mistake of their method, they should be hailed with a still tenderer love. The pain in their own hearts is keen enough. In secrecy they have known the very bitterness of death. To such men the promise of being guided into all truth becomes a personal torture. They yearn for its fulfilment: they are straitened until it be accomplished. Other men can wait, but their waiting is a grace rather than a virtue. Enthusiasm is unknown by them. Temperamentally they know nothing about time; and there is no future to them because they have no idea of the suspense and occasional anguish of expectation. Such men are sure to have a kind of advantage over those who are made impatient by a great promise, because, having themselves risked nothing, they may thoughtlessly indulge self-felicitation at the expense of men whose shoe latchets they are not worthy to unloose. Martyrdom thus comes without the tragic surroundings which bring with them their own alleviation : it is inward agony, often unconfessed, but terrible as the pains of hell. Little enough is known about such martyrdoms, and perhaps the less the better, because theirs is a suffering which would be aggravated by the very touch of unsympathetic hands.

4. "*He will show you things to come.*" The word translated "He will show" is ἀναγγελεῖ, He will announce to you; the word in the Vulgate is *annunciabit*. Such a promise would seem to imply that secret communications about the future will be made to the church; yet this construction of the promise must be admitted with extreme caution, if admitted at all, because of the dangerous uses to which it may be put. Men would in some cases mistake prejudices and frenzies for inspiration, and in others they would inflict needless trouble upon themselves and upon society at large. Limited to the immediate hearers of our Lord, of course the promise is exhausted and the results are to some extent recorded in apostolic history; but it cannot be so limited without impairing the worth of the promise by taking it away from the category of assurances which are to enrich and stimulate the church through all time. Merely to "show things to come" in the sense of prevision is a blessing greater in appearance than in reality; but *to prepare the mind*

for things to come—to show the mind how to deal with new and perplexing circumstances—to give the perception which sees God everywhere and the affection which thankfully accepts His discipline—is an advantage which cannot be expressed in human terms. Whatever the promised "announcement" may include, it must involve this supernatural preparedness of mind and heart or it will merely excite and bewilder the church.

That the Holy Spirit did "show things to come" in a prophetic sense is proved by instances circumstantially reported in the New Testament: for example,—" The Holy Ghost witnesseth in every city, saying that bonds and afflictions abide me;" " Agabus took Paul's girdle and bound his own hands and feet, and said, Thus saith the Holy Ghost, So shall the Jews at Jerusalem bind the man that owneth this girdle, and shall deliver him into the hands of the Gentiles ;" " Now the Spirit speaketh expressly, that in the latter times some shall depart from the faith, giving heed to seducing spirits, and to doctrines of devils." In one case this is purely personal; in the other it is almost vague. Seeing, however, that the Comforter is to abide with the church "for ever," and seeing that as a matter of fact the church is not gifted with prevision, we are thrown back upon the gracious and all-sufficient assurance, that whatever may come, and with what violence soever its coming may be attended, the church will be prepared to withstand every shock and surmount every difficulty.

Out of this assurance comes rest; the future is no longer a trouble; the clouds that lie upon the remote horizon will be scattered by the brightness of the image of God.

We have thus pointed out four aspects of the ministry of the Holy Ghost, which may be described as *universal*. There is a fifth aspect which belonged to the disciples alone, which is yet of supreme consequence to ourselves: "He shall bring all things to your remembrance, whatsoever I have said unto you." There is an inspiration of memory. Readers of the gospels must have been surprised by the minuteness of recollection which is shown in their pages. Conversations are reported; little turns of dialogue which seem to be merely artistic are not omitted; records of occasions on which the disciples were actually not present, and of which they could only have heard from the lips of the Lord himself, are presented with much particularity and vividness: how, then, was this done, and especially done by men who certainly were not conspicuous for the kind of learning which is needful for the making of literary statements? The explanation of this artless art, and this tenacious memory, is in the promise of our Lord—"He shall bring all things to your remembrance, whatsoever I have said unto you: you shall live it all over again: the scene of which I have been the centre shall be set before you in vivid detail, and you shall be so taught how to gather up the fragments that nothing of all its minuteness shall be lost."

VIII.

THE CONVICTIVE WORK OF THE HOLY GHOST.

THERE was a tone of sorrow in the voice of our Lord when He said that the Spirit of truth " will reprove the world of sin because it believeth not on Me." Our Lord knew that viewed outwardly, as a question of station or numbers, His personal ministry upon the earth had been a failure, yet it was to be proved by another, whom He Himself would send, that the failure was due to the very sublimity of His character. A character like His was not to be compassed and honoured by the public mind in three short years. With less grandeur He might have drawn around Himself a wider homage; or with a grandeur undegraded by Nazarene associations He might have carried that homage to the very point of superstition, and so have wielded an influence the more commanding from its being spectral and mysterious. But to be just what He was—divine yet human—the supreme anomaly and contradiction in the whole range of history—proved the stumbling-block and rock of offence against which His contemporaries bruised themselves by their obstinacy and unbelief. In withdrawing from the world He said that His case would be completed by the ministry of the Holy Ghost, who would so operate upon the moral nature of mankind as to establish a perfect righteousness and an incorruptible judgment, and in so doing would show the absolute need of Himself as Mediator and Saviour. This would seem to be the purport of the words "because they believe not on Me." The world has never cared to own its need of the Son of man. He has always been a stranger, viewed with suspicion and listened to with reluctance. He came unto His own, and His own received Him not; He was despised and rejected of men, a man of sorrows and acquainted with grief, and we hid as it were our faces from Him. The world has never known exactly what to do with this stranger in the house, it has approached Him, and recoiled from Him : it has owned Him, and discarded Him in a breath ; it has hailed Him as king, and crucified Him with thieves ; He has been at once the spell and the dread of all who have known Him. He was aware of this, and said in effect :—You will not come unto Me ; you are determined to go to the Father through some other way ; I cannot remain longer in the body, but I will send the Spirit of truth, and when He is come He will convince you of sin because ye believe not on Me. To this point we shall come again, after some analysis and reasoning.

To convince the world of sin is much more than to convince the world of crime. The world is satisfied with rough definitions, and therefore it has unhappily used the words "crime" and "sin" as equivalent and interchangeable terms. In the higher reasoning this is a fatal error. There may be sin where there is no crime, but wherever there is crime there is sin to account for it. Society is organized to defend itself against crime, yet every member of it is guilty of sin. This has to be made clear by the Holy Ghost, and has already in a measure been made clear to every one of us. Thus: Society condemns *murder;* so in his reasoning with us the Holy Ghost begins with this admission, and proceeds to say—You condemn murder, but this is merely a gross and vulgar morality, little better, indeed, than selfishness stimulated by fear; you must find out how murder begins,—it begins in unholy *anger;* that anger may never have spoken one word or shown one sign of impatience, yet by so much as you have given way to it in the secrecy of your inmost heart you are guilty of murder in the sight of God! It required a *Ghost* to teach us that. We had no moral instrument of our own fine enough and keen enough to make so delicate a distinction; we could only get so far as to make some difference between murder and manslaughter, or between murder with extenuating circumstances and murder without them. There society paused, being unable to go further; and precisely *there* the Spirit began His work, taking the crime to pieces, tracing it back to its origin, and finding that origin in a secret and perhaps long-hidden excitement of the heart, and having found it, the Spirit said—*This* is the murder;

the outward deed was a social outrage, an odious and revolting vulgarity; *this* movement of hatred in the heart, this unbridled passion, is the murder. "Whosoever hateth his brother is a murderer." Thus we are brought to subtler definitions than have hitherto satisfied our rude morality, and the measure of our assent is the measure of our self-conviction. Those of us who have walked up and down in society as blameless men suddenly find ourselves in the presence of a new law of judgment, and are compelled to own that if murder is traceable into the region of motive, feeling, latent or unconfessed abhorrence of a man, it is more than possible that we ourselves may be murderers in the sight of God. To accept such a doctrine is to invest life with a most solemn and tragic grandeur, and is to do something further which will appear as the analysis proceeds.

Society has made murder penal, but it has not been able to set *falsehood* amongst the crimes which are to be punished by the magistrate. By society itself falsehood is treated more spiritually than murder; so we come into a higher region of the operation of the Holy Spirit. We ourselves make further admissions in this case than we were prepared to make in the other. We own, for example, that a man may *act* a lie as well as *tell* one: that he may use words with two meanings: that he may guard himself and mislead others by mental reservations. These are great admissions, far more spiritual, it will be observed, than were made in the case of murder. What more can the Holy Ghost Himself do? It is not indeed needful that more be done if the object be merely to secure self-conviction. Yet more is possible. The Holy Ghost says that a form of words may be true, and yet it may express a lie! A conversation may be reported *verbatim et literatim*, yet, by a mere change of tone, by the omission of a facial expression, by a skilful variation of pause or emphasis, the report may be a falsehood from beginning to end. Farther and deeper still, a man may be false to *himself*. He may actually have treated himself so dishonestly as to have suspended or destroyed the very power by which he knows right from wrong. His conscience is "seared as with a hot iron," and human speech has lost all value and use as a moral medium. Some men are spoken of as "given over to believe a lie;" that is to say, the natural conscience itself, the primary element of responsible life, is dispossessed of its proper function, and belief has become an instrument of self-delusion. Under such circumstances the man is something more than a *liar*, he himself is actually a *lie!* When a man is guilty of lying there may be some hope of his restoration because of certain counterbalancing virtues on other sides of his character; but when the man *himself* is a living lie, the whole nature is in so false a condition as to leave no hope of penitence and recovery.

Under such difficulties who but the Spirit of God can undertake the work of convincing the heart of sin? There must be a process in a heart so lost, which can only be typified by the most terrible displays of power which take place in the material world,—eruption, and earthquake, and lightnings like the glance of God.

But the process becomes still more spiritual. Murder and falsehood are at all events nominally condemned by every man who has any sense of social decency; but what of virtues which are praised as the very security and crown of human society? The Spirit of God seeth not as man seeth; for man looketh on the outward appearance, but the Lord looketh on the heart. The form of godliness is to be distinguished from its power. An illustration taken from every-day life will help us to see the meaning of this. Take an act of almsgiving, and let it be outwardly the choicest specimen of its class: the gift is large, most timely in its presentation, and most deservedly bestowed; many a heart was made glad by the donation, and many an anxiety was set at rest; the gift was given with such cordiality too: the tone of the giver was cheerful, and gladdening to all who heard it; altogether the charity was marked by every desirable beauty. Beyond this point society does not carry its judgment,— man looketh on the outward appearance. Where man ends, the all-searching Spirit begins: He holds the candle of the Lord over the secret places of the heart; he tries the motives of the soul by the fires of the supreme judgment; and having done so, He says in effect to the applauded man, —" Your love went not with your gift; had you been left wholly to the motion of your own will you never would have given it; it was an oblation to your own vanity; it was a bribe by which you bought reputation and goodstanding amongst men; it was not given to the poor, it was given to *yourself.*" This conviction may be made so clear to a man, and brought to bear upon him with such urgency, as to cause him the most painful suffering at the very time when human applause is most general and vehement. Here, then, is the point of departure from such cases as murder and falsehood, the point of excellent appearance where the informing spirit is vicious and detestable.

We are now upon the line every point of which adds to our knowledge of spiritual realities as distinguished from formal facts. How near, for example, are we to the point which shows that prayer itself may be a lie! We turned from murder with disgust, and from falsehood with a sense of shame, but what of the prayers so much approved for every charm of expression and tone? May our *religion* be the chief of our immoralities? You prayed in the house of your friend, and made your prayer the medium of personal compliment to his supposed excellences and deserts; you praised the creature to the Creator, making mention of his virtues, but not daring to hint at his sins; with many a complimentary reference you lingered upon the case of the master, but you dismissed the servants in one hurried and shallow sentence: would you have *so* prayed for the man if he had not been listening to you? Answer that question distinctly. Would you have called him God's "*dear servant*" if he had been a mile away? Would you have prayed *at all* if you could decorously have escaped the duty? Not only does the Holy Ghost ask these questions, He compels you to answer them to your shame, nor does He cease His piercing and destructive ministry until you own that you have turned your religion into a crime and uttered blasphemy at the very gate of heaven. So, the period of mere definition is passed, and the time of direct and irresistible application has come.

More: even if we are unassailable at any of the great points now indicated—crime, falsehood, selfishness, impious prayer—yet there is another kingdom wherein the divine judgment is set up, the kingdom of unuttered desire and thought. Every man has two lives—the life of motive, and the life of behaviour, into the first of which none can enter but the Spirit of spirits. "He knoweth our thought afar off," before it is a complete thought, when it is too dim an outline to have any relation to the uses of human speech, and before it leaves the shadows of its inception He declares its quality and metes to it the judgment of righteousness. So solemn is life, so perilous, so painful! Through your heart there shot a desire which scorched you, though no human eye will ever see the blister which it left, and the very memory of that desire will make you dumb whilst others sing; it will sting you, humble you, and make a coward of you all your days. Into your mind there came what was only *the hint of a thought*, yet it struck you like a thunderbolt, so evil did it seem to be even in its incompleteness! These are the visitations which, when rightly understood, show a man that there is something worse than crime, and make him impatient with the deceitful comforters who would "heal his hurt slightly."

Thus we come back to the point with which we started, viz., "The Spirit of truth will convince the world of sin,—of sin because they believe not on Me." The Holy Ghost will so vividly and thoroughly show the nature of sin, that those who thought themselves the best examples of human society will be afflicted with the keenest compunction because of what they know themselves to be in the presence of God. It will no longer be a question of comparison as between one class and another, or between one man and another; the judgment will lie wholly between man and God, and every heart will see itself as if it were the only heart in all the universe. This personal consciousness is to be so vivid and intense as to become painful; a man will see himself as he never saw himself before, and feel the burden of life with a new and intolerable oppression. His moral sense will be so purified and perfected that he will feel even an evil *thought* to be an unpardonable sin; and so humbled will he be by finding that even his best deeds are tainted, and that his very prayers are but a refinement of impiety, that all strength will go out of him and all self-hope will expire. Can he in that moment of despair turn to others for help? No; because they are in the agonies of the same experience, groaning because of a common paralysis and helplessness. The hour is too solemn to admit of trifling by comparing one degree of sin with another; there is no question of degrees; whatever difference there may be in the mere *accidents* of crime, under all surfaces there is the terrible fact that every heart has broken away from the rule of the Divine King. What then? When the conviction is so keen and relentless, when every concealing shadow is chased from the inmost life by the fierce light of infinite purity, the heart will begin to know that in turning away from Jesus Christ, that strange and tormenting middle quantity by which it was so fretted in the days of its own haughtiness and self-sufficiency, it turned from the Son of God, the only mediator of the covenant of peace, and then the agony will be like the very pains of hell. This is the conviction of sin which the Spirit of God is to work in hearts which have not believed in the Saviour of the world. Jesus Christ cannot be understood until sin is understood. So long as sin is regarded from a merely social point of view, the cross of Christ must appear to be an exaggeration,—justice assuming a sensational attitude. Why do with blood a work which could be done as well with water? Why sacrifice a man when the blood of a beast would answer every purpose? These inquiries are legitimate so long as *sin* is underrated or misunderstood, but the moment that sin is seen under the illumination of infinite holiness, the cross of Christ alone is equal to the tragic awe and appalling horror of the situation. The first clear view which any man gets of the sinfulness of sin marks the crisis of his life. From that time he elects his destiny. It is questionable whether there can be any repetition of that view, so intense, so intolerable, is the light. Jesus Christ, then, would seem to say, in the words now under discussion, something to this effect :—" You do not understand Me now; you think you can do without a mediator between yourselves and God; so little do you know of sin as God knows it, that you suppose yourselves equal to every occasion which can arise in working out all the dispensations of divine righteousness; so must it be for a little while, but not for ever; when the Spirit of truth is come He will give you such views of the sinfulness of sin, and show you so clearly the true condition of your own hearts, that under His ministry you will cry out for mediation, and remember in the anguish of your pain that you would not come unto *Me* that you might have life."

In the light of this exposition we may see the way clear to some practical conclusions.

1. All attempts to establish a satisfactory life on the basis of what is commonly known as morality, must be given up. Morality has become one of the fine arts. It is an attitude, a fine balancing of calculations, a tacit understanding with evil powers, at best but an armed neutrality. The surface of society is not ill-conditioned; its politeness was never so polished; its laws of giving and taking were never so admirably codified. This social behaviour is only the fit expression of individual virtues which conspicuously abound, and which are properly used as bonds of intercourse in carrying on the business of daily life. But what if morality be only an art,—the most cunning and profitable of tricks? What if the partitions which we call our "rights" be saved from destruction merely because it pays better to repress the fire of passion than to give it free course? This is not said cynically, but rather with bitterness of sorrow. The Holy Ghost teaches that we cannot be right with one another until we are right with *God*. He says we must be *religious* before we can be profoundly and truly *moral*. By being religious the Holy Ghost means that the human will must be under the control of the will of God; and it is precisely at this point that a great controversy arises between the human and divine. By so much as a man subtracts anything from the sovereignty of God's control, and transfers it to himself, he assumes that it is possible to create a satisfactory morality without divine help. The Holy Ghost says, "No; you must be

born again—you must come into thorough newness of life, and not into a mere readjustment of habits and behaviour—you must die unto yourself, that you may live unto God." His work is thus fundamental. He will not attempt to do anything that is merely on the outside; He says that the very nature of man must be born again, and that until regeneration takes place, so-called "morality" is but a well-contrived device of selfishness. This is clearly a magnificent basis of life, supplying as it does eternal guarantees of purity and nobleness. In the absence of such a basis there can be no dependence upon the loudest professions of confidence and friendship; they must be taken for what they are worth, as very pleasant to the outward ear, but as liable to be blown away by the first cross wind which assails our popularity. On the other hand, where the heart has been born again, and as a consequence draws all the considerations which govern it immediately from the will of God, there must be incorruptible truth and invincible constancy. If we plead that when thrown entirely on our own resources we can develop a very beautiful life, the Holy Ghost says, " No ; your results are *artificial;* they express study and contrivance on your part; they are rather a group of negations which attest a more or less severe discipline, they are not the natural outcome of a moral condition which cannot be changed by outward circumstances ; you make clean the outside of the cup and platter, but the inside is full of rottenness and death."

So the very morality which we boast may be, as already said, the last aggravation of our wickedness. Recollect how severe Jesus Christ was with the "righteous" men of His day; He never spared them; He never had one approving word for them; when they gathered up their ceremonial skirts and ran away from the path of the "sinner," He damned them with infinite condemnation as hypocrites, devourers, and whited sepulchres. This ministry of His is continued by the Holy Ghost,—"He shall take of Mine, and shall show it unto you,"—and the ministry thus continued cannot cease until man throws down his artificial morality as a burden and a lie.

2. All hopes founded upon what are thought to be different degrees of sin must be abandoned. There are, of course, different degrees of crime, but the question does not turn upon crime at all. The murderer is undoubtedly a greater criminal than the pilferer; but the murderer is *something more* than a murderer, and the pilferer than a pilferer. The murder and the theft are accidental forms, nothing more. For all the purposes of criminal law it may be sufficient to classify men according to the mere accidents of their mischievous behaviour, so that punishment may be assigned with some degree of proportion to the shock which public feeling has sustained; but another standard must be set up when the offence is between man and God. "Would you send a murderer and a

speculative sceptic to the same hell?" it may be asked. But stop! It is *not* the murderer, accidentally as such, that is sent to hell, nor the speculative sceptic, accidentally as such, that is shut out of heaven. The question is one of *death* not of *disease*, of the heart not of the hand. According to the teaching of the Holy Ghost it may be (even considering the question as one of degrees) that the heart through which has passed an unholy desire may be in a worse condition than the heart whose momentary passion has vented itself in murderous vengeance. There is an iniquity which is rolled under the tongue as a sweet morsel, a secret enjoyment of sin; and there are also moments in which is revealed to the soul a horrible *possibility* of sin where such possibility was least suspected, a revelation known only to the soul because too dreadful to be put into words and communicated to a stranger. The first time, in our sunny youth, we realised this awful possibility, can it ever be forgotten? It was only a shadow that swept over the heart, not a thing for words at all, yet the very memory of it chills us like the touch of death. Or it was a demand of the heart made at a time of festivity, it came upon us without warning, it made the heart bound as if it had been secretly touched with fire,—in that moment we saw that our life is being daily spent on the edge of an abyss. Left to ourselves as a community of men, we can set up comparisons and contrasts, and actually shudder at enormities which secure for themselves a bad eminence; but introduced into the presence of God, and searched by the Holy Ghost, we feel that a look may be blasphemy and that unkindness may be cruel as murder. The thing to be understood is that sin is spiritual, and that it is to be judged spiritually, without reference to the vulgarity or noise which may make it socially noticeable.

3. Under such realisation of sin the work of Jesus Christ is seen in its true light. On this point some remarks have just been offered, but we may recur to it as the chief point in the discussion. Here it is emphatically true that " they that be whole need not a physician but they that are sick." The analogy will help us to higher truths. A man who has never known the agony of pain or the prostration of weakness may feel himself at liberty to treat very lightly the claims of men who follow the profession of medicine. From his own point of view he may feel himself entitled to sneer at such men and may plead his personal robustness as an argument against their pretensions. He may, if of a narrow and obstinate nature, even go so far as to contend that other people might all be strong as he is, and consequently to withdraw his sympathy from them. But let that boastful and austere man awake to the fact that in his own body there is a slowly developing disease, painless in its early stages, but surely advancing upon his very life; let him come to the *conviction* that at any moment his pulse may

cease, and instantly his attitude towards the medical profession may be totally changed. A new *conviction* has given him a new feeling and compelled him towards a new policy. Ask him the reason of the change, so complete and striking, which he has undergone, and at once he will justify himself by his new consciousness. Jesus Christ makes use of this very experience to throw light upon His own ministry: "I am not come to call the righteous, but sinners to repentance;" "They that be whole need not a physician, but they that are sick." Everything, therefore, is made to depend upon *conviction*. Where there is no conviction there will be no pressure of necessity. Where there is no thirst, who cares for the fountain; but in the desert, under an intolerable sun, who can calculate the value of a cup of cold water? Jesus Christ awaits the demands of spiritual necessity. He knows that the Holy Ghost will so torment the heart with a sense of sin as to compel the sufferer to pray for mercy, and at that point of anguish He will show Himself to be the Saviour of the world. Jesus Christ cannot work in the absence of *conviction*. When the physician lays his finger upon the strong man's pulse, the strong man smilingly anticipates an exclamation of surprise and congratulation; but when the pulse of the dying man is felt, it is amidst the silence of anxiety and fear. Tell the Pharisee that Jesus Christ died for him, and the man is shocked; but tell the sinner who knows the torment of remorse that the Son of God died to save him, and the statement becomes " the glorious gospel of the blessed God." Through his remorse he sees what he never could have seen through his philosophy. For years he may have vainly studied the Cross as a controversialist, but in a moment he saw all its meaning when his heart was broken because of his sin. In the light of these reflections we may see how far removed from the region of mere controversy is such a doctrine as the atonement. It does not express a controversial result, so how can it be reached by controversial means? It came out of *feeling*—that is, out of the tender pity and love of God—and cannot therefore be understood but by the aid of feeling. The logician is out of his beat here. The broken heart will see farther than the keenest intellect. It is only for a moment now and then that any man really and truly sees *himself*, and such moments are times, not of equable and serene complacency, but of intense excitement and passion,—times of madness which the world cannot understand : how, then, can a being who can see *himself* only now and then, see *God* always, and explain in easy words the sorrow and the grace of the Eternal? No man could bear the strain of continual conviction of sin. It kills him, that he may be made alive again by the Spirit, and ever afterwards he speaks of it as a memory rather than as a current experience. The agony upon the cross was soon past, and it could come again no more. It is so with this *conviction* which reveals the cross : however long the preparation, it is but momentary in the final

The Convictive Work of the Holy Ghost.

pain, yet long enough to show sin, God, and salvation. This being so, the atonement cannot be dealt with in coolness and patience, like a problem which appeals but to one set of faculties, it must be seen *at once*, through the agony of broken-heartedness, or it can never be seen at all. Though soon seen it is never forgotten. It rules the life evermore. Fruits of the Spirit will attest by noble confirmation the reality of the Spirit's ministry. The anguish of the birth is forgotten so soon as the man is born, but the man has to live under discipline and to be the willing and grateful scholar of the Spirit to whom he owes HIMSELF.

The conviction of sin is to be accompanied by the conviction of righteousness and the conviction of judgment,—*accompanied by*, rather than *followed*, for these great spiritual quickenings and movements would often seem to involve many simultaneous experiences which are only in *appearance* separated by intervals of time. It may be taken that the convictive work of the Holy Spirit is one great act, describable, however, by a threefold effect, and that such work is initiated *at once* in all its complexity. Commentators have not found it easy to give a clear and satisfactory rendering of our Lord's words upon this subject, nor are we bold enough to hope that we can simplify what they have found it so difficult to explain. The meaning of the words would seem to be substantially this; The world has its own notion of wrong-doing; the world has its own notion of propriety, or justice as between man and man; the world has its own notion of moral differences, of right and wrong, of good and bad,—but when the Spirit is come, He will seize upon all these notions, and with convincing refutation will show them to be only names, to be superficial, shallow, altogether inadequate, fallacious, and misleading; having done this negative work, He will proceed to His affirmative mission, and in doing so He will replace the word "wrong-doing" with the word *sin*, the word "propriety" with the word *righteousness*, and the word "differences" with the word *judgment;* He will show the spiritual essence and reality, of which the world has but a dim and imperfect notion; He will throw the world into discontentment with all its own moral theories, and bring it to see that it has been mistaking appearances for realities; thus, negatively and positively, the Spirit will carry out a profound and vital work of spiritual conviction. But the point which is to be specially observed is that the convictive mission of the Holy Ghost *is entirely identified with the name and ministry of Jesus Christ.* The conviction, regarded simply as the result of spiritual argument, might have been accomplished in the very first ages of human history; it must, therefore, be something more than an intellectual conviction, and for its accomplishment it must have required every aid that is implied in the gift of the Son of God as the minister of salvation. Mark the statement and the reason: The Comforter will convince the world of sin—*because they believe not on Me;* the Comforter will convince the world of righteousness—*because I go to the Father;* the Comforter will convince the world of judgment—because the prince of this world is judged (is cast out) for, for this purpose was I manifested that I might destroy the works of the devil. In the light of this connection the whole passage may be treated in free paraphrase thus: When the Comforter is come He will convincingly refute the world's theory of wrong-doing by showing God's idea of sin as proved by the shedding of My blood, which blood the world has trampled under foot and accounted an unholy thing; in future when men want to know what sin really is (not merely in its accidental expression but in its essence) they will see God's revelation and estimate of it in My cross. When the Comforter is come He will convincingly refute the world's theory of righteousness, which relates wholly to appearances, and is more or less a successful adaptation of expedients, and this He will do by taking up and continuing My work which I now lay down that I may go to My father. I have spoken the word, I have also shown the example; now a great spiritual process must set in, and My outward and visible work must receive spiritual illumination and exposition. When the Comforter is come He will convincingly refute the world's theory of judgment, which is founded upon the most obvious differences only, and has no reference to those deep spiritual elements and facts which underlie and account for all human conduct; He will show the meaning of My temptation, the purport of My answers in the wilderness, and the discriminations with which I startled the men of My day—such as preferring the publican to the Pharisee, and the mites of the widow to the gold of Dives: all this He will do, and then will be seen that My work is not the broken column which it now appears to be, not a failure, not a humiliating overthrow, but the beginning of a kingdom fair as the sun and everlasting as the heavens.

This conviction is being wrought out by many instrumentalities; as, for example, by the wise exposition of the living Word; by loyal obedience to the statutes and ordinances of Jesus Christ; by holy and unblamable lives, whereby ungodly men are silently rebuked and instructed; by startling developments of spiritual power by which the people are now sobered by great fear and anon made glad with sure and exultant hope; by good coming out of evil; by sudden and terrible reproofs of powers haughty and defiant in their self-sufficiency; by the honour of methods and plans thought to be feeble and useless; —in all these ways, and in others many and wonderful, a great work of spiritual conviction is proceeding in society, and is showing itself in the higher legislation and the keener discipline of mankind.

Such work is necessarily slow in its progress. Conviction is probably the slowest of all work. By its very nature it is both negative and positive; that is to say, it has to penetrate error and prejudice, and actually to destroy them, before it can begin its constructive processes. This is the very force of the word ἔλεγχος as employed by our Lord in this passage,—a word which involves condemnation, remorse, penitence, and better-mindedness and health of soul. Work of this kind is not to be done in a day, or if so done it may be as quickly overthrown. The kingdom of heaven is in nowise to be hurried in its construction, and inasmuch as it is the highest of all kingdoms it is the least susceptible of impatient influences. It resents them. For a time, godly labour will seem to disappear in nothingness, and to leave the labourer without reward or joy; but afterwards there will come up signs and tokens which cannot be mistaken for aught but the hire and honour of those who do well. Sin, righteousness, and judgment, are not to be seen objectively, or the work would be easy enough; they must be revealed subjectively, in much painfulness, self-accusation, and controversy of heart, for thus only can they become part of our very consciousness and live for ever amidst the ruling memories of human life. Jesus Christ commits His great work to the ages, and to the ministry of the Eternal Spirit, assured that in the long run the world will trace its true ideas of sin, righteousness, and judgment, to the Golgotha of His sorrow and the Olivet of His ascension. "He that believeth shall not make haste." "Thou fool, that which thou sowest is not quickened except it die." "Verily, verily, I say unto you, Except a corn of wheat fall into the ground and die, it abideth alone: but if it die, it bringeth forth much fruit."

IX.

REGENERATION.

ACCORDING to the gospel of St. John, our Lord taught the doctrine of regeneration at an early period in His ministry. It is remarkable, as illustrative of a point insisted upon at the beginning of this essay, that this fact should have been noticed by John alone, showing, as it does, the intensity of his spiritual nature. The narrative given in the third chapter is evidently written *con amore*, being, as to its tone and purpose, quite in the vein of John's own sympathies and aspirations. It is certainly made clear that our Lord attached primary importance to the doctrine of the second birth, and that He identified it with the special function of the Holy Spirit. What, then, is this new birth,— this being born again, or born from above?

Regeneration, as our Lord explained it, was evidently a novel doctrine to Nicodemus. "How," said he, "can a man be born when he is old? Can he enter the second time into his mother's womb and be born?" Considerable light is thus thrown upon the intellectual character of Nicodemus: he was a master without mastery, a Horeb without a burning bush,—a fact of which our Lord availed Himself in an *argumentum ad hominem* which must have had a humiliating effect upon the ruler in Israel. When physical facts are set forth as the types of spiritual realities, the success of the figure depends upon the intellectual constitution of the student. One mind reasons upwards, another downwards; so whilst one man seeks the theology of a flower, another is content simply to know its botany. Nicodemus had only one idea of birth, and with all the simplicity of ignorance he instantly applied it to the kingdom of heaven. It would seem as if our Lord always used what we (mistakenly) call common words in their primary signification, and that consequently there was frequent confusion between Him and His hearers. For example: "I will give living water," is an expression which was taken to mean water out of the well; "Beware of the leaven of Herod," was regarded as a reference to ordinary bread; "Be born again," was considered as limited to physical generation. What if *our* uses of these words should be but secondary and relative, and if a reproof of their misapplication should come from heaven? Our sense of the term "water" or "bread" may be but a convenient misuse of words whose meaning points towards the most solemn necessities and desires of life; in that case *we* become the offenders by materialising and limiting words current as between the highest spiritual experiences throughout the universe. We say that when our Lord said "bread" in the instance just quoted He was speaking *figuratively;* why may not *our* use of the word "bread" be figurative? Who taught man language? Is it inconceivable that God may have lent man an eternal symbol by which to describe a temporary necessity? So with the word "born:" we limit it to one act, whereas it may describe the progressive transitions by which men and angels pass "from glory to glory" in the highest heavens. It is convenient in a case like this that a man so literal as Nicodemus proved himself to be should lead the conversation, because he will ask questions in their baldest form, which we shall all wish to have answered, but which some of us may have too much pride or too much caution to propound. A dull and candid man often lays his superiors under considerable obligation without knowing it. The presence of such a man in certain companies is invaluable.

A grave difficulty arises on the first reading of our Lord's doctrine, which may be thus generally expressed—" As a man had no control over his first birth, so he can have no control over his second; the question of regeneration, therefore, is one with which he need not concern himself, for it is entirely beyond his province: if he is to be born again, he will be born again; if not, not; and whether one way or the other, he himself is wholly without will or responsibility." It has been attempted to support this view of the case (more or less modified) by such quotations as these: " Born, not of blood, nor of the will of the flesh, nor of the will of man, but of God" (John i. 13). " Of His own will begat He us with the word of truth, that we should be a kind of first fruits of His creatures" (James i. 18). "Being born again, not of corruptible seed, but of incorruptible, by the word of God, which liveth and abideth for ever" (1 Pet. i. 23). These words would seem to destroy the action of the human will in regeneration, and to leave man literally without choice or alternative. This would be of small concern where the act of regeneration *does* take place and all its dignities and inheritances are secured, but it is another matter where no such act transpires and no such enjoyments are realised. What of the men who are not born again, and are consequently excluded from the kingdom of heaven? Let us look at two theories;—

1. Regeneration belongs wholly to the region of divine sovereignty; it leaves the will of man without choice, election, concurrence, or movement of any kind; in this matter man is simply as clay in the hands of the potter; whether born again or not he is wholly without responsibility. And—

2. The act of regeneration transpires with the consent of the human will, that will having first been moved by the Holy Ghost, or had brought to bear upon it all the motives which are accessible to the most cogent and persuasive appeals, and the man having affirmatively answered the inquiry, Dost thou believe on the Son of God?

Now are these theories as mutually hostile as they appear to be? Or are they identical in the sense of one being the doctrine and the other its application? Most decidedly, in our opinion, the latter.

We view the subject in this way: The *idea* of regeneration is essentially and absolutely God's, without the slightest admixture of human thought; it never came—it never could have come—within the range of man's intellectual province. Man could have proposed reformation, satisfaction by penalty, repetition of life on the basis of experience, but at some such point his inventiveness would have ceased and determined; what, then, was to be done? From the *human* side, nothing; from the *divine* side what? The question involves an agony. It can be answered only by a revelation, for the soothsayer is dumb and the seer is blind. God answers the inquiry: He says, Ye must be *born again*. The very phrase took the world by surprise. It was astounding. Nicodemus exclaimed in amazement when he heard it, How can these things be? Let this surprise on the part of a ruler of Israel be carefully observed as showing that the most cultivated and trusted minds had never risen to the discovery of such an idea as the possibility of a *second birth*. When Nicodemus spoke, he spoke not for himself alone; he expressed the bewilderment and confusion of the whole world. Now that we are familiar with the phrase "born again" we may lose much of its proper force; but put back the mind to the night on which it was first used and we shall understand something of the concussion by which Nicodemus was stunned. Coming thus suddenly upon the human mind, without consultation with any human counsellor, the idea of the second birth is so entirely God's that we are constrained to say, "Of His own will begat He us: not by works of righteousness which we have done, but according to His mercy hath He saved us, by the washing of regeneration and the renewing of the Holy Ghost." No other words would do justice to the case, so complete and absolute is the sovereignty which interposed the possibility of regeneration between sin and death. So much for the first theory. It is in its substance philosophically and theologically sound. Regeneration is as exclusively a divine idea as is creation, and not the less so that it adds the mystery of grace to the mystery of power.

But how is this proposition, so manifestly divine in its originality and beneficence, to be brought to bear upon mankind? First of all it must, of course, be declared; being declared as a fact, it must in the next place be expounded as a doctrine; but it separates itself so immeasurably from all the tracks of finite thinking, that the mind cannot lay hold of it,—it is like a star which lies beyond the field of the telescope; how then? In the absence of a connecting medium it will mock and trouble every aspiration and every dream of human hope. Is there, then, such a connecting medium? Our Lord says there is, and He proceeds to indicate it to Nicodemus. He preaches redemption by the sacrifice of Himself, as completing all the typical processes with which Israel was familiar. Redemption was intelligible; it seemed to carry with it the principle of equivalents; it did, indeed, touch the tragic element of human life, yet it presented a great practical aspect which easily secured attention and confidence. It is of the first consequence to observe that our Lord connected regeneration inseparably with His own priestly work: apart from this it would, as in the case of Nicodemus, have confounded all human thinking and troubled all human effort by a spectral and indefinable influence. Our Lord proceeded to the divine mystery along the line of the divine love. He said in effect: You must begin with the known and find your way to the unknown; you must first study the work of the Son, and then proceed to study the work of the Spirit; if I have told you earthly things and ye believe not, how shall ye believe if I tell you heavenly things? But if you cannot at once realise the purpose of My coming, you must go back to Moses, and study afresh the spirit and method of his administration. He did something which will help you to understand what I am about to do, "for as Moses lifted up the serpent in the wilderness, even so must the Son of man be lifted up, that whosoever believeth in Him should not perish, but have eternal life,"— in other words, should be born again. The ground of primary inquiry is thus distinctly defined. We cannot understand Christ until we understand Moses, nor can we understand the Spirit until we understand Christ; "understand," indeed, in no pedantic or exhaustive sense, but with that tender love which is the best teacher of the intellect. Still, another link is wanting. How is man to lay hold upon the ministry of Jesus Christ so as to secure its advantages and submit to its discipline? Our Lord Himself is a mystery, how then can He be known? Undoubtedly He is a mystery, yet nearer to the nature of man than any purely spiritual being can be. What does He Himself say as to the method of approach? He never changes the condition upon which the blessings of His redemption and fellowship are to be secured—"whosoever *believeth*," "he that *believeth*," "be it unto thee according to thy *faith*." That this condition was emphatic and unchangeable is shown throughout the whole ministry of the apostles whose exhortations may all be expressed in the words of one of themselves—"*Believe* on the Lord Jesus Christ, and thou shalt be saved." But is not faith itself the gift of God? True: yet "God hath dealt to every man the measure of faith" (Rom. xii. 3); that is, He has given to every one of His responsible creatures a germ, an initial power, call it what you please, on the right use of which depends the destiny of the soul. Every man has something with which to begin the world,—to begin eternity!

Our Lord did not attempt to explain the mystery of regeneration: "The wind bloweth where it listeth, thou hearest the sound thereof, but canst not tell whence it cometh or whither it goeth, so is every one that is born of the Spirit." Our Lord does not mean to say that the wind is lawless, or that it blows according to the whim of an arbitrary power; He simply illustrates the limitation of human knowledge in the physical world, and suggests that the same limitation is as actual in a world much higher. Yet as Nicodemus would not think of denying the existence of the wind because he did not know its origin and could not trace its destination, so he must not deny the reality of the second birth simply because he was baffled by its mystery. We ourselves are daily testifying to the soundness of this very reasoning. Are we not the subjects of many processes which may be described as births, and do we not accept the results without pleading the mysteries as a ground of unbelief and inaction? Thus: is not the child born into the man? How? At what precise moment does the child disappear and the man assert his status and dominion? No man can answer the question. Again: is not *thought* being continually born and re-born in the mind? Who can explain, beyond all mystery or doubt, the origin and succession of ideas? How do thoughts combine, repel, modify each other, or correct and enlarge themselves? Who can measure the eccentricity of the orbit through which the mind daily passes? Of such experiences it may be truly said, The wind bloweth where it listeth, thou hearest the sound thereof, but canst not tell whence it cometh or whither it goeth, so are the movements of thine own mind. In every man there seems to be another master than the man himself,—a genius, an angel without a name, with whom he often wrestles, but against whom he may not always prevail. And again:

Is there not a similar experience in the development of the affections? Love has never known its own secret. Why not love all persons alike? By what law do hearts claim kindred, and know one another afar off? What is the law of antagonism and recoil amongst persons marked largely by the same general characteristics, and presumably equal to one another in education and status? How is it that a conversation in the highest electric sympathy and confidence, can be thrown into disorder by a person who is a nonconductor? The wind bloweth where it listeth, thou hearest the sound thereof, but canst not tell whence it cometh and whither it goeth, so are the currents of thine own sympathies and affections!

Regeneration must be its own witness. It is not to be discovered by a spiritual chemistry known only to a few, but to be proved by a life which the rudest observers cannot but distinguish by its virtue and nobleness. The fruit of the Spirit is manifold, yet it is of one quality and worth throughout: it is described by the Apostle Paul with very remarkable minuteness—" The fruit of the Spirit is love, joy, peace, longsuffering, gentleness, goodness, faith, meekness, temperance." Why use so many words? Would not the one word "goodness" have sufficed? No. Because spiritual growth is often in individual *points* rather than in the central substance of the character, and it is helpful to have many lights by which

L.

to judge of progress. Regeneration does not destroy the primary individualities of human nature: Peter is as ardent and Paul as courageous after spiritual renewal as before, but each must be taught to add to his original characteristics a culture which may seem to lie far beyond his strength,—Peter must add self-control to his ardour, and Paul must attemper his courage by long-suffering and gentleness. Not so much by the development of his specialities as by a movement towards new graces will the wise man determine his personal regeneration.

In laying down the doctrine of the new birth, our Lord showed how fundamental and complete was the change which human nature must undergo as the condition of entrance into the kingdom of heaven. He did not propose to effect merely what is known as a social reformation. He had not to treat the question of external decay but of spiritual death. This statement to Nicodemus is our Lord's doctrine of what is known as the fall of man; instead of saying in so many words that Adam fell, He stated the fact in an infinitely more comprehensive and impressive form when He said, "Ye must be born again." All hope of self-reformation was destroyed, and man was sent back to God for new life on the ground of being already dead in trespasses and in sins. Christianity has no other than the same fundamental message to deliver to every man. When its preachers speak any other language the gospel falls below its mission, and misleads its hearers. Given a humanity only partially dismembered and enfeebled, and Christianity is altogether in excess of the occasion; but given a humanity "born in sin and shapen in iniquity," then Christianity alone can invest it with eternal life. Man may be staggered by the doctrine of personal and absolute depravity, in the early stages of his serious thinking; it will probably appear to him to be a doctrine of violence; he will point to a grace here and there in his own character which will practically contradict the fierce impeachment; but when he is "born again," and looks back upon his old self, he will see in the doctrine a truth which has been but too feebly stated. Some truths, like some objects in nature, are best seen by contrasts. The doctrine of what is commonly known as "original sin" is in some respects the hardest of all doctrines for unrenewed man to receive; it assails him so desperately; it shuts up his mouth when he would plead his cause; it divests him of all status in the sanctuary of God; it will not grant him a single postulate with which to start an argument in his own defence: what wonder then, if he be goaded to resentment, and retire within the security of his own pride? When, after many an hour of agony, he yields to the pleading of the Holy Ghost, and becomes "a new creature in Christ Jesus," he will see himself by contrast, and confirm a doctrine which once made him mad.

Regeneration gives its subjects a new standpoint from which to view all outward things,—in a more than poetical sense it gives them new heavens and a new earth. We know how all outward things vary in aspect and value according to the spiritual condition through which we regard them. The world is shadowed or brightened by our own heart rather than by anything in itself; our joy makes the cloudiest day glad, and our grief finds night in the sunniest sky. In that supreme moment when man is first conscious of his regeneration, there is no miracle in all the life of Christ that does not appear to him simple and easy, and the removal of mountains by faith as a grain of mustard seed is only the sober expression of an ordinary truth. Such removal is startling to us in our spiritual coldness and languor,—quite extravagant and absurd indeed,—but the reason is in our ourselves. In a moment of high spiritual realisation St. Paul exclaimed, " I can do all things through Christ which strengtheneth me." Exactly so. Let a man feel that the case is not measurable by his own strength but by the power of Christ, and he is at once delivered from the prison of so-called impossibility; he will know that all things are possible to him that believeth, and gird himself to great occasions by offering the all-inclusive prayer, " Lord, I believe; help Thou mine unbelief." Measuring ourselves by ourselves, miracles are incredible because impossible: animated by "the power of an endless life," miracles are to us but the large letters in the Bible of nature. If a man be but a *critic* of the things that are about him, he will not see them as they really are. He will defeat himself by his own cleverness. His self-consciouness will isolate and impoverish him. But when a man is "born again" he sees that what he calls the universe is but a speck in a higher kingdom, and that what he calls "the laws of nature" are but constabulary forces intended to keep fools in their places and help honest men to do their work in security.

X.

PENTECOST.

A CAREFUL study of "the day of Pentecost" will properly introduce an examination of the apostolic doctrine of the Holy Ghost. It will be remembered that our Lord delivered a farewell message to the disciples in these words : "And behold I send the promise of My Father upon you; but tarry ye in the city of Jerusalem until ye be endued with power from on high." It appears that almost immediately upon this injunction, the apostles put to their Master a question which was meant to develop His plan, or to elicit some notion of His purpose as the national Saviour : "Lord, wilt Thou at this time restore again the kingdom to Israel?" This would seem to be the greatest question which they had to ask,—a question which shows how far they were from understanding the relation of the particular to the universal. So at the very last, when human strength usually breaks down, our Lord had to speak an apparently ungracious word; at the very moment of supreme tenderness, when He would not have withheld anything from them that could have comforted the few hearts that had trusted Him, He felt it to be right to speak a word which must have fallen coldly on their expectant patriotism : " It is not for you to know the times or the seasons, which the Father hath put in His own power." That was indeed a cruel repulse. In one moment more He healed the wound: in effect He said, "You have asked for little, you shall have much; you have been living within the narrow circle of your curiosity, you shall live in a larger sphere; I say *No* to this inquiry, but hear what a promise I give you,—'Ye shall receive power, after that the Holy Ghost is come upon you: and ye shall be witnesses unto Me both in Jerusalem, and in all Judæa, and in Samaria, and unto the uttermost part of the earth.'" This is the law which seems to govern the divine answer to prayer,—a great, holy, beneficent law which disregards the keen prying of mere curiosity, and sends down upon the whole life baptisms which renew the energy and bloom of its youth. It was not the *Jew* but the *man* that was to be satisfied: the politician belongs to the state, the man belongs to the universe. This is no new turn in the method of our Lord. He never dwarfed Himself within the limits of local questions,—He was never less than the Son of man.

It will be convenient to make some parts of the narrative of the events which took place on the day of Pentecost very prominent. The narrative is given in the second chapter of the Acts of the Apostles:—

"*And when the day of Pentecost was fully come,*

they were all with one accord in one place." That place was (according to the most careful authorities) neither the temple nor any room belonging to the holy edifice. The time of distinct separation had come. Yet with a beautifulness of consistency, divine in its delicacy, the event took place at the time of one of the great Jewish festivals; it touched the historic line of Jewish worship, yet escaped the glittering point which would have localised and debased its significance. Already the shadow of doom lay across the temple roof; hence it was better that the living and indestructible church should not be identified with a building marked for destruction, and yet that it should touch, though by mere coincidence rather than by sympathy, a hallowed feast which preserved the most gracious and pathetic memories of Israel. God does thus curiously interweave human recollections, and run on into massive completeness the scattered paragraphs of human experience.

The apostles were all with one accord in one place. This was the period of silence and expectation, in which no man had aught to say to his brother, the period of suspense and wonder known to every man who lives a deeply spiritual life. Life has its hours of exhaustion wherein one of two events must happen,—death, or renewal of youth. Every line of the old commission has been worked out, and the soul sickens at the thought of repetitions for which it has neither desire nor strength. The soul prefers death to repetition. When there is no more juice in the grapes, why tarry at the press? Again and again this question has been put in various forms by men who have outlived the dispensations into which they were born. Devout men who had "waited for the consolation of Israel," had waited so long that their expectation had sharpened itself into a pain: they went into the temple wearily; Zacharias had grown old in the priestly office; Simeon wondered why he was kept so long out of heaven; and Anna the daughter of Phanuel was groping for the gates which opened upon the city of her desire. A strange lull has always gone before the greatest shocks in personal and imperial history. What man is there, who has any knowledge of the holy mysteries of the inner life, who has not passed through these hours of waiting and troubled wonder, as if an expected angel had been delayed and his soul would die of weariness? We must remember the quietness of the particular time marked in the narrative, if we would appreciate the contrast which is instantly developed.

"*And suddenly there came a sound from heaven as of a rushing mighty wind.*" From heaven! Every wind comes from heaven, and so, primarily, does every sound, yet some winds travel along the dust and come with much earthliness, whilst others seem to come down from the way of the stars and the paths of light. The suddenness of divine appearances is expressly noted in the Scriptures. Thus: "The Lord spake suddenly unto Moses and Aaron;"

the Lord is to come suddenly to His temple; suddenly there was with the angel of the annunciation a multitude of the heavenly host; and in this case, the rushing mighty wind came suddenly from heaven. All great events appear to come with suddenness, even when long-expected and wearily waited for. When did *death* come other than suddenly, though the watchers thought themselves prepared for the solemn presence ? In every line there is a climacteric point. Intellectual illumination is sudden, but intellectual education is always slow. In a moment the mind sees the vision, and is consequently tempted to describe the disclosure as sudden, how laborious soever the process of study and self-preparation. Even Archimedes felt that the wind came suddenly from heaven, and he shouted *Eureka* like a slave bounding from constraint into liberty. From the divine side there can be nothing sudden. This pentecostal baptism had actually been foretold by one of the prophets of Judah; the *fact* was declared, the *hour* was concealed. Soldiers advancing to battle know that the word of command will be spoken, yet so sudden will be its utterance that it will come upon them like a shock: they know the *fact*, they do not know the *time*. God proceeds by this method. He gives the great promise, but keeps back the knowledge of the precise hour of its fulfilment ; thus : " the kingdom shall be restored to Israel, but it is not for you to know the times and the seasons of the restoration : I will come to the world in judgment, but it will be as a thief in the night; of that day and that hour knoweth no man, not even the Son, the Father alone knoweth: the Son of man will come at an hour when He is not expected." So in this case: far back in time, even when Azariah was king in Judah, the prophet had said—" It shall come to pass in the last days, saith God, I will pour out of my Spirit upon all flesh; and on my servants and on my handmaidens I will pour out in those days of my Spirit, and they shall prophesy," and Peter claimed the scene at Pentecost as the fulfilment of words so old. In this way men are trained to live by faith, and in this way is reserved for them the keen joy that comes of suddenness and surprise.

"*And there appeared unto them cloven tongues like as of fire, and it sat upon each of them.*" A fulfilment of the word of John the Baptist: " He shall baptize you with fire." Consider the beautifulness of the consistency which combines a sensation of *ardour* with a gospel of *love*. Fire indicates the point at which love reaches enthusiasm. A church without fire is a church without enthusiasm, and consequently without adequate credentials and authority. Not only, however, was there fire in the general sense in which there was a rushing mighty wind, the fire resembled cloven tongues, and it sat upon each of the apostles, so that there was something more than a glow of hallowed delight and thankfulness in the heart—an ecstasy deep but mute, which proved its presence by a rapt and glistening expression of countenance—there was that outgoing power which is called *utterance*, showing that what every man in the apostolate had of divine fire and unction he held for the benefit of others as well as for the profit and comfort of his own soul. Consider, too, how impossible it would be to mistake an apostle for a common man, when the fire of God was burning upon him, as it burned in the bush on Horeb! Does not fire distinguish genius from mere ability? Is not fire the great distinction of all men of supreme power? When a speaker makes men's hearts burn within them, he has known the sanctification and joy of the higher baptism. Were it our business now to preach we could utter many words which would affright the empirics who have taken the name of apostles, but whose incantations are unanswered by the fire of heaven.

"*And they were all filled with the Holy Ghost, and began to speak with other tongues, as the Spirit gave them utterance.*" An effect instantly followed which was peculiarly suited to the circumstances: " There were dwelling at Jerusalem Jews, devout men, out of every nation under heaven. Now when this was noised abroad, the multitude came together, and were confounded, because that every man heard them speak in his own language. And they were all amazed and marvelled, saying one to another, Behold are not all these which speak, Galileans? And how hear we every man in our own tongue, wherein we were born? Parthians, and Medes, and Elamites, and the dwellers in Mesopotamia, and in Judæa, and Cappadocia, in Pontus, and Asia, Phrygia, and Pamphylia, in Egypt, and in the parts of Libya about Cyrene, and strangers of Rome, Jews and proselytes, Cretes and Arabians, we do hear them speak in our tongues the wonderful works of God." It should be pointed out that the observers of this pentecostal spectacle are distinctly characterized as "devout men;" men of sober and religious judgment, who would look upon the scene without any disposition to fanaticism. These men, then, testified that they heard the apostles speak "every man in his own tongue, wherein he was born;" and the testimony is specially valuable as going to the point that the speech was rational and religious; not a mere mouthing, groaning, sighing, or raving, but a declaration of "the wonderful works of God." So that though the tumult was uproarious as viewed from an unsympathetic point, yet in reality it was controlled by the very spirit of order and directed to the highest edification of the church. Looking at St. Paul's discussion of the doctrine of tongues, it has been suggested that this pentecostal utterance was not the utterance of foreign languages, but a strange and mysterious mingling of sounds of whose meaning the speakers themselves were ignorant. We cannot agree with this criticism, which is undoubtedly just as directed to the "tongues" referred to in the epistle to the Corinthians, but (in our opinion) as undoubtedly without point as bearing upon this case. First of all, this was a fulfilment of prophecy;

secondly, the speech was understood without the aid of an interpreter; thirdly, some preparation would certainly have been given in the prospect of such scenes as St. Paul describes, otherwise the apostles must have been regarded as the subjects of lunacy; and fourthly, whilst a distinctly valuable object might be secured by the intelligible utterance of foreign languages, it is difficult to see what could be gained by exposing the apostles to the suspicion of insanity. The scenes described by St. Paul would, if they have any connection with Pentecost (which may be doubted) rather suggest the decay of this power than give any idea of its original dignity and use, or sanction any attempt to recover a gift which the Lord designed to be but temporary. Very wonderful in its suggestiveness is the fact that this miracle should have operated in the direction of *language*. What separates nation from nation so completely as ignorance of each other's speech? Even where sympathies might be supposed to be identical, as between painters, poets, astronomers, and the like, reciprocal joy is almost impossible where there is no medium of common speech. A gospel intended to be universal should have the mastery of all language. This was a sign, a beneficent token of the sublime future. It seems to us that a continuance of this power would have facilitated the conversion of the world by making the universal publication of Christian truth comparatively easy. Where a case appears to be so vividly evident, the probability is that human reasoning omits some element which if known would determine a contrary conclusion. God mercifully shows, now and again, some startling glimpse of the fulness of His power, and thus points out at once the way that is to be taken and the fountain of sufficiency upon which His servants have to rely. This was done on the day of Pentecost. In giving this manifestation of the Spirit, Jesus Christ said in effect to His apostles—" I have told you to teach all nations ; to go into all the world and preach the gospel to every creature ; the commission is wide ; you may indeed be confounded by its scope, but tarry in the city of Jerusalem until you are endued with power from on high ; I will show you that all language as well as all truth is at My disposal ; for a moment only will I keep the vision at the miraculous point, but that momentary glimpse will do two things for you : it will show you a sublime possibility, and assure you that power equal to the occasion is lodged in the right hand of our Lord." Men must sometimes be taken out of themselves in order to know both their power and their weakness. In moments of exaltation they may propose to build on the quiet heights and remain there for ever, but they will learn from the Lord to go down hill again, and help those whose life is a daily distress. We have been on the mount of Pentecost, and now we are in the valley, speaking the word of redemption and hope,—not " we " individually, but the church. That is enough, if we seize its meaning aright ; we not only divide the inheritance but utterly fritter away the spiritual lineage and the holy estate if we fail to connect ourselves with the earliest experiences of the church and to call them our own. In this high sense we were present at Pentecost, and have known the mystery of speaking all tongues.

Mark the great significance of this mastery of speech. As a matter of fact, Christianity is the universal language. This pentecostal sign was symbolical of that gracious reality. By addressing the heart in the name of purity, love, and peace, it speaks to man in all places through all time. It speaks to the trained intellect and the untutored mind, to the old man and the little child, to every hope and every fear, it is the one speech which is self-interpreting the world over. Here, then, is the inward and spiritual grace, of which the miracle on the day of Pentecost was but the outward and visible sign. Why cry for the sign to reappear when the holy grace is manifest to our hearts? Why go in quest of the burning bush when the Holy Ghost is present in the very springs and outgoings of our life? Every departure from the spiritual line is a movement towards elements that are "beggarly" and useless.

In explaining the events of the day, the apostle Peter took care to make three things very distinct :—

1. That the prophetic word spoken by Joel had been fulfilled, and that therefore the Christian doctrine claimed to have exhausted ancient prophecy. It is clear that prophecy cannot have two separate

and contrary fulfilments. If Christianity is the fruition of the prophecies, no party of theologians can build itself upon the Old Testament as in contradistinction to the New. With very noticeable consistency the evangelists point out how Jesus Christ claimed to have fulfilled the prophecies, and one of them expressly records how immediately upon the resurrection, He began at " Moses and all the prophets, and expounded unto them in all the scriptures the things concerning Himself." These challenges in respect of prophetic fulfilments are remarkable as having been addressed to people who had charge of the oracles of God ; they addressed themselves immediately to this grave issue—Christianity must be a true revelation because it completes and glorifies the word of prophecy, and therefore he who rejects Jesus Christ rejects also the prophets of the Lord. A bold demand, yet not too bold if the facts can be shown to justify it. Demands of this kind are most perilous because they must encounter the slow but terrible hostility of *time* if unjust or irrational. Prophecy *will* be fulfilled, and if fulfilled contrary to the claim of its interpreters they must be covered with confusion and shame. In no case did the evangelists or apostles hesitate when they claimed the realization of a prophecy, and it is but just to say that two thousand years have not impaired their integrity or their wisdom.

2. That the gift of the Holy Ghost proceeded

from Jesus Christ, and was therefore to be regarded as the seal of His testimony and service. Peter's words are very emphatic: "Jesus of Nazareth whom ye have taken, and by wicked hands have crucified and slain, being now by the right hand of God exalted, and having received of the Father the promise of the Holy Ghost, hath shed forth this which ye now see and hear." Explanation of circumstances so remarkable was needed, and all the more so that there does not appear, on the face of the evidence, to be anything *distinctively Christian* in this marvellous display of divine power. Look at it. There was a sound from heaven as of a rushing mighty wind; there were cloven tongues like as of fire; there was such an utterance as led some hearers to exclaim, "These men are full of new wine." For a time there might have been reasonable hesitation on the part of devout observers as to the meaning of the event, and it is not inconceivable, especially if the apostles were uttering words of which they themselves did not know the sense, that some of these observers might have felt that the Christian cause had been condemned by a special token from heaven. The rushing mighty wind, the flaming tongues, the confusion and tumult of utterance, were rather out of keeping with the kind of life which Jesus Christ and the apostles customarily led as amongst themselves, than consistent with it. How to treat the occasion, then? Peter would have been put *hors de combat* if he could not have seized the ancient prophecy, and connected it with the promise and mediation of his Master; but being able to do this, he showed by his own sobriety and complete self-control that the spirit of order was supreme. Had Peter been unequal to the exigency, an acute and determined enemy of the Christian cause might have said,—See the confusion to which these unsuspecting dupes have been reduced. The very winds fight against them, and the stars in their courses mock their imbecility; time has answered them, and events have confounded their hopes! But the enemy was anticipated. Instantly the man whom they all knew to have denied his Lord stood forth and claimed the event as a proof of His divine truthfulness and sufficiency. And he did more than this: he showed—

3. That the gift which had been shed upon the apostles was offered to all men, upon conditions easy of comprehension: " Repent, and be baptized every one of you in the name of Jesus Christ for the remission of sins, and ye shall receive the gift of the Holy Ghost; for the promise is unto you, and to your children, and to all that are afar off, even as many as the Lord our God shall call." How different would have been the case had Peter said —We alone are involved in this matter; it is not for you,—a special class has thus been created, and endowed with privileges which can neither be explained nor communicated; henceforward we stand apart in a citizenship which no other men can attain.

Instead of a speech so self-congratulatory and monastic, he said—" Men and brethren, this great gift is ready to come upon you also ; there is nothing arbitrary in its distribution ; it follows conditions which you can all observe ; save yourselves from this untoward generation." The *universality* of the Christian appeal will always be, as it has ever been, an argument impossible to refute. A religion without money stipulations, without invidious social distinctions, speaking to the sinful, the weary, and the despairing, words of infinite hope and pathos, is presumably such a religion as would be propounded by a God of righteousness and mercy. Peter's exposition was not, as to the effects of his doctrine, limited in time. It holds good to-day. Men may test it for themselves, seeing that the residue of the Spirit is with God, and that the Father will give it " unto them that ask Him."

In making these three points clear, Peter set himself in a new and impressive light. The speech actually glorified the speaker. As an exposition it is remarkable as well for intellectual grasp as for spiritual unction. As it proceeded it was felt that the taunt, " these men are full of new wine," was a poor sneer.˙ The exposition goes back to the solemn days of ancient prophecy, it gathers the events of current activity and thought around the Cross, and it penetrates into scenes afar off and ages yet to come. It was a speech in every respect equal to the occasion, and in no particular more so than in the intensity of its *ardour*. Every word of it might have been uttered with a tongue of fire. We shall know now the standard by which apostles and apostolic doctrine are to be measured : there must be no falling below this original type ; no man must be less ardent, less liberal, less hopeful; every man must of course retain his own stature and his own accent, but if he abate aught of enthusiasm and nobleness the validity of his spiritual baptism may be denied. Strange, yet beautiful, is the arrangement by which Peter thus becomes the typical man of the apostolate. Contrast this speech with the statement made by this same Peter before the fire fell upon him. At an early meeting of the church it was proposed to fill up a vacancy in the office from which Judas by transgression fell. Peter laid before the "men and brethren" an explanation of the case, and the election was determined by the giving forth of lots. Lame and impotent conclusion! Had Peter waited a little longer he would have looked with contempt and shame upon this miserable shift. Matthias was elected to the apostleship, and to *obscurity* : he was never heard of more; a rebuke which properly finished an old and poor way of doing things, without utterly disregarding the prayerfulness and religious impatience of honest men who were anxious to keep forms and numbers in perfect order. After the descent of the Holy Ghost, no lot-drawing was needed to enable this same Peter to see in Cornelius the Gentile an elect saint, and to detect in Simon the sorcerer a child of the devil. So much for a true spiritual instinct. We hear no more of lot-casting, or of the formal tests which many Old Testament men delighted to set up in times of perplexity. A new and higher order has been established; they who live in the Spirit know what is right by a sympathy sensitive and unerring, and when they come into practical difficulties, instead of resorting to signs and tokens which are not far removed from jugglery, they quietly wait for the salvation of God.

XI.

THE WITNESS OF THE SPIRIT.

JESUS Christ taught the doctrine of regeneration by the Holy Spirit, and St. Paul, "an apostle of Jesus Christ by the will of God," taught the complemental doctrine of a direct personal *witness* of the same Spirit to the soul that had become renewed,—" the Spirit itself beareth witness with our Spirit, that we are the children of God." In a sense, then, which is evidently as probable as it is consolatory, the act of regeneration is succeeded by the act of confirmation; which, indeed, would seem to be the divine method even in nature itself, seeing that not only did God create the heavens and the earth, but He followed each act of creation with the assurance that it was "very good;" thus, as creation was followed by approval, so the higher act of regeneration is attested by a special witness and seal. It is quite true that the works of nature are continually vindicating their own goodness, and it is not less true that spiritual sonship is its own witness in the presence of all men; yet the soul which has passed through the agonies of penitence and reconstruction—having known all the sinfulness of sin, and felt that self-redemption is as impossible as it is blasphemous—needs just that word of tender assurance and comfort which is expressed in the doctrine of the Witness of the Spirit. It is not enough that great events be merely accomplished, as if by a great strain which has taxed every power ; their accomplishment is often followed by a wonder that stuns the beholder ; a wonder so great, indeed, that it is not unlikely to settle into doubt and fear unless the mind be well fortified and watched ; and so a beneficent revolution may collapse and leave behind only memories of disappointment and pain. Take the case of the New Birth : a man has been born again, a new world is round about him, new impulses animate his conduct, new hopes enlarge and brighten his future,—the probability is that the very completeness of the change (seeing that he is limited and embarrassed by the old physical conditions) may be attended by perilous excitement. In view, then, of such possibilities, an extension of the divine ministry is required : re-creation must be followed by assurance, benediction, clear and tender witness that the change is a reality, not a dream, and that all exigencies are more than provided against by the infinite sufficiency of God. So, the mind is stayed ; superstition is warded off, and the fear which often succeeds paroxysms of joy, is not allowed to descend upon the newly-born and newly-illumined soul.

Thus, the Witness of the Spirit brings with it the most gracious and nourishing *comfort*, in which sense it may be well to consider the doctrine for a moment. In all the great experiences of life we need a voice other than our own to give us confidence, and to complete the degree of satisfaction which begins in our own consciousness. For current action in common affairs we may be strong enough without external encouragement; even our mistakes in such affairs may be a part of our education; but when life is sharpened into a crisis, and the whole world seems to have become our assailant, we need something more than is possible to our unaided powers. Even where by a violent strain we could encounter opposition single-handed, it is most strengthening and comforting to have the support of a second witness. There are times when we need to hear our own convictions pronounced by the voice of another; we know they are right; death itself could not affright us from their avowal; yet when we hear them spoken aloud by a friendly voice, we seize them with a still firmer grasp, and strengthen our heart in God. Let that second witness be *greater* than ourselves, and his testimony will bring with it proportionate comfort; let him be the *wisest* of men, and still the consolation is increased; let that witness be not a man but *God* Himself, and at once we are filled with peace that passeth understanding, with joy unspeakable and full of glory! According to this view of the case the renewed man is entitled to talk to himself in some such fashion as this :—" I know that I am born again because of the complete change of my convictions, sympathies, and habitudes; old things have passed away and all things have become new; still, I am often tempted, and often sorrowful on account of sin; when I would do good, evil is present with me; I delight in the law of God after the inward man, but I see another law in my members, warring against the law of my mind, and bringing me into captivity to the law of sin which is in my members; yet through all my conflict there comes a voice which tells me that my divine sonship is a fact, but that not until resurrection has done for the body what regeneration has done for the soul can I have perfectness of spiritual release and enjoyment; this is the witness of the Spirit which calms me with ineffable tranquillity." The witness is not that the whole work is done, but simply that it is *begun;* and after all, *that* is the great difficulty. As to progression and sanctification there is a great law of movement; but how to re-establish *life* itself was the question which astounded and baffled the universe. Possibly, men may be occasioning themselves grievous pain by mistaking the scope of the witness: they may be expecting too much all at once; it is not that we are already in heaven, but that we are the children of God, that the Holy Spirit testifies in the experience of regenerated men.

Still, the very divineness of this comfort clothes the witness with the severity of inexorable *discipline.* Apostolic teaching will not allow man to settle down into the enjoyment of spiritual comfort, as if sonship had no responsibilities. " Know ye not that ye are the temples of the Holy Ghost?" Will any man make the temple of the Lord a temple of idols? Will the Holy Ghost share the heart of man with the spirit of evil? There is to be no balancing between the comparative advantages of two rival dominions, for "no man can serve two masters." We are to walk in the Spirit; to mind the things of the Spirit; and to bring forth the fruits of the Spirit. Otherwise there can be no comfort! If there is sweetness in the mouth, it is the taste of stolen honey. The comfort is not a spiritual luxury, a genial condition of feeling which has no relation to moral health,—it is the assurance of a true standing before God, the summer which descends out of heaven from the Spirit of righteousness. The apostolic doctrine is that the promises of God should move the heart towards more and more purity; thus St. Paul's says, "Having these promises, dearly beloved, let us cleanse ourselves from all filthiness of the flesh and spirit, perfecting holiness in the fear of God." That is, do not let your comfort from heaven be lost upon you, but let it encourage you towards the very highest progress possible to earthly conditions; if you are living trees, the sunshine will help you to grow; if you are dead plants, it will hasten your corruption. A terrible thing to have the witness of the Spirit as to newness of life, if men do not *grow* in grace and in the knowledge of our Lord Jesus Christ! God's purpose as to character is *growth*. Let the sacred germ lie dormant in the heart, and the witness of the Spirit will decline in vividness and emphasis, and the germ itself will perish beyond all possibility of restoration : " For it is impossible for those who were once enlightened, and have tasted of the heavenly gift, AND WERE MADE PARTAKERS OF THE HOLY GHOST, if they shall fall away to renew them again to repentance;" " If after they have escaped the pollutions of the world, through the knowledge of the Lord and Saviour Jesus Christ, they are again entangled therein and overcome, the latter end is worse with them than the beginning." Their spiritual state is not to be described by mere negations. No man can blaspheme so consummately as the man who once knew how to pray ; therefore, says the apostle, " Pray without ceasing," because to " cease " is to recall the dominion of the devil. Once interrupt the communion of the soul with the Father, and the soul may never be able to resume the fellowship : then (the apostle would say) "Pray without ceasing" if you would enjoy the permanent witness of the Spirit. Thus the argument arising out of Divine comfort in the human soul points steadfastly towards *discipline*, " If we live in the Spirit let us also walk in the Spirit ; " " If ye through the Spirit do mortify the deeds of the body, ye shall live ;" " They that are after the flesh do mind the things of the flesh, but they that are after the Spirit do mind the things of the Spirit,"—a high law of discipline given for the preservation and ennoblement of the sons of God upon earth.

Yet with all the comfort is there not an aspiration hardly distinguishable from discontent, and with all the discipline is there not a secret but most gladdening hope which makes it easy? The explanation is found in the fact that the present enjoyment of the Spirit is but an *earnest*,—a gift beforehand,—a pledge of the coming fulness. In his Epistle to the Romans (viii. 23) St. Paul speaks of those "which have the first fruits of the Spirit;" and in his other epistles he uses equivalent expressions: thus—" After that ye believed, ye were sealed with that holy Spirit of promise, which is the earnest of our inheritance;" —" Now He that hath wrought us for the self-same thing is God, who also hath given unto us the earnest of the Spirit;"—" Whereby ye are sealed unto the day of redemption." What can be meant by such words but that the spiritual life is a continuous progression, receiving, with its widening capacities, richer gifts of the wisdom and holiness of God? The church by mistaking the " earnest" for the " fulness," runs the risk of stating incomplete truths as final revelations, and then follows a sensitiveness lest the enlargement of its own dogmas should involve an offence to the Spirit of truth, utterly forgetting, in its unreasoning veneration, that self-correction is a moral necessity of spiritual expansion and enlightenment. The " earnest" of the Spirit constitutes a lien upon the future service of the receiver; if the service be unperformed, the " earnest" will be withdrawn; whereas if the service be lovingly rendered with the whole might of the heart, the measure of the gift will be filled up even to the sanctification of the "whole body, soul, and spirit." The church is in its infancy as to realisation of spiritual blessing. It is, too, so much engaged in controversy, that it can hardly be preparing itself for the completion of the holy promise. By mistaking the part for the whole it is in danger of settling itself into premature satisfaction, as if it had exhausted the possibilities of prayer! Will it be uncharitable to suggest that the church is too much engaged in that worst and most cankering of all worldliness, the elevation of one sect above another, and the angry defence of forms which are but transient conveniences? What is delaying the outpouring of the fulness of the Spirit? There is, indeed, a still sterner inquiry, which cannot be put without emotion, yet it may not be honestly suppressed, *Is not the Presence of the Holy Ghost in the church less distinct to-day than in the apostolic age?* Without encroaching upon the function of the preacher, it may be well to urge this inquiry, and so force the church in the direction of self-examination or penitence. Certainly there is not much appearance of pentecostal inspiration and enthusiasm in contemporary Christianity. Can modern piety enrich its history with such a passage as this:—" When they had prayed, the place was shaken where they were assembled together; and they were all filled with the Holy Ghost." Or this: " And they were all filled with the Holy

Ghost, and began to speak with other tongues, as the Spirit gave them utterance"? Is the church baptized with the Holy Ghost and with fire? (Matt. iii. 11.) Is it honourable to escape the challenge involved in such inquiries by suggesting that such manifestations were confined to the early church? It was *after* those manifestations that the apostle Paul described the measure of the Spirit already given as an "earnest," and if only an earnest, where is the fulness which there is not room enough to receive? Christianity is nothing, if not *spiritual;* yet its spirituality is not to be shown by its adroitness in substituting refinements of wickedness for the gross vulgarities of crime, but in that heavenly-mindedness which can neither be tempted by vanity, nor disturbed by such accidents as shake the world of the atheist. With a felicitous accommodation of himself to human ideas God speaks of the gift of the Holy Ghost in terms of measure and quantity; hence we read of "first fruits," "earnest," "double portion,"—terms which do not impair the personality and unity of the Holy Ghost, but describe rather our human realisation and enjoyment of His presence. We may be said to receive more and more of the sun as noontide approaches, and to receive a "double portion" of the spirit of every author whose writings we study with admiring affection. Now, why has not a church eighteen hundred years old a fuller realisation of the witness of the Holy Ghost than had the church of the first century? Has the church accomplished all the purpose of God, and passed for ever the zenith of her light and beauty?

It is true that believers in the Holy Ghost have been guilty of the opposition of *fanaticism*, which is probably more mischievous than are the assaults of disbelief. Macedonius openly degraded the ministry of the Holy Ghost to a level with the ministry of angels; and Pelagius, whilst confessing the Holy Ghost, actually disowned His grace. On the other hand, Montanus not only claimed to reproduce the phenomena of Pentecost, but to represent in his own person a larger effusion of the Divine Spirit than had ever been realised in the history of mankind. After Montanus arose his disciple, Tertullian, who claimed for his master at least an equality of inspiration with St. Paul. In the great African schism, distinguished by the name of Donatism, the most arrogant claims to exclusiveness of inspiration were asserted; and the Paulicians, of the seventh century, insisted upon a spiritual pre-eminence not less vain and impious. What has to be found, then, is the point between hostility and superstition,—the doctrine of a simple and joyous communion with the Father and with His Son Jesus Christ. How, then, are men to know that they enjoy the witness of the Spirit? Partly by the anxiety with which they put the question, and partly, too, by the occasional comforts which suffuse the soul with inexplicable gladness, but mainly by the daily sacrifice of loving service, and the disquietude of an unutterable and enrapturing expectation which sometimes touches the very point of agony. How is it, nevertheless, that men who do enjoy this holy witness have to confess many sins, and to humble themselves in the deepest abasement because of many omissions? Were the inward witness genuine and reliable, surely the heart which received it would be incapable of coldness or disloyalty towards God, would it not? But as a matter of fact, no heart has attained to the high estate of unblemished and incorruptible piety; of what value, then, is the spiritual witness? Can any man be both good and bad at the same time? This is a question which requires a special exposition and argument, which shall be given immediately.

XII.

THE HUMAN SPIRIT LIMITED BY THE HUMAN BODY.

EARLY in this discussion we said, Man *has* a body but he *is* a spirit. We have now reached a point in the argument where it becomes necessary to get some understanding of the hindrances which the physical constitution of man throws in the way of his spiritual progress. It is too obvious that the body and the spirit seldom act in common and happy consent; yet it is supremely difficult to say which is right and which is wrong in any strife that may arise between them. The spirit may seek release from some of its highest obligations by an unjust reproach of the body, and the body may complain of the ignoble and mischievous uses to which it is put by the spirit. So there is a war in every man, a war which enfeebles and, probably, vitiates the whole nature. What, then, is the reality of the case, in the light of scriptural evidence as interpreted by human consciousness and experience? It is quite certain that the body does limit the capacities and functions of the spirit. Taking human life as a whole, and having regard to infancy, disease, sleep, and occasional prostration, it is more than probable that half the *time* of the spirit is engrossed by the body. When, therefore, seventy years are spoken of as the limit of human life, the body must be regarded as having decidedly the larger share of the lease, and from this very circumstance the body must charge itself with great influence and responsibility. The spirit may wish to work all the twenty-four hours of the day, but it must deny itself that the body may have needful rest. In like manner, the spirit may desire to free itself of the limitations of time and space as known to us, and to penetrate with reverent boldness into things that are hidden from sense; but the body detains it here with a vulgar force which chafes and humbles the soul. Fierce passions thrill along every nerve; unholy appetites madden the senses; the very blood seems to be set on fire of hell; the question is, whether in the midst of such excitements the spirit is sitting in its hidden place like an injured angel, mourning the corruption and waywardness of its companion, or whether with subtle, though unexpressed consent, it is not really the cause of the riotousness which it affects to deplore? It would certainly be most convenient if we could at once set down the criminal side of life to the credit of our untamable flesh; but would it be just? Can spiritual discipline be so perfected as actually to subdue and even sanctify the flesh? Or, after all that is possible to spiritual discipline, will there remain a fleshly despotism which can only be destroyed by death itself? These questions are discussed by St. Paul in the most candid and fearless manner, especially in a very graphic passage in his Epistle to the Romans. The seventh chapter of that epistle presents a very complete summary of the strenuous contention in which all earnest men are engaged; it is a universal spiritual biography; the apostle therein showing that when any true man speaks distinctly the innermost secret of his spiritual experience, he becomes a citizen of the world and an interpreter of human nature in its totality. Let us look carefully at the minute and persistent analysis :—

"*I had not known sin, but by the law; for I had not known lust, except the law had said, Thou shalt not covet.*" The sudden change to the first person singular which takes place here (ch. vii. ver. 7) gives very keen interest to the statement, taking the question, as it **does**, out of the region of mere speculation, and **investing** it with all the vividness of actual experience. But what is it that *does* "covet"? Is this "desire" a bodily or a spiritual act? An answer seems to be furnished by the fifth verse : "For when we were in the flesh, the motions (incitements) of sins, which were by the law, did work in our members to bring forth fruit unto death." And yet this is hardly an answer, for are we not "in the flesh" still? The meaning may be that though we are "in the flesh" we are no longer under its dominion, but are conscious of a new and better mastery, that is to say, the control of a *spiritual* director. Human life is begun in an animal condition. The animal has, so to speak, the first chance upon human destiny. Possibly the animal nature may never be subdued; the spiritual kingdom may never supersede the fleshly dominion; and consequently the man will always be "in the flesh," and will always be victimised and befooled by the importunity of sinful incitements. How is the animal tendency in human nature to be assailed? By a spiritual *law*. The law may not succeed, still there it is, as a new fact in life, bringing with it new chances and new responsibilities. Whilst the lower nature is seeking nothing beyond its own gratification, it suddenly encounters opposition in the form of a law which authoritatively says, "*Thou shalt not covet.*" At once the flesh has to adjust itself to this definition of liberty; that is to say, the flesh must set itself in a distinct relation to it, a relation of acquiescence, or of open and violent disregard. The apostle accepted the former position, and therefore declared himself to be no longer " in the flesh," in the sense of obeying and gratifying all its desires. There was set up within him a new and holy power which held his passions under beneficent control, and thus the body was degraded from mastery to servitude. But the body did not accept the degradation without resistance; on the contrary, sin took a still firmer hold of the flesh, and wrought in Paul all manner of concupiscence! Who can accept the limitation of enjoyments without rebellion? The flesh can never do so. Its only idea of liberty is licence. To say to it, "Thou shalt not," is to infuriate all its passions, and to add to its strength the violence of desperation. Still, this must be done, or the motions of sins in the flesh will "bring forth fruit unto death," and at all risks death must be escaped. So, then, the apostle would argue, we are *in* the flesh yet not *of* it, as we are in the world itself yet superior to its maxims and vanities,—and even the letter, "Thou shalt not," is superseded by "newness of spirit." How, then, does the controversy stand? Thus :—

"*It is no more I that do it, but sin that dwelleth in me. . . . To will is present with me, but how to perform that which is good I find not: for the good that I would I do not; but the evil which I would not, that I do: now if I do that I would not, it is no more I that do it, but sin that dwelleth in me.*" Here is a strange but most positive duality, the proof of which is in the consciousness of every man. Commentators appear to have misspent much industry upon the exegesis of these words. Are they not fulfilled in the experience of every one of us? Is not every man's life a self-contradiction? We smile at the notion of a man talking to himself, yet all men do this very thing, and *must* do it, in obedience to a sovereign law. What expressions are more common than, "I reproached myself," "I corrected myself," "I blamed myself," "I was angry with myself,"—confessions of self-reproct which are much more numerous than con fessions of self-complacency. The question to be determined by every man whose self-complaining is honest, is simply, What is the direction of my *will?* As soon as Paul was able to say, "To will is present with me," he was also able to add that his evil deeds were not done by himself, but by "sin that dwelleth in me." So there may be in a man a power in some respects superior to his own will, dragging him into forbidden ways, and blotting the most carefully written pages of his highest life! What, then, is the consequence as to divine judgment? Will God visit the overborne man with frowning and wrath, or will He come to the struggling soul with benediction and succour? The question is answered by St. Paul himself :—" There is therefore now no condemnation to them which are in Christ Jesus, who walk not after the flesh but after the Spirit ;"—they are *in* the flesh, yet they do not *walk after it;* whenever they seem to have yielded to it, they have been momentarily dragged from the sanctuary of their delight, and their soul is inflamed with indignation and sorrow. But if a man be divided against himself, can he stand? St. Paul answers, that he is *not* divided against himself; he himself is wholly on one side, hence he says, "It is no more I that do it but sin that dwelleth in me ;" what evil he did was done against his will, and therefore he denied that his spiritual individuality was involved.

Where, then, is responsibility? The responsibility is entirely towards God : " Thou knowest our frame ; Thou rememberest that we are dust." Where social offence has been committed, social responsibility has been incurred ; but the question of social offence does not arise in the apostle's argument, which lies wholly between himself and the idea of divine sanctification which has been shown to him by the Holy Ghost. The man cannot reach his ideal. His most vehement prayers fall short, and his severest self-discipline is incomplete. He seems to be within reach of the prize, yet misses it by less than a hair's breadth. Out of all this, there comes complaining which is very bitter, and there sets in a war which turns life into a spiritual tragedy,—" O wretched man that I am, who shall deliver me from the body of this death? I thank God through our Lord Jesus Christ. So then with the mind I myself serve the law of God; but with the flesh the law of sin." But no man can serve two masters ! True ; nor does Paul attempt this impossibility,—*he himself* served one master, yet another mastery had laid hold of his outer and inferior self; that is to say, the flesh on which was written the condemnation of death.

A more thorough understanding of the influence of the body on the mind would modify the fearfulness of many honest spirits, and create a tenderer charity in all social judgments. Religion is affected by temperament. It is not equally easy for all men to *pray;* nor is it equally easy for all men to *hope;* and the reason simply is, that it is not equally easy for all men to *live.* Life is one thing to the man who never had an hour's pain, and another thing to a man who never knew the joy of health. The sanguine temperament and the bilious temperament will express religious convictions in two almost totally different languages. The one will have long sunny days of gladness, and the other will walk through life covered with clouds and oppressed with burdens, and possibly the one might be to the other a temptation and an offence, because of the want of a common language of interpretation and sympathy. Summer must be a great mystery to winter; and the fern, thriving in the moisture and shadow of its cool grot, must wonder how the rose can bear the hot sun on its face all the day long. It should be pointed out that the difference which is seen so conspicuously under the action of religious sentiment, is after all not a religious but a *natural* characteristic; that is to say, religion does not change temperaments, but works through them, and takes its tone and colour from their distinctiveness. The man whose spiritual life is gloomy, will be found to be gloomy also in business, and even his family love may be tinged with a melancholy which may often cause it to be misunderstood and undervalued. Such reflections as these, arising out of the most obvious facts, should lead to the exercise of a nobler judgment of human life. We do not know through what suffocation some poor broken hymn of piety may have struggled; and we may give the loud songster credit for religion which ought to be given in no small degree to the healthiness of his lungs and the redness of his blood. Under all circumstances it should never be forgotten that the minor as well as the major key is part of the music which expresses the gladness of all things.

Then the body is to be treated as an incorrigible criminal, and to be held free of all discipline and subordination? No. The apostle Paul is never more precise and emphatic than when he states the course which every follower of Christ is bound to pursue in the matter of physical control. The proof of this might be established by the most copious citations from his writings; for example:— "They that are Christ's have crucified the flesh with the affections and lusts;" "Put ye on the Lord Jesus Christ, and make not provision for the flesh, to fulfil the lusts thereof;" "Our old man is crucified with Him, that the body of sin might be destroyed, that henceforth we should not serve sin;" "Glorify God in your body;" "As ye have yielded your members servants to uncleanness and to iniquity unto iniquity; even so now yield your members servants to righteousness unto holiness;" "Mortify therefore your members which are upon the earth;" "Now the works of the flesh are manifest, which are these . . . of the which I tell you before, as I have also told you in time past, that they which do such things shall not inherit the kingdom of God." When Paul explained the anomalousness of his moral condition, in the seventh chapter of his epistle to the Romans, was he not describing his pre-christian state? Did he undergo the same conflict after he had been crucified with Christ? It would distinctly appear that he did, and consequently that the seventh chapter of the epistle to the Romans is part of his actual Christian experience. What other can be the meaning of his exhortation "unto the Churches of Galatia," viz.: "Walk in the Spirit, and ye shall not fulfil the lust of the flesh, for the flesh lusteth against the Spirit, and the Spirit against the flesh, and these are contrary the one to the other, so that ye cannot do the things that ye would" (Gal. v. 16, 17). A collation of these passages will show that even the renewed life is a daily conflict, and yet that he whose will is strenuously on the side of holiness will be accounted victor in the strife, even though he may be weakened and impeded by many bodily infirmities. Judge a man by the lower side of his nature, and there may be found room enough for taunting and discouragement; but judge him by his best efforts, his purposes, and his sacrifices, and on all the ruggedness of his difficult way there will be seen a light which could have come from heaven only. The Christian is not in heaven, yet he is often judged as if he were an angel. Faults and slips on his part are aggravated into great sins, and men who point them out imagine that to indicate the failings of others is to exemplify perfections in themselves.

But what of that great prayer of the apostle's, found in his first epistle to the Thessalonians :— "And the very God of peace sanctify you wholly; and I pray God your whole spirit and soul and body be preserved blameless unto the coming of our Lord Jesus Christ"? The answer is, that it *is* a prayer. Prayer is the ideal rather than the actual life; it shows what we *would be* rather than what we *are;* and it calls up every disciplinary act to the highest point. It is in the religious life what high and urgent aspiration is in other objects and services. The painter who *desires* (prays) to reach perfection will excel the sloven who never knew the compulsion of a pure ambition; so he who desires, with all the vehemence of unceasing prayer, that his body may be preserved blameless unto the coming of Jesus Christ will, as a reward, be enabled to realize the highest possible degree of self-control and chastity. That is the great and beautiful life which confesses its faults and turns each of its mistakes into a reason for more critical self-watchfulness; and that is a poor and superficial existence which declines all hard tasks and all severe exposures, lest so much as a flaw should mar the polish of its respectability. It should be remembered, too, that higher holiness always brings with it higher sensibility, so that where once an evil *action* could be looked upon without self-reproach, now even a questionable *thought,* in its most transient passage through the mind, leaves in the heart a sting of shame and self-hatred. That is proof of growth. It is worth while to say these things, because they may help others towards a godly cheerfulness in passing through the sharp discipline of a life which is assailed and torn through the weakness of the flesh.

XIII.

THE GIFT OF THE HOLY GHOST CONSIDERED AS THE CULMINATION OF THE GOSPEL.

To understand the meaning of the proposition that the culmination of the Gospel is to be found in the gift of the Holy Ghost by Jesus Christ, it will be needful to get at least some general notion of what is known as the Gospel scheme,—scheme, novel as may appear this application of the term, for the Gospel has a distinct though often a hidden or unprojected method; that is to say, it is not a mere congeries of assertions and emotions, but a vital system of thinking and service though with next to nothing of framework or technicality. In other words, the Gospel is stateable in distinct and progressive propositions, and consequently it can be treated methodically for expository and argumentative purposes. This is what we mean in applying the word "scheme" to the Gospel, and it is of such scheme that we now propose to get a general notion.

I.

In the first place, the Gospel proceeds upon *a most distinct and exceptional theory of human nature.* If this theory be mistaken or disputed by the student, there will be a succession of difficulties and angry controversies along the whole of that historical and doctrinal line which terminates in the cross of Jesus Christ. No point in that line can have its proper relation and value assigned if this theory be unknown or unaccepted, a fact which shows that the doctrine of human nature as held by the Gospel is fundamental; that is to say, is neither tentative nor potential, but absolute and unchangeable. Herein is one of the permanent difficulties of Christianity, namely, that its students too generally approach it upon the divine rather than upon the human side. Thus, they begin with the cross; they invert the natural and self-explanatory process; and in doing so, the mind becomes unbalanced by the pathos of the spectacle, and is tempted to suggest that surely something less awful might have sufficiently met any exigency that could have arisen in the growth and discipline of moral life. In this way a prejudice is set up. The inquirer is troubled too much to be able to look calmly at the whole argument; the shadow of the awful cross accompanies him and darkens all subsequent study: he owns himself at a loss to imagine the fundamental theory of a movement which has culminated in so distressing a catastrophe, and thus he comes upon the mystery from a wrong level, and probably may be either revolted by its extravagance or tempted to regard it as a merely dramatic agony. Instead of beginning with the cross, he should have begun with *himself;* that is, with human nature. Undoubtedly the Gospel theory of human nature is one which involves severe and unmitigated accusation; so severe and unmitigated, indeed, that if we did not already know every step of its progress we should wonder how such a theory could be succeeded, argumentatively, by anything short of perdition. What is that theory? It is expressed with infinite simplicity and terribleness by Jesus Christ in one word; according to the teaching of our Lord, human nature is—"*lost.*" At this moment we are not asking whether the Gospel theory is true or untrue; we are merely asking what it *is*. Let us keep to this one point closely, resisting every temptation to mix up with it something for which we are not yet ready. We must completely understand the impeachment before we accept or reject it.

Christianity teaches that all men have erred and strayed like lost sheep: "all we like sheep have gone astray, we have turned every one to his own way;" it insists that all men are morally alike: "there is none righteous, no not one;" it pronounces mankind to be "dead in trespasses and sins." Never, even for one moment, is it tempted to relax the severity of its charge, so as to modify what it has to offer in the way of salvation. It acknowledges the accidentally or temporarily beautiful aspects of human life, but, fundamentally, includes it in one condemnation that it may afterwards recover it by a common process. We speak of the fall of Adam, and baffle ourselves by wondering what that Fall was, and what it can have to do with the men of to-day. Instead of talking of the fall of Adam, let us think of the *self-revelation* of Adam; and in place of the word "Adam," let us take the generic term *Man*. We know ourselves more thoroughly through our *sins* than through our supposed excellences. Adam would never have known sin but by the law, and not to know sin is not to know the whole capacity of human nature. Every man must fall for himself that he may have his own measure of self-revelation. We may indeed be shocked or grieved by the fall of others, but not until our own hand has touched the forbidden tree, and the poison has mingled with our own life, can we tell how much is concealed in that greatest of all earthly mysteries—the human heart. Every man (according to the Christian theory) has done substantially what Adam did; whatever there may be of difference is merely nominal and accidental. But it is precisely in this region of accidental differences that the supreme difficulty of Christian appeal and persuasion is found. We distribute offences into primary and secondary orders, conveniently and properly enough for social purposes, but involving a profound fallacy when regarded as sufficient and ultimate. "Sins" is itself a misleading word, unless specially limited; it invites comparisons, it calls attention to lights and shades which modify each other, and it so exaggerates one class of enormities as to make another almost re-

O

spectable. For "sins" say *sin*, and then degrees and modifications are abolished. So long as a man limits the inquiry as between himself and some other man, he is incapable of handling this great controversy; moreover, such a limitation (except for merely social purposes) is itself an offence, for we are not at liberty to separate ourselves from the race, and to set up isolated humanities. All men are branches of a common root, and are to be spoken of in their corporate qualities and powers. Individuality there will of course always be; but even individuality presupposes a common life. By typical instances we are to learn the nature and scope of the entire mass. We must look beyond the mere *names* of Adam, Cain, Noah, Abraham, and Moses, and think of the whole quantity *man*, which they partially represented, if we would know our own nature, and turn to right meanings and uses the current of human history. "But *I* did not fall in Eden!" says the objector. No; but you *would* have done just as Adam did had you been placed in the same circumstances, and therefore you *did* (not historically but morally) do the very thing that was done in Eden. There is nothing but meanness in the suggestion that *you* would have done better than Adam. Consider the case again, and you will see that the only other thing beyond meanness is a charge against God himself. Adam represented God's own idea of *manhood;* to suppose that He made *you* a stronger man than He made Adam, and yet that He risked the destiny of the whole race upon the weaker man, is undoubtedly to bring a grave charge against the divine administration. But the charge recoils upon the accuser. He ought to be a very pure man who suggests that if *he* had been at the head of the race mankind would have been in a happier position to-day. He compels attention to himself, and forces from society an inquiry into his quality, disposition, and achievements. And if he be mean, covetous, hard, unsympathetic, selfish, he gives but a poor guarantee that he would have been a better Adam than the first! More than this: if there is so much as *one* weak point in him, whatever be the stern strength of other sides of his character, through that one weakness he would have perished in the great struggle. And who is there who will declare himself exempt from every weakness, and claim for his own character the actual perfection of God? We know precisely how such a claim would be treated by the common-sense of mankind,—it would be ridiculed with laughter rather than with anger, so thoroughly would men understand its monstrousness and insanity. When men are every day touching forbidden trees, breaking holy laws, giving way to evil tempers and desires, and proving to themselves the need of incessant watchfulness lest they stumble irrecoverably; and when it is being shown by the most tragical and startling instances that there is but a step between life and death, honour and dishonour, heaven and hell; it is, to say the least of it, irrational and indecent to suppose that the first man was weaker than ourselves. A terrible thing to have been the first man! Without experience, without history, without an equal, without a footprint on all the road,—this was itself a temptation, or a sorrow which could not put itself into words.

Do not instances of personal nobleness—heroism and sacrifice in all their varieties and degrees—contravene the theory of human nature on which the gospel proceeds? Surely such instances ought at all events to modify the accusation which Christianity brings against human nature! The gospel distinctly answers that such instances confirm the accusation instead of impugning or disproving it. In reference to such instances, the gospel would first of all examine the ostensible nobleness in a dry and pure light, and show how far it was merely apparent, how far it was relative, and under what pressure it would utterly break down; and in the next place, the gospel would properly ask why such nobleness is exceptional, or how it comes to be so marked as to draw any attention to itself, and whether this would be so were human nature fundamentally sound and true. Moreover if the argument of numbers be introduced (a fallacious argument generally, but in this case utterly vicious) the gospel will logically insist that the proofs of its own theory are, taking the whole world into account, innumerably more than can be quoted by its opponents. The gospel will continue the argument by denying that any one man (whose judgments must of course be affected by the necessary limitations of his personality) can know human nature in its totality ; and will follow up the denial by protesting that *human nature is, in its own degree, quite as much a revelation as is the divine personality itself.* Day by day the progressive man is more and more fully revealed to himself; men must likewise be revealed to one another; and even after the widest collation of instances there will always remain a further something—distinctly felt, but too subtle for the treatment of words— which further something is the very essence of what we know as the nature of man. It would appear to be commonly thought that whatever mysteries becloud the divine identity, we can undoubtedly see and measure the whole quantity of human life; but that is the very thing which is denied, and certainly is the very thing which is contradicted by the best psychology and metaphysics. Who is there that is not often self-surprised by the course of his own thoughts, volitions, and sympathies ? A new self would seem to come every day, or foretokenings of a self other and better than we now realise; so much so that our whole being is yet unmeasured, or we have not yet come into full possession of ourselves! What, then, if it be a mistake to suppose that we can test the whole question of human nature exhaustively, and if the principal fact in our history be the fact of an ignorance hardly relieved by the illumination of twilight? The gospel distinctly says that human nature is to be revealed to itself, and that the proper revelation of its moral condition is to be found in such words as "corrupt," "lost," "dead in trespasses and in sins." Suppose that this revelation is not believed by mankind? Such disbelief would be a strong presumptive proof of its truthfulness; for what man is predisposed to believe evil of himself, or to do other than resent every suggestion of impotence or dishonour? And if the gospel have any propositions to make to man, the probable truthfulness of its first unwelcome disclosures is infinitely increased by the fact that it would simply stultify itself by first setting up a needless but most proper and righteous antagonism, and then offering what it supposes to be the greatest of all blessings for the acceptance of mankind. Who would accost a man with unfriendly and even scurrilous epithets in order to conciliate his attention or get a lien upon his confidence? On the other hand, what physician would be credited if he trifled with the gravity of a disease merely to create false hopes, or to get some temporary advantage from his patient? Looking at these considerations, and other reflections from which they are inseparable, the probability would appear to be that the disbelief of mankind would be a strong presumptive proof of the truthfulness of the gospel theory of human nature.

"It would appear, then," the dissatisfied reader may say, "that we must not go to the Gospel for a high estimate of humanity; it will try to humble us by the most emphatic assurances that we are 'lost,' 'dead,' and 'corrupt,' but it will never speak of our greatness and value as men." Precisely the contrary is the case! Instead of making these declarations a ground of contempt, the Gospel says that notwithstanding these things *man is worth saving!* How great, then, must be its estimate of the value of human nature! Given any state (even though only imaginative) which can be described as "lost," "dead," and "corrupt," to find out the appropriate treatment. Who can hesitate to answer that the appropriate treatment is *destruction?* Yet the Gospel says—"No: the appropriate treatment in the case of mankind is salvation." So, in this very Gospel which was supposed to treat human nature with contempt is found an estimate of its worth unparalleled for benevolence and hopefulness. And consistently so, if the scriptural testimony be carefully studied throughout. Nowhere in that voluminous testimony is there one derisive tone, or one signal of divine contempt; everywhere there is poignant grief, yearning of love over the prodigal, a cry as of bereavement and loneliness, the lament of a broken heart. Still, not one word of the accusation is withdrawn or softened. The impeachment is, so to speak, written upon the whole front of the heavens, that the universe may be confounded with astonishment in learning the ingratitude of man,—yet God cries out for His child, and follows up the mystery of sin with the higher mystery of forgiveness. Compare this with the poor flatteries which other theories of human nature have addressed to mankind; the selfish compliments which have been paid to the genius and strength of man; and say whether viewed simply as an intellectual conception the highest tribute ever paid to human nature was not paid by One calling Himself the Son of God, who avowedly came into the world to seek and to save that which was lost. Have the flatterers of human nature ever suffered anything on its behalf? Consider what the flattery of human nature is, and at its very core will be found the idolatry of self. No wonder that men who live in an atmosphere of mutual applause resent the violence of a theory whose primary principle is that there is none righteous no not one! The first destructive ambition of man was to be *as God*, and to this day he is falling over the same rock, and madly kicking against the same pricks. He is very sensitive as to his dignity. You wound him when you tell him of his weakness, and yet you cannot so far delude his consciousness as to get him beyond a changeful and troubled joy even when you most effusively assure him of his glory and strength; even then a ghost dilutes his wine, and challenges him to a battle which he knows must end in his own death. The Gospel reads the riddle to him: with loving frankness it reveals his failures, and shows him that all outward blemish is but an imperfect expression of his inward corruption. It does not tell this with harshness or with the slightest refinement of cruelty, but with the explicitness of incorruptible honesty, and with a tenderness which means that presently it will have something better to say. What that something is we shall now endeavour to define : meanwhile, to the charge that Christianity takes a low view of human nature, the Cross of Christ is the answer of God.

II.

It will be seen that the Gospel has (taking the objector's word) by its very *extravagance* brought a heavy responsibility upon itself by proposing to deal remedially with a nature which it has with persistent austerity described as "dead," "corrupt," "lost," "born in sin and shapen in iniquity ;" it should have spared its epithets if it had any misgiving of its strength, for by this free, and almost riotous, use of condemnatory words it has determined its own tests and there can be no escape from their judgment. What can be more incautious (not to say unjust) than to exaggerate a disease, and then boastfully to propose remedies which are monstrously inadequate ? And what can be more cruel than to dilate upon the horrors of an affliction for which it is known that cure is impossible ? If from this moment—now that it has been allowed to state the case in its own way—the gospel forget one item of its impeachment, or prove itself (as weakness always does) more energetic in condemnation than in the provision of adequate help ; it will not only provoke the most indignant reprisals but be justly chargeable with the most atrocious cruelty. We are, therefore, if in earnest in this argument, intensely excited to know the precise remedy which the gospel has to propose, and we have been prepared, by its own condemnatory tone, to receive the proposition with aggravated and resentful jealousy : nor do we apologise for this, for men ought not to allow themselves to be first damned with the most odious epithets, and then to be trifled with by speculative suggestions or empirical nostrums. As the gospel has come to the point on the one side, so it must at once come to the point on the other. The question which urges itself after hearing the indictment is—*Does God Himself believe it?* Or, has He magnified the disease that He may glorify Himself by an easy and inexpensive arrangement on His own part? We shall get the answer in the proposed remedy. What is it? This : " God so loved the world, that He gave His only begotten Son, that whosoever believeth in Him should not perish, but have everlasting life." Now (even from an imaginative point of view) it may be fairly claimed that how awful soever the impeachment this answer transcends it in solemnity and pathos. At this moment we are not affirming either this or that theory to be either true or false, we are simply getting hold of a case as it is outlined in history, and our submission on strictly literary grounds, is that the impeachment of human nature was so terrible that it seemed to defy everything like an answer or a mitigation, and that this answer, found in the love of God and expressed in the mediation of Jesus Christ, fills up and overflows the measure of the occasion, and is the sublimest sentence in the literature of mankind.

A very curious question, however, arises out of the construction of this answer. Is there not an abrupt and most unsatisfactory turn in the language? We are told in the first place that God loved the world, and in the second place we are told the exact degree of His love; but, strange to say, that degree is not measured by God *Himself* but by the gift of His Son! We do not read that God so loved the world that He gave Himself, but He so loved the world that He gave some one else! A great gift, no doubt (the greatest indeed to any giver), but still secondary, and bringing with it many difficulties which would appear to be insuperable. It will be seen that a case of this kind, involving humiliation so deep and other consequences so disastrous and intolerable, could not be met by any degree of mere *consent* on the part of the Son. Consider what is involved in any arrangement by consent of parties: however full the degree of the consent, it is evident that the Son, if an inferior Person, could only regard the salvation of the world as an idea which had been suggested to Him by the Supreme Mind, and which had, either by force of argument or force of sovereignty, laid such hold upon His understanding and affections that He yielded to it, and for the time being became the very slave of this great thought. Now such arrangement, regarded from a human point of view, must be seen to be painfully insecure. An idea of this kind, so vast in its scope and so costly in its execution, cannot, in the very nature of the case, be realised derivatively and secondarily Such realisation may be *attempted*, indeed, but the attempt must end either in blasphemy or madness. If Jesus Christ could have had an idea suggested to Him then He was less than omniscient; if He was less than omniscient He was less than God; and if He was less than God He was exposed to all those counter considerations which modify and re-arrange finite judgments, and which, therefore, might impair His resolution to be the instrument of the world's salvation. But what if He was so inspired and ruled by the Almighty as to render His faithfulness invincible? Then He was no longer a voluntary agent. A man may be overborne by inspiration as well as by meaner forces; and to whatever extent he is under the dominion of influences which he can neither understand nor control, he loses sympathy with those who do not share his elevation, and in fact, cuts himself off from their approach and their petitions. The term inspiration is, of course, variously understood and applied, and therefore it may be worth while to point out the exact sense in which it is used in this argument. In a sense far from inconsiderable *every man* is divinely inspired; some men (as the highest thinkers, whether philosophers or poets) are *specially* inspired; a yet smaller number of men (as Isaiah and Ezekiel) have been the subjects of an inspiration more peculiar and distinctive still. Our contention is that in not one of these senses was Jesus Christ inspired, but rather that He Himself was the actual *Inspirer* of these very men! To say that He was *inspired* is to put Him into a secondary position; because if inspired He was of course inferior to the Being from whom He derived His inspiration. Say rather that Jesus Christ was *self-inspired;* that His whole ministry was self-originated and self-directed; and though He is thus argumentatively set infinitely above the race which He redeemed, He is yet left in full possession of that power, which happily is inseparable from God, by which He can with infinitely pathetic condescension stoop to the meanest of His creatures. In saying that such a Being is unapproachable we do not, even theoretically, destroy His ability to do on His side what without His aid is impossible on ours. He can come to us; He does come to us every moment; thus the thing which may be even unthinkable in theology is one of the continual and necessary facts of daily human experience. When we say that the *sun* is unapproachable, we do not mean that his *light* cannot come down to the meanest of human habitations.

Is there, then, a serious decrepancy between the first part of this marvellous answer and the second? If we take Jesus Christ's estimate of Himself we shall see the answer in another light. Speaking of Himself He said, " I and my Father are one;" if only one in sympathy and purpose He was in reality saying nothing, for this is a commonplace which applies to many human covenants and enterprises; any holy angel could have said the same thing, and even some devoted men might use the very words. If, however, we regard the words as expressing not only sympathy but equality, we come at once to a new and satisfactory reading of the answer now under discussion; thus: God so loved the world that He gave Himself in human form, Emmanuel, that whosoever believeth on Him should not perish but have everlasting life. How far, then, is this reading supported by other scriptures? Is there any evidence to show that Jesus Christ claimed originality and voluntariness for His own interposition? If He derived the idea from God, and held it (with whatever tenacity) as a suggestion only, He would be careful to give God the glory in terms so distinct as to render any reference to Himself that was not guarded with jealous rigour, an act of profanity and blasphemy. What, then, do we find to be the tenor of apostolic teaching as to Christ's part in the proposed scheme for the salvation of the world? A few citations will show this clearly:—"The great God and our Saviour Jesus Christ who GAVE HIMSELF for us" (Tit. ii. 13, 14). "Our Lord Jesus Christ who GAVE HIMSELF for our sins" (Gal. i. 4). "The Son of God who loved me and GAVE HIMSELF for me" (Gal. ii. 20). "Christ Jesus who GAVE HIMSELF a ransom for all" (1 Tim. ii. 6). There is no qualifying clause, as for example, "at God's suggestion," or "in deference to a higher will;" the terms are simple, unencumbered, and absolute; and therefore the following paraphrase of the answer would seem to be wholly justified—"God so loved the world that He gave Himself, embodied in the form of Jesus Christ, that whosoever believeth in Him should not perish but have everlasting life;" and herein is it true that "he that hath seen me hath seen the Father;" and, "it is not I that do the works, but the Father that dwelleth in Me, He doeth the works." A mystery, indeed, on every side, not to be dispelled wholly by any explanation, yet so to be expounded as to prove, without one broken link in the evidence, that when God so loved the world as to give His only begotten Son, He so loved the world as to give *Himself.*

But Jesus Christ was a man? Undoubtedly: to forget His manhood is to forget half the gospel, and to overlook one of the reasons which originated the scheme of saving the world. It is in the highest degree remarkable that when God proposed to come to earth to save the children of men, He did not attempt to improve the plan upon which man was originally made, but on the contrary He reproduced it so completely that Jesus Christ was actually known as the *second Adam.* This should be remembered as a proof that the first Adam fully represented manhood as it existed in the divine conception, and was not set forth as the type which was to be matured by the progress of ages. Jesus Christ was "made in all points like as we are;" as much as to say, that God could not have added another element or feature to His original idea of manhood, without having completely changed it and really made something other than man; and therefore when He purposed to constitute a new head of the race, He actually made it on the first plan. But whereas the first man was made only in the image and likeness of God, the second man was God Himself, the Lord from heaven. Jesus Christ adopted a remarkable method in the treatment of His own humanity; He challenged men to destroy it, and He would raise it up again in three days; He said that it was His Father who did the works, at the very moment that He was in the act of doing them Himself; He said that He came from God and went to God. So the alphabetic letter says—" I am but a form, a medium; I do not give wisdom, the *Spirit* which I represent gives life and understanding: the wise man uses me, and so does the fool, yet how different the spirit of the one from the spirit of the other! When the eyes of your understanding are enlightened you will see me as I really am, and then, having seen me, you have seen my spirit and meaning also." The treatment of His personal humanity which Jesus Christ adopted was more needful and important than may at first sight appear. Why did He so carefully separate it from godhead? Why did He show His exhaustion, His hunger, and weakness to the men who were round about Him, and openly say that He had not where to lay His head? Because it is in human nature to worship itself, and to look no farther than the range of its own power and wisdom. From the very beginning this has been its temptation—"Ye shall be as gods." On this ground, therefore, it became Him who was the second Adam, and the head of a new race, to define the proper limits of human nature, to separate the formal from the essential, and to be for ever pointing men away from the physical and the visible to Him who is a Spirit and must be worshipped in spirit and in truth.

Jesus Christ was so careful to assert His proper humanity, that he called Himself by no less singular a name than "the Son of man," a name which is not only most distinctive, but one which by its very delicacy admits of easy perversion and impoverishment. Its meaning would be destroyed were it *a* son of man, or the son of *a* man. The fact is, the name so precisely expresses what it was intended to convey, that it cannot be re-arranged or varied in any degree without sustaining injury and dishonour. If we want God's idea of *man* we must go back to the creation of Adam, (God created Adam [man] in His own image, in the image of God created He him), and then the name "Son of man" will be equal to son of Adam, and the meaning of the name will probably be that Jesus Christ was, merely as regarded His bodily manifestation, what the son of Adam would have been had the estate of innocence been retained. That is to say, he was God's ideal of humanity realised in all points; as human as any other man *yet without sin*, really and properly human, touched with a feeling of our infirmities,

P

and in all points temptable though invulnerable. A beautiful condescension this, on the part of God; coming all the way to us, and actually laying hold of our very nature. And a marvellous answer to the difficulty of sin! An answer after this fashion —" Sin has brought human nature into captivity and death, and so far has to all appearance successfully challenged my divine dominion; I first set up humanity in my own image and likeness, and sin has defaced the work of my hands. But the day shall be surely turned upon the enemy: through this self-same humanity shall come redemption and immortality, and the serpent shall be crushed by the seed of the woman,—the Son of man shall be the *Saviour* of man, and human nature shall thus be protected from the charge of weakness and failure." So it can only be a false theology which puts into a secondary place the proper human nature of Jesus Christ. We separate ourselves from His most helpful influences by magnifying His divinity at the expense of His humanity; and by our very eagerness to worship His godhead we exclude that subtle and tender sympathy by which He seeks to get His first hold of our confidence and love. We are, too, tempted to narrow the term Godhead, and to set up unitarianism on another than the common basis; that is, we are so vigorous in our assertion of the proper Deity of Jesus Christ, that we overlook both the Father and the Spirit. Probably the principal reason why the humanity of Jesus Christ is not acknowledged with sufficient distinctness and honoured with appropriate homage is, that the very term "human nature" has lost its true meaning; it is not thought of as God's own highest idea of earthly existence—a translation of Himself into form—but as something almost self-created, corrupt, contemptible, and worthless. This is not God's view, nor is it a view which is held with God's approbation. At best it is but the *accidental* condition of human nature,—a rough and tragical episode, revoltingly and mournfully true within certain limits,—not the divine idea which is yet to be reclaimed and vindicated, and covered with glory ineffable and everlasting. When we see human nature as God meant it to be, pure, strong, loving, wise, clothed with its original dominion, and moving up the immeasurable altitude to which it is called in the purpose of God, we shall see how lofty is the title Son of man, and that to be a *man*, is to stand at the right hand of God.

III.

Upon these two points our conception of the gospel scheme is tolerably clear; at all events we know that as a matter of fact it presents a distinct and exceptional theory of human nature—a theory so obviously *sui generis* as to be substantially original, and originality on *such* a subject is equivalent to a revelation—and proposes to meet the human condition which it describes in terms so graphic and humiliating by a method which, if true, *is*, on the face of it, transcendently sublime,—the incarnation, the sacrifice, the resurrection and priestly mediation of God the Son. But, how to bring this method to bear? Not only how to bring it to bear as one great act, for the time being eclipsing everything else and smiting the universe with a terrible surprise, but how to give it nearness and influence in all lands and in all ages even until time shall be no more? Just now we were excited to know how such a condition of human nature as had been described could possibly be met by obviously *adequate* remedies, and we have at this point precisely the same excitement arising out of the inquiry, How can this work of Jesus Christ overflow the limitations of time and space, and extend its advantages to all generations and all the habitable places of the earth? It is clear that the continued bodily presence of Jesus Christ could not have met the case, and that beside falling short of it, would have created difficulties not only insuperable but most mischievous. Who would have believed in His proper humanity if He had lived five centuries and five more, and then added a thousand years, and promised to live as a man for ten thousand more? By the mere lapse of time He would have destroyed all confidence in His claim to be regarded as "made in all points like as we are," and would in His professed humanity, have become an infinitely greater mystery than in His claim of equality with God. How then, according to the gospel theory, whether true or untrue, did He propose to secure duration and universality for His work? This is the brilliant and astounding answer—*He ascended up far above all heavens, that He might fill all things.* All things, all time, all space, all hearts, all kingdoms and masteries. " Therefore being by the right hand of God exalted, and having received of the Father the promise of the Holy Ghost, He hath shed forth this, which ye now see and hear." The inquirer will be able to say whether the sublimity of the second answer equals the sublimity of the first, or whether the gospel scheme outwits itself by the creation of difficulties which it can only meet by impotent expedients. Has that scheme created an ideal Christ which it cannot universalise?

By the inspiration of the Holy Ghost there is a human ministry of the Gospel in the world. Men are specially called to that ministry by the Holy Spirit; they are qualified by appropriate gifts; their living word is accompanied and confirmed by the power of God; their hearts are quickened by an enthusiasm which can find no sufficient expression but in the proclamation of the truth as it is in Jesus. The Holy Ghost creates a church,—companies of men who live in the Spirit, walk in the Spirit, pray in the Spirit, and bring forth the fruits of the Spirit; men who are the temples of the Holy Ghost, and whose union is a continual testimony to the power of Jesus Christ. That they are despised and rejected of men is true, but true only in so far as the fact connects them with the history of the Lord, whose name they bear. Unquestionably the church is at a discount in the world : to belong to it other than nominally, is to provoke opposition and sneering; to be earnest in the cause of the Cross, is to invite the charge of fanaticism or the insinuation of hypocrisy. Still, the church lives, and its ministry is resuscitated from age to age. A continual resurrection thus supervenes, and the morning freshness reappears in spite of all the centuries and their impairing power. By the action of the self-same Spirit, the Atonement is saved from all the disadvantage of merely historic distance, so that, to the spiritually earnest man, the Cross of Jesus Christ is as near to-day, as if the crucifixion had just transpired. Herein, truly, is a marvellous thing, that men are *now* preaching Christ crucified. What do they know about the crucifixion ? Yet they preach it as if they had but just left Golgotha after seeing the blood of Jesus ; and no story so deeply moves the human heart, or so mightily stirs the energies of mankind, as the story which takes us back nineteen centuries, and translates itself out of a strange tongue.

Now, mark the effect of this Spiritual ministry upon the doctrine of Human Nature and the doctrine of Incarnation and Sacrifice just stated. We have been told that human nature is "lost," "dead," and "corrupt," and by the very fact that it is so, it is clear that its condition can be effectually reached only by *Spiritual* influence,—that is by influence that is superior to the nature on which it acts, and that is *quickening* or life-giving,—"And so it is written, The first man Adam was made a living soul; the last Adam was made a quickening spirit." "The letter killeth but the Spirit giveth life." "It is the Spirit that quickeneth; the flesh profiteth nothing; the words that I speak unto you they are Spirit and they are life." Surely, such provisions wonderfully fulfil the conditions on which the gospel theory proceeds; the theory is rescued from the fate of mere intellectual abstractions, and applied in the direction of revitalised and sanctified human nature, and so is shown to be founded upon reality and adapted to experience. Still, there is the inquiry, Can this quickening power be brought to bear upon human nature without the interposition of material instruments? And to this inquiry the scriptural answer is distinctly in the negative. Human nature could not, in its lost condition, be communicated with directly by absolutely spiritual agents. Its ears were waxed heavy that they could not hear, and its eyes were made dim and sightless by unrestrained transgression. Then must the Almighty thunder if He would be heard, and spare not His lightnings if He would be seen even in roughest outline: the "still small voice" would be wasted music. There must first come that which is natural, afterward that which is spiritual,—first the earthquake, the fire, the sounding storm beating on the mountains and sending the horror of darkness and a noise of trouble through the valleys ; and then must come the sweet peace of a spiritual ministry—a harmony too exquisite for the ear of the flesh, but ravishing the soul with refinements of music indistinguishable from the praise of heaven. We have more than once in the course of this essay claimed that this is precisely what has been done in that administration of human affairs which culminated in the gift of the Holy Ghost; and this brief review enables us to reaffirm that the gospel theory is, even in the most subtle and delicate points, consistent from beginning to end with itself, and is therefore presumptively *true.* It can only be with a feeling of grateful surprise that we observe how graciously it has been provided that this entire scale of revelation, so to speak, should be available, in all gradations, to mankind as much to-day as at any period of the history of Christianity. To preach the high doctrine of the Holy Ghost to the heathenism which surrounds the piety of the most enlightened countries would be simply to speak an unknown tongue, and, indeed, to speak the language of heartless irony. So also with lands which are visited by the Christian evangelist. He may begin his ministry with the words, "God is a Spirit," but he will soon find that he will have to take his heathen hearers through almost literally the course which runs through the Old Testament and the New, and terminates in the gift of the Holy Ghost. To the heathen must be spoken the commandments, and revealed the exacting "law," which more than anything else can teach man the poverty of his moral resources. The alphabet and the picture-book will be found indispensable by the missionary. Then will come the narrative of Jesus Christ's outward life—miracle, parable, and startling word—then the prætorium and the cross—then the Holy Ghost. There is no escape from this line: it is, as we have endeavoured to show, the line of intellectual growth and of social development, as distinctly and unchangeable as it is the line of spiritual training and progress. On the other hand, to be preaching the "first principles" to congregations who have been listening to Christian exposition for a lifetime is to the discredit either of the preacher or the hearer. Perhaps, however, there is some excuse for the preacher, seeing that he is conventionally compelled to address all classes in a common speech, instead of being permitted to address each class in its own language, and according to the degree of its spiritual enlightenment. Christian teaching regarded in its proper distribution would furnish a magnificent picture if we could command the whole in one clear view. Far away in the distance are heathen nations taking their first lessons (in large and highly illuminated letters) under the direction of the Christian missionary; nearer still are little children to whom the divine word is being spoken in its utmost simplicity with all the aid of parable and story; still nearer are groups of partially enlightened inquirers who see men as trees walking; interspersed amongst many other classes are persons who can be approached only through their sensibilities and emotions, and who can constitutionally never have any strong hold of truth apart from its most pathetic objective expression; but at the centre of all, there should be a class of inquirers specifically different from all the rest,—a class whose studies are far beyond miracle, picture, ritual, and the limited "letter," intermeddling with "the deep things of God," and breathing the air of a higher world. But how is any preacher to address all those classes when they come together in common assembly, except in generalities which will hardly satisfy any one of them? To speak with edification to the last would simply be to speak an unknown tongue to all the others, and to speak with edification to the first would be to offer "milk" to strong men, or to fret philosophers with recollections of the alphabet and primer. Out of the working and conflict of classes so varied, and apparently so little related (yet between which there is a constant inter-transition) come charges of heterodoxy, rationalism, mysticism, and transcendentalism! What wonder? Surely the child who is in dissyllables must think the mathematician a heretic and the metaphysician a madman for spending his nights and days in quest of the "cosmic reason." And probably the tyro to whom the multiplication table is a mystery would hear of algebra with shuddering and horror. A wise word is that, here as elsewhere, "Judge not that ye be not judged, for with what judgment ye judge ye shall be judged, and with what measure ye mete, it shall be measured to you again." It is a long way from the letter which killeth to the Spirit which giveth life, and the progress from the one to the other must always be a mystery,—a mystery to the advancing man himself, and a mystery to those who take an interest in his growth. Yet what great reliefs accompany the mystery! The fruit of the Spirit is not unintelligibleness, self-inclusion, scorn of backward learners, and latent disdain of human nature generally; the fruit of the Spirit is love, joy, peace, long-suffering, gentleness, goodness, faith, meekness, temperance. The better the scholar, the deeper his humility. If any man say, " I walk in the Holy Ghost," his claim can easily be tested by the inquiry, What are his *fruits?* " By their fruits ye shall know them."

XIV.

THE MIRACLES OF THE HOLY GHOST.

WE are so accustomed to connect the word "miracles" exclusively with the name of Jesus Christ that it may startle us to associate it with the name of the Holy Ghost, especially if we do so for the purpose of showing that the word is only partially and temporarily applicable to any ministry but His own. The miracles of Jesus Christ were well called "signs" by Himself and by others. That is precisely what they were, and nothing more,—outward and visible signs of great spiritual realities. If we reverently regard them in this light we may talk freely about them, and come to a just understanding of their import and value. No man showed so clearly the worthlessness of miracles as Jesus Christ showed it. Beyond a very limited line He made no account of them, and how properly so is evident enough. Jesus Christ healed a lame man, but what of it? Is it a great thing to mend a bone whether by much surgery or by one quick word? Is it not mocking a man to raise him from the dead, when he must needs die again in a war from which there is no discharge? We say that Jesus Christ suspended the laws of nature, but we forget to add that nature showed herself greater than all her laws by resuming everything that had momentarily been taken from her dominion. The lame man was restored, but in the long run nature smote him with a deadlier infirmity. The dead body was reanimated, but nature waited and won. Let this be thoughtfully observed, as not only explaining the cessation of what is called the "age of miracles," but as showing the worthlessness of the physical wonders which once made men wild with much astonishment. Jesus Christ did no physical miracle which remains until this day: lameness, blindness, deafness, are still at hand, and the sea is as noisy as if He had never spoken to it. In effect, Jesus said about His own mighty signs and wonders, "You see that these things do not satisfy you. I no sooner do one miracle than you ask Me to do another, and the more miracles I do the greater is your bewilderment, and not a whit the less is your scepticism. Now let Me tell you the meaning of what I do, and so lead you away from the outward to the inward—from the sign to the thing signified. I have healed, for a while, your lameness, blindness, and dumbness, but all your physical disadvantages will recur with aggravation in the hour and article of death. The thing I aim at is *spiritual* restoration, *spiritual* completeness, *spiritual* immortality. I have come to give you life, and to give it more abundantly; and if you miss this meaning of My miracles, your vague and tumultuous wonder will do nothing for you. I gave you bread in the desert, but you must eat *Myself* if you would hunger no more. My Father giveth you the true bread from heaven. I am the bread of life; he that cometh to Me shall never hunger. I have found water for you in dry places, but you must drink the water that I shall give you if you would never thirst again." In this way Jesus led the observers from the mere sign to the eternal grace that was signified. In the same manner He taught the inner circle of His apostles the true value of astounding deeds : " the seventy returned again with joy, saying, Lord, even the devils are subject unto us through Thy name :" Jesus answered, " Rejoice not that the spirits are subject unto you, but rather rejoice because your names are written in heaven." If miracles, as that term is generally understood, could have answered other than temporary and intermediate purposes, they would have been permanently established amongst the ministries of the church. In their place they had a high use, but beyond it they were of no value. Jesus provided for the development of true and abiding miracles by the promise, " Greater works shall ye do because I go unto My Father." And in drawing the attention of the disciples and others from the outward miracle to the inward truth, He did exactly what He attempted when He taught the disciples to see in *all* outward things some hint of spiritual meaning or care; as, for example, in the lilies of the field, the fowls of the air, and the impartial benediction of the sun and the rain. He referred to these as points from which spiritual reasoning might start, and suggested that if the spiritual truth of these symbols escaped the observer, the great purpose of the type was lost. If God care for the grass of the field, how much more will He care for men ? If He feed the fowls of the air, will He neglect His children ? It is nothing to admit that He gives the young lion his prey, you must go further, and allow that in doing so He is proving that " no good thing will He withhold from them that walk uprightly." All these outward instances of beauty, patience, care, and government, are but so many superscriptions on the envelope ; the seal must be broken by man, and the inward writing must instruct and gladden his heart. We are not to be letter carriers but letter readers.

Bearing upon the point which indicates the spiritual uses of the outward and visible, there are some remarkable scriptural expressions. The appostle Paul teaches that " the invisible things " are to be understood from " the things that are made;" and the author of the epistle to the Hebrews—an anonymous writer of great power in spiritual interpretation, as shown in his reading of the Levitical ritual—says that " things which are seen were not made of things which do appear." The meaning would seem to be that what we call the universe is only a symbolical expression of a spiritual power which cannot otherwise make itself known to us under present conditions,—but a foothold, indeed, from which we may see only that there is yet everything to be seen. Were either of those writers to accompany us in our physical studies he would probably address us to this effect: What you call Nature is only a mode of the Divine Personality; not, indeed, that the Divine existence is either limited by it or synonymous with it, but it is God's first manifestation of Himself to you,—His pictorial alphabet, large enough and vivid enough to make you wonder, and to get you to ask questions. You cannot see God Himself (neither, indeed, can you see your *own* self; but you can see this symbol of His brightness and power, as you can see your own figure and identify your physical individuality. See how wonderful all nature is, how calm, how vast, how rhythmic; "day unto day uttereth speech, and night unto night showeth knowledge." If you could get one glance behind the veil you would be blinded by the essential light. What is required of you is that you walk by *faith*, that you live *as if* you saw the invisible, that you wait patiently for the fuller revelation. When He who is your life shall appear, you shall be like Him, for you shall see Him as He is. Now you see what you call light; it is God's garment; you are amazed by the *profusion* which is characteristic of Nature; not merely a star here and there, but millions beyond all conceivable number; not flowers enough for one year only, but for all ages, yet so economised that each flower is the garner of its successor; not one or two varieties of living form, but endless types and degrees: all this profusion is but a hint of God's unsearchable riches. Look at Nature in this way, and you will not err. You know in part, and you can therefore only teach in part; but when that which is perfect is come, that which is in part shall be done away. This would seem to be the teaching of the writers of the epistles to the Romans and the Hebrews, and it clearly commends itself as wise and modest. Sir William Hamilton tells us that a concept would fall back again into the confusion and infinitude from which it has been called out, were it not rendered permanent for consciousness by being fixed and ratified in a verbal sign. It is so with our highest idea, the idea of *God;* we should lose it, or walk for ever in confusion and vexation, but for this alphabetic sign, the gross and palpable universe.

It is interesting to notice how in some instances *spiritual* miracles were done by Jesus Christ, and in others *physical* miracles were done by the Holy Ghost. Yet in a marvellous manner the functions of the Son and Spirit were kept from mutual encroachment. Look at the case attentively in order to prove this. It appears that the Spirit wrought miracles which were distinctively physical, as when Ezekiel says, "The Spirit lifted me up and took me away;" and as implied in the words which Obadiah addressed to Elijah, "The Spirit of the Lord shall carry thee whither I know not." This same manifestation of power was seen in the case of Philip, recorded in the book of the Acts of the Apostles: "The Spirit of the Lord caught away

Philip, that the eunuch saw him no more." These were the *physical* miracles of the Holy Ghost; on the other hand, there are *spiritual* miracles by Jesus Christ. For example, Jesus saw Nathanael under the fig-tree,—a circumstance which so impressed Nathanael himself that he yielded homage to the Messianic character of Christ. Jesus also revealed so minutely His knowledge of the history of the woman of Samaria that she exclaimed, "Sir, I perceive that Thou art a prophet." There is a yet more notable instance of spiritual power: Jesus had forgiven the sins of a man sick of the palsy, whereupon "certain of the scribes reasoned in their hearts, Why doth this man thus speak blasphemies?" The reasoning was not audible. Not a word was uttered, nor was any sign made, yet "Immediately when Jesus perceived in His spirit that they so reasoned within themselves, He said unto them, Why reason ye these things in your hearts?" A spiritual miracle truly, and far more exciting than the cure of blindness or palsy. It should be further observed that though the miracles of Christ were almost wholly physical, yet He always magnified what may be called their *spiritual* aspect, and so trained the observers from curiosity to worship. It is well worth while to look at the proofs of this. When Jesus was called upon to interpose in the storm lest the disciples should perish, He rebuked the wind and the sea, and instantly there was a great calm. But what was the meaning of the act which Jesus intended to convey? Evidently this.—" The sea was not disorderly; not a wave was out of its place; but your fears were excited, and so much excited that only what you call a miracle could allay them. I have therefore only quieted the wind that I might quiet your *hearts*,—objectively the miracle is wrought upon the sea, but subjectively it is wrought in your spiritual nature,—all things are for your sakes." A great thing to rebuke the sea because of a man, instead of sacrificing a man to the "laws of nature"! And if one sea, all seas; and if all seas, all nature: for "heaven and earth shall pass away, but My word shall not pass;" all things must give way before spiritual claims and moral necessities. In this fashion did Jesus Christ press upon men's attention the true meaning of the mighty signs and wonders which He wrought. He went even further still in this spiritual direction, and spoke words which may well amaze and confound mankind. When He restored sight to the blind man, or recovered the woman of her plague, how did He account for the result? Did He sound a trumpet, and say to the astonished observers, "Behold My power! Look upon Me with awe! Fall down that I may trample upon you"? He actually made no reference to Himself, but said to each of His beneficiaries: "Thy faith hath made thee whole"! As if they had done the miracle *themselves*, He being but the medium through which they found access to omnipotence. So, then, the physical result came through a spiritual process, and was intended to convey spiritual meanings. Miracles were not ascribed to faith in a merely isolated instance, but continually; that is to say, not by accident but on principle: "Thy faith hath made thee whole;" "Be it unto thee according to thy faith;" "He could not do many mighty works there because of their unbelief;" "How is it that ye have no faith?" "If ye had faith as a grain of mustard seed, ye would say unto this mountain, be thou cast into the midst of the sea, and it would be done;" "All things are possible to him that believeth." In the face of testimony so direct and positive there is no escape from the conclusion that through every miracle Jesus Christ intended to educate the *spiritual* nature of mankind, and specially to reward and strengthen the faith without which it is impossible to please God. But what faith? Faith in destiny? What? "*By faith that is in Me*,"—faith in Christ, —"Without Me ye can do nothing:" so when Jesus Christ credits a believing man with having made himself "whole" by his faith, He is careful to explain that He Himself is at once the inspirer and rewarder of that wonder-working belief. "Lord, increase our faith." *

---

* "When our Lord said to His disciples, 'If ye have *faith*, and doubt not, ye shall not only do this which is done to the fig-tree,' but also, if ye shall say unto this mountain, 'Be thou removed, and be thou cast into the sea, it shall be done,' it is plain that the faith, which in this and in several other passages, He was inculcating on them, is not to be understood of mere

The Miracles of the Holy Ghost.

In His self-resurrection our Lord repeated all His miracles in one inclusive act. So in the ministry of the Holy Ghost, regeneration is the spiritual grace of which physical resurrection is the outward sign. Regeneration sums up all the miracles of the Holy Ghost. The minor miracles are intellectual stimulus, prevision, the upward movement of the will, interpretations, tongues, groanings that cannot be uttered, manifold solaces and helps for which there are no corresponding words; but the supreme miracle is the NEW MAN! "If any man be in Christ Jesus he is a new creature, old things have passed away and all things have become new." This result has been vividly stated by St. Paul in another passage—" Fornicators, idolaters, adulterers, effeminate, thieves, covetous, drunkards, revilers, extortioners ; "

---

belief in Jesus as the Messiah, or in the doctrines of His religion, or of trust generally in divine power and goodness. It evidently has reference to miraculous powers, such as are not bestowed on all Christians; though faith, in another sense, is required of all But in this and other declarations of like import, there can be little doubt that our Saviour had in view *confidence in those admonitions and injunctions which His disciples and many others of the early Christians from time to time received, authorising and empowering them to work certain miracles.* Their extraordinary gifts were not (as those of Christ Himself were) at their own command. Even Paul, who performed so many mighty works, and, among others, possessed the gift of healing in a high degree, yet was not always permitted to exert this gift, even in favour of his dearest friends (2 Tim. iv. 20). A special commission seems to have been requisite to enable them to exercise their delegated powers. And this was conveyed to them,—their commission and call to perform miracles was announced to them,—in various ways."— *Archbishop Whately.*

what can be made of such a list? put in a parallel column the kind of difficulty with which Jesus Christ had to deal—halt, blind, withered, maimed, deaf, dumb, leprous, palsied, dead,—look at the two lists together in one view, and say which is the one upon which *non possumus* may be most distinctly written! We know how Jesus Christ succeeded in the latter case; now we have to ask as to the success of the Spirit in the former. Recall it: " fornicators, idolaters, thieves, drunkards, revilers, extortioners," —" Such were some of you, but ye are washed, but ye are sanctified, but ye are justified, in the name of the Lord Jesus, and by the Spirit of our God." This is the supreme miracle, and the proper rendering and completion of all the miracles of Jesus Christ. This, too, is the *enduring* miracle. We have reminded ourselves that all the wondrous works of Jesus Christ were redemanded by Nature; but in the instance of the Spirit's miracles we find continuance and immortality. Observe how appropriate is the distribution of the service. The human Saviour does the outward and visible work; the Eternal Spirit sets up the inward and spiritual kingdom; the *man* heals the body, the *Spirit* renews the soul. This is not only the logic of history, it is the music of vital and indivisible consistency. A healed leper may appear to be a greater miracle than a renewed soul, but in reality, in comparison, he is hardly a miracle at all! Which is greater, to quiet the storm or to give peace to "a mind diseased"? The inquiry answers itself in favour of the work of the Holy

Ghost. It is remarkable, too, as showing the ever-dwindling importance of merely outward and physical miracles, even as wrought by Jesus Christ Himself, that they are scarcely so much as referred to in the apostolic writings. A fact this which is full of meaning, and helpfulness in the way of interpretation, if we lay hold of it properly. Nothing made of the miracles even by the apostle Peter who had seen them all! Here and there just a pregnant reference (as notably on the day of Pentecost—" Jesus of Nazareth, a man approved of God among you by miracles and wonders and signs"), but soon away again to spiritual interpretation and spiritual comfort! In the epistles of Peter there is probably not a single reference to the mere *miracles* of Christ. Yet how full are these epistles of spiritual exposition and application! It is Peter who speaks of " obeying the truth through the Spirit," and of " being born again, not of corruptible seed, but of incorruptible, by the word of God which liveth and abideth for ever,"—a sentence fit for the pen of John. It is Peter, also, who tells us that " the Spirit of Christ was in the prophets," and who insists that " the prophecy came not in old time by the will of man, but holy men of God spake as they were moved by the Holy Ghost." As for Paul, on whom a miracle had been wrought, the whole of his argument is intensely spiritual, so much so that he expounds the Christian doctrine as if no miracle had ever attested the claims of Jesus. But the miracle of regeneration was the central fact in his ministry, as thus—" We ourselves also were some time foolish, disobedient, deceived, serving divers lusts and pleasures, living in malice and envy, hateful and hating one another. But after that the kindness and love of God our Saviour toward man appeared, not by works of righteousness which we have done, but according to His mercy He saved us, by the washing of regeneration, and renewing of the Holy Ghost." If Paul had been asked for miracles in proof of his apostleship, he would have pointed to those who had believed his testimony and become temples of the Holy Ghost,—to dead men born again, to aliens enfranchised in the Jerusalem from above. The best miracles, surely! Jesus does not want to see the repetition of His signs, He waits to be satisfied with *the travail of His soul*—the sons which He will bring to glory. Yet Paul's case is remarkable for the fact that he never loses sight of *himself*, as the one great miracle wrought by Jesus Christ. He could never forget that a blasphemer and a persecutor had been put into the ministry. And if for a moment the merest shadow of a doubt fell upon his faith, he instantly chased it away by reminding himself of his journey to Damascus, "with authority and commission from the chief priests." Paul had the witness in himself, so much so that to have destroyed his Christianity would have been to obliterate his consciousness; even if his logic could have been answered his *life* would have remained. Christianity repeats this same work to-day in supreme and undecaying power. Why deny the spring when buds and blossoms are bursting forth on every hand? Why doubt the authority of Christian doctrine when the proofs are so abundant of Christian *life?*

So, then, the age of miracles, supposed to be gone, is now in the very zenith of its glory. There is indeed no more natural sign, but there is the actual thing which was signified. Is it a miracle to give a man new physical power, and but a commonplace act to give him new dispositions and desires? Is it a great thing to open his eyes, and nothing to renew his life? The miracle of miracles is this—"A new heart will I give you, and a new spirit will I put within you: and I will take away the stony heart out of your flesh, and I will give you an heart of flesh." When the proud Brahmin has received the truth as it is in Jesus, and extended the right hand of Christian fellowship to the meanest member of the lowest caste whom he has met at the Cross, a greater miracle has been wrought than in the healing of the lame or the raising of the dead. To put the law "in the inward parts" and to "write it in the heart," is more than to fill the firmament with stars.

XV.

HOLINESS.

It would appear, then, that the great miracle is *Sanctification*, variously described as Holiness, a New Creature, and a New Man. The demand for this, on the part of Christ and His apostles, is unequivocal,—it is, indeed, the very life of their word ; thus : " Be ye therefore perfect, even as your Father which is in heaven is perfect :" " As He that hath called you is holy, so be ye holy in all manner of conversation;" " That ye may stand perfect and complete in all the will of God." The Christian affirmation is that there is a Holy Ghost, and that His function is to regenerate and sanctify human nature : and the question arising out of that startling statement is, How far has the Holy Ghost succeeded in His work ? If He has completed it there must be facts enough on every hand to prove the completion ; or if He has not fulfilled His purpose there must be some ascertainable reason for the failure or delay. Let us say at once that the Christian church, as we now know it in all evangelised countries, is as perfect as God Himself is perfect. The very statement would be received by the church itself, not only as ironical, but as an impious taunt. Yet the Holy Ghost has been working in the Christian church for many centuries. Other miracles were done instantaneously, but this miracle lags with stubborn reluctance. Why? Is the word of the Lord without power, or is the prey taken from the mighty? We have not to answer the mockery of bad men, or to repel the charges of false accusers, but to meet the honest and humbling confession of the church itself that sanctification is a miracle not yet accomplished.

But society is better than it was, say, a century ago? Probably; but everything depends upon the exact meaning of the word "better." Manners have certainly undergone a favourable change in several respects, and many gross social enormities have been outgrown, yet society may be only outwardly not inwardly the better. Morals may be artificial, and as for manners they may have been treated merely as a branch of the fine arts. Your host no longer considers himself bound to conduct you to the point of intoxication and helplessness in order to show the generousness of his hospitality, but that he is therefore a better man, in the Christian sense of the word, does not follow. The disease which showed itself in a noisome form may be reappearing very subtly. It may be a critical question in the correlation of moral forces, whether the force "bacchanalianism" has not its equivalent in the force "covetousness" or "hypocrisy." Possibly enough, as every man knows, a passion may not have been extinguished, but only, so to speak, put further down in the heart so that it is not so easily awakened as it used to be, and certainly not so noisy, but still *there!* A man boasts that he is not so irritable as he was twenty years ago, but he does not say that his self-control is used as an element of strength in doing bad deeds with a steadier hand and a calmer effrontery. In the old days he would have fumed and made himself heard in angry words; but now he waits, he strikes with cold steel. He has replaced fury with a heartless and bitter sneer, and he boasts that he has grown in the grace of self-control! He gets credit, too, from society for marked improvement. His acquaintances who now see him under provocation, say that they have seen the day when he would have flown into a rage for one tenth of the reason, and they wonder at his patience and forbearance! They do not know that what they praise so much is the result of calculation, and has in it a strong infusion of malignity. Their friend has said to himself, "My opponents get the better of me when I am in a rage; I miss my aim; my blows are wasted in the air; I must hold my temper down with a strong hand, and bide my time, and then I can do more with one finger than I can do now with my whole strength; I will be cooler now." If such reasoning precede the self-control which society applauds, the self-control is not only vicious in itself, but is actually an aggravation of the original offence. It may be the same with other social changes and judgments. The reformed drunkard no longer dishonours public decency, but if he has sunk into miserliness he is not a whit the better for his reformation. We change our vices and call them virtues. We have cleansed the skin, but driven the impurity back upon the heart.

Christian men will honestly say so in speaking about themselves; they will own that in their heart of hearts there is a root of offence and bitterness, and that beyond all their prayers there is a shadow which can only come from the presence of the devil. Yet the Holy Spirit has been operating in the church for centuries, and in the hearts of those very Christians it may be for most of a lifetime!

We may get further knowledge if we give full liberty of speech upon this whole subject to a cynical critic; he shall have his own way of stating the case, and it will be for each of the parties adjudged to say how far the disagreeable observations are true. We shall imaginatively invest our cynical critic with the largest conditions of relationship, confidence, and insight, and thus invested he shall find speech for himself:—

"Take my own spiritual adviser, and see what the Holy Ghost has done for him. He is an ordained minister of Jesus Christ, and his profession of godliness is distinct and emphatic. He goes amongst men for a good man, and is respected in the most respectable circles. Yet look at him. When he composes his sermons he writes between the lines that he is a clever man, and that no one can hear such sentences without applauding their taste, their beauty, or their rhythm; he chuckles over their shapeliness and grace, and is pleased, as a child is pleased with a toy, when he hits upon some novel conceit in phraseology: he says it will strike, it will gratify, it will be talked about, it will be declared original and piquant. His sermons are all composed for a selection of his hearers, not for his congregation as a whole. He calls an eclectic circle round his desk, and nods to them and receives their smiles, and he says, 'If *you* be absent when this discourse is delivered my labour will be lost. I am making it for *you;* I am studying your taste and measuring everything by your judgment; *you* are my real hearers, the others are but so much padding; if they can get any good they must get it through *you.*' He preaches self-denial, but secretly leaves no appetite ungratified; he denounces worldliness, but insists upon 'the pound of flesh' for which he himself has bargained; he bears other people's trials with elaborate and pompous patience, but yields to fretfulness and petulance when the sting of care pierces his own life; he will unctuously mourn the decay of his intellectual power, but if any man even seem to believe him that unhappy man will be marked and distrusted. My spiritual adviser boasts of the high respectability of his cure; he says that the educated and the intelligent are his most appreciative hearers, and it is known that he will change any appointment to meet the wishes of the chief attendant upon his ministry,—the parishioner who comes to church in the sumptuous chariot, or the pewholder who dictates the decisions of the leading bank. This is my spiritual adviser! He will talk by the hour to his rich visitors, and assure them that his delight is to know his parishioners more and more intimately; but when a poor man calls upon him he is just at that moment going out to an appointment, or is in the agony of composing his next brilliant discourse. Am I to believe that this man has been baptized into the spirit of Jesus Christ, or that he is living under the special benediction of the Holy Ghost? You tell me that he has all the appearance of being a most amiable man, and so he is when all things go his way; but oppose him, and you will find that his words are no longer softer than butter. Many a man who makes no profession of religion, and whose voice has no pretence of amiability, has in reality a far more genial and noble nature. He speaks with tender softness when all things are sunny and blooming, but he can frown like night when his grain is reversed. I want to know if this man is a temple of the Holy Ghost and a specimen of Christian sanctification?"

Again—

"Take literature as it is conducted by avowedly Christian men, and observe what degree of holiness it represents: that literature is professedly conducted for the 'glory of God,' as in the first instance it was projected at the bidding of conscience: the editor is in high office in the temporal section of one church, and the reviewer is as dignified in another; an unpopular cause, however, is never espoused; it is agreed that nothing be said about the circulation, so that the advertising agent may draw upon his imagination when seeking for 'clients.' It is a standing rule in the office to proclaim the ever-increasing and unexampled popularity of the publication, and to encounter the appearance of every rival with the bold announcement that such appearance has been followed by a twofold or a tenfold extension of its own constituency. The reviewer determines his criticism by his liking or dislike of the author; he sneers broadly at unpopular or struggling men, and kicks with great vigour the cause that is down; he endorses the most worthless trash if it issue from a successful or influential school, and snubs with rude audacity the efforts of men whose very shadow he is intellectually unworthy to touch. And the publisher is equal to his colleagues in duplicity and meanness. He never speaks the truth wholly and simply; he has meanings which are unknown beyond 'the trade'; he pays his advertisements by one scale and charges the unhappy author by another; he inserts a dozen advertisements for a guinea, and then charges a guinea to the account of each writer; he promised me 'half profits' for my book, and returned a statement showing that at the end of the year my profits were exactly nothing, and I know that in the case of a dozen other writers the result was precisely the same; yet he rides in a carriage of his own, and we have hardly the necessaries of life! All these are strictly religious men. They combined in an anti-ritualistic movement, and denied slumber to their eyelids until a reredos was taken down and the table of commandments set up in stead; they hunted one clergyman out of the diocese because of his cloudy notions respecting the Fall of

Adam, and they protested against another on grounds which they were too indignant to explain. Are these holy men? Is this the work of the Holy Ghost? When we ask for sanctification, are *these* its living tokens and symbols?"

Again—

"Take the case of general business as it is conducted by professional Christian men. There the one law is, 'Every man for himself:' the pure truth is never told; yea never means yea, and nay never means nay; business is a process of sounding, tempting, luring, compromising, and sharp practice. I bought a house, and immediately I had paid the money I was told that one thing had slipped the memory of the vendor, namely that the foundations were giving way at one corner; and when I asked him to return the money, he said, 'Business is business, and you should have asked more questions,'— yet this man 'takes the communion' regularly. I had a horse to sell in order to meet a pressing obligation; I knew the horse to be sound in wind and limb, and to be in every way good and useful. I offered it to a church-going man, violent in the no-popery controversy, and fond of the uppermost seat in the synagogue, and he told me that in his judgment the animal was not worth more than about half the sum I was asking; the animal was wrong in the knees, faulty in the neck, not up to the mark in the hind quarters, and, in short, not to be compared to a horse which he himself had almost given away. I was pressed for money, and the man took the horse at his own price. Next day he told his friend that he had bought the best horse in the county, and that he would not take twenty pounds for his bargain. Knowing this, I asked him if he was satisfied with the arrangement, and he told me that I had just got rid of the animal in time! The next thing I heard of this benevolent and public-spirited man was, that he was about to preside at the annual meeting of a great missionary society. What is true of one business man is substantially true of all. They vary in method, in tone, and in several particulars, so that the one can blame the other, and point to himself as a model of commercial honour; but in spirit and purpose they are in reality all alike, and all bad."

We have not restrained the speech of the cynical critic, for it is better to know all sides of a case than to be deceived by the flatteries of partisans. Instead of asking the cynic to bate something of his harshness, let us take his statement exactly as it is given, and in full view of it let us ask, Is the miracle of sanctification ever likely to be accomplished in human life? Its progress is slow, we admit. St. Paul himself did not claim that it was completed in his own case: "I count not myself to have apprehended, but this one thing I do, I press toward the mark for the prize of my high calling in Christ Jesus." And in the same connection he says, "Not as though I had already attained, either were already perfect, but I FOLLOW AFTER." As for those whom the cynical critic has just described, it must never be forgotten that nowhere are they condemned with severity so keen as in the very book by whose precepts they profess to be ruled. It is important to repeat the observations we have already made upon this point, to show that it has not been left for an enemy to find out that Christian professors are often inconsistent and unworthy. " Many walk of whom I have told you often, and now tell you even weeping, that they are the enemies of the cross of Christ " (Phil. iii. 18). " By good words and fair speeches they deceive the hearts of the simple " (Rom. xvi. 18). " These are spots in your feasts of charity; clouds they are without water, carried about of winds; trees whose fruit withereth, without fruit, twice dead, plucked up by the roots; raging waves of the sea, foaming out their own shame; wandering stars, to whom is reserved the blackness of darkness for ever" (Jude 12, 13). The cynical critic never rose to *that* dignity of accusation. He pointed out with cruel care his details and particulars, but where he used the point of a pin the apostles used the edge of a sword. We thus first of all dispossess the cynic of all claim to originality; for in his criticism he is only putting into vulgar terms the lofty impeachments of infinitely superior men. In the next place, we have to remind him that how great soever may be the inconvenience which he suffers from the imperfections of professing Christians, the one great sufferer in this case is God Himself. If God can be patient in the outworking of this holy miracle, is it a great thing that man should be asked to restrain his tongue from unwise and unmerciful judgment? It was in some such light that God stated the case of Nineveh to the petulant and sensational prophet. "Thou hast had pity on the gourd, for the which thou hast not laboured, neither madest it grow; which came up in a night, and perished in a night: and should not I spare Nineveh?" This is the principle upon which the sanctification of the world proceeds,—spare mankind; spare the tree yet another year; do not break the bruised reed; do not quench the smoking flax! God requires *time* for this last all-crowning and all-glorifying miracle, simply because man is indisposed towards the highest goodness: partly good he is quite willing to be; good for the occasion, and then at liberty to return to his old ways; but to be good as God Himself is good is not in his heart, for then, he thinks, his whole pleasure would die, and he would mope and chafe under a harsh discipline, with no relief but the promise of a remote heaven.

But *this* is the miracle, that any man should ever have felt any *desire* towards holiness! Consider the view of human nature which is given in Holy Scripture, and then hear that same human nature pray, "God be merciful to me a sinner," and *there* is the miracle which outshines all other wonders. We need not wait for absolute holiness, for holiness is a growth; the miracle is at the *beginning*, not at the end,—in the prayer for mercy, not in the completed character. We hear of people in India who would rather perish in time of famine than accept relief under conditions which would even seem to compel them to become nominal Christians. Now, suppose that such people could be brought to see the meaning of Jesus Christ's cross, and to seek Jesus Christ's mercy, at *that* point the miracle has been wrought, —a very wonderful miracle considering the stubbornness of the original conditions. As to falling short of the completeness and glory of perfection there may be some aspect of a miracle even in that failure; for it is of the very nature of holiness to be dissatisfied with its attainments so long as there is any accessible point beyond; holiness always has some further prayer to offer; and so long as there is any desire towards God unsatisfied must there be a sense of shortcoming and imperfection. But the divine promise abides to soothe and assure the soul; those who are now afflicted, tossed with tempest, and not comforted, shall yet rest on foundations of sapphires, their windows shall be of agates, their gates of carbuncles, and all their borders shall be of pleasant stones (Isa. li. 11, 12).

The Christian aspirant says that he sees holiness afar, in the figure of a shining angel, and that he longs with ardent desire to seize the prize. Then why not seize it instantly? Because between himself and the angel there is a wide battle-field on which a deadly fight is proceeding without break or pause, and the combatants are his own passions and his own better nature. The miracle is that he still wishes to penetrate the opposition and find his way to the other side; the temptation is to surrender, but he is saved from that humiliation by the assurance that he that endureth to the end shall be saved, and that he who overcometh shall eat of the tree of life, and live for ever. "Holiness" is a word not easily written on the rugged surface of human life, but it shall in the long run be graven upon it indelibly. It is to be written upon the bells of the horses, and to be inscribed upon the lintels and the doorposts of human dwellings. All unrighteousness is to be driven away by its benign power, and all weakness, and all death. It aims at no partial empire,—at nothing less than universal dominion! It is now the one condition of seeing the Father Everlasting: "without holiness no man shall see the Lord." It is the peculiar characteristic of the sanctuary in the heavens: "Nothing that is unholy shall enter therein." It is the appellation of the Inhabitant of Eternity: "His name is Holy." Towards "holiness" human life is being moved, how slowly soever, by the ministry of the Holy Ghost, and when the end comes there will be no such miracle in the universe. Is this a picture? Meanwhile perhaps it is. But how poor the world would be but for its pictures! They are prophecies and promises; inspirations towards high action and noble patience; and presently, even whilst men are looking upon them, they will cease to be pictures by becoming real and immortal.

XVI.

INCIDENTAL TESTIMONY.

No survey of the biblical field of evidence can be complete without reference to passages which are full of suggestion as to the function of the Holy Spirit, yet which hardly admit of formal classification. As in the case of Jesus Christ, so in the case of the Holy Ghost, there is a great deal of incidental allusion and illustration, of the utmost importance as bearing upon the argumentative harmony and completeness of the doctrine, yet singularly difficult of effective treatment, and the more so where, as in this case, the exaggeration of details would be fatal to perspective and unity. There is, of course, no one scriptural book, or section of a book, devoted to a special statement of the doctrine of the Holy Spirit; the doctrine permeates the whole field of revelation, here and there, indeed, very broadly, but for the most part in a subtle and assumptive manner, as of power without form. Let us show this by examples :—

"*The Spirit searcheth the deep things of God.*" Are not all the things of God deep, hidden in secrecy and veiled in awfulness? Clearly not. In many places His name is written plainly, and His hand is almost seen; in all goodness, in all pitiful and tender regard for the life of His creatures; in all condescension and healing grace,—a ministry not to be explained in words, yet to be felt with sereneness and joy. On the other hand there are mysteries which fill life with uneasiness, as if the very earth would break under our feet, and as if enemies beyond number were hovering in the darkness; in our thinking, too, we come to great deeps that have no explanation, and to fierce contrasts which bewilder our moral sense and tempt us towards atheism and madness. Do we not ourselves often do things which we cannot explain to the young, the foolish, the unsympathetic, or the feeble, yet which we know to be right and wise? Have we not the power of hiding ourselves from the very people who think they know us best, and of concealing our reasons from men who think they comprehend our actions? It was in view of these realities of human consciousness that St. Paul wrote the words before us: " For what man knoweth the things of a man, save the spirit of man which is in him? even so the things of God knoweth no man, but the Spirit of God." It is impossible that the existence of spiritual mystery can, as was pointed out in a former chapter, be more explicitly recognised than in the Bible itself. The very book is itself a mystery, and from end to end it cautions its readers against such apprehensions and conclusions as are flattering to human reason. It is the more needful to repeat this even at the risk of tediousness, because it would appear as if some persons were under the impression that by uncommon sagacity on their own part they had discovered that there is something like mystery in the Bible. The Bible says in effect, " I am a mystery ; I am a light, touching but a point or two of infinite secrecy; I can give but small satisfaction to Reason, but I can detain Faith in exercises of wonder, expectation, and worship." When we would go into the sanctuary whose door is sealed, the Bible warns us off with the words—" These are the deep things of God." And when we complain of exclusion, it quiets us with the analogy of our own inner life—" What man knoweth the things of a man save the spirit of man which is in him, even so———" Thus we are to reason upward from the flutter of our own heart towards the pulsations of the infinite I AM. Yet this pressure upon the sealed sanctuary, when controlled and sanctified, is the inspiration of that hopeful and watchful patience which lingers near the hallowed portals that it may catch the first glimpse of the King.

" *The manifestation of the Spirit is given to every man to profit withal.*" No man begins life without a spiritual dower,—without sagacity, moral sense, and power of spiritual discrimination and election. *How* it is given to man is a secret. But no greater secret, we repeat, than the beginning of that merely *intellectual* life whose existence is universally acknowledged. At what period does the child become a man in thinking, or is he liberated from the small world of circumstances, and introduced into the illimitable kingdom of philosophy and speculation? Spiritual transitions would seem to be immeasurable as to time, yet what can be more positive as to reality and influence? The apostle, in making this declaration, is but putting into words one of the chief facts of our own consciousness; that is to say, we *know* that we are controlled by a discriminate and elective power, though we might not be able to express in words its name, origin, and quality, yet when we hear fit words we can claim them and attest their propriety. The "manifestation of the Spirit" spoken of by St. Paul, distinguishes human life from all other creaturedom below it. Given a case where a child shall be treated merely as an animal, being deprived of education and of all the ministries of human love, it is not improbable that the child might, in the end, be found speechless and irrational. But if that proves anything it proves too much. Its application would destroy the most beautiful distinctions in floral life, and turn the healthiest houses into noisome dungeons. But, apart from this, any inference impugning the dignity of human nature which may be drawn from so violent a hypothesis is at once deprived of all value by an inversion of the terms: instead of degrading the child, exalt the animal; put them, as far as possible, under the same influences, give them the same lessons, send them to the same universities, and the argument shall stand or fall by the results. For what purpose "the manifestation of the Spirit is given to every man " should be carefully observed, viz., *to profit withal*, to profit himself and to profit others; for "to him that hath shall be given, and he shall have abundance," and out of that abundance will come an overflow for social benefit. The Spirit dwells with every man, first as an individual illumination, and secondly as a public light,—as an *individual* illumination (for in the Greek the emphasis is on ἑκάστῳ) and as a public light, that others may be guided and blessed. The passage has been variously rendered by critics, yet every rendering proceeds on the doctrine that each man has his own individual gift of God. Hence—

"*Know ye not that ye are the temple of God, and that the Spirit of God dwelleth in you?*" The appeal is to those who have received spiritual enlightenment, and not merely intellectual sagacity. It must be borne in mind that every man has the awful power of deciding whether he will be a temple of the Holy Ghost or a synagogue of Satan, —as to the mere *fact* of his manhood he is irresponsible, but as to its *uses* he is an accountable steward. Human intellect would seem to be rather the start-point than the completion of human nature. What are we to do with it? Regard it with a contentment which shall degenerate into idolatry, or use it as the organon by which we are to acquaint ourselves with God, and lay hold upon a spiritual inheritance? To create an intellect is to create a will, and to create a will is to impose certain limitations upon the Creator himself. You control your dog by force, you control your child by consent; in the one case you insist, and in the other you reason. So God commands the stars, but He entreats and persuades the hearts of men. Where, therefore, there is an acceptance of the presence and rule of the Holy Ghost, the man has consented to become a temple of God. But is it individual man or collective man that is the subject of St. Paul's inquiry? Clearly both. The individual spirit is regenerated; the individual spirit is sanctified; the individual spirit is renewed in strength and comfort day by day; there can, then, be no violence in carrying the process to its completion, and speaking of the individual heart as the temple of the Holy Ghost. It is true also that the *church* is the temple and dwelling-place of God, for He loveth Zion, and sets Himself in the minds of them that fear Him. God speaks to companies of men as He never speaks to solitary watchers and students; there is a fuller tone, an intenser fervour in Pentecostal revelations than in personal communion, and, as we ourselves know, there is a keener joy in sympathy than can be realised even in the devoutest solitude. The argument of the apostle is more self-consistent and more powerful, and therefore more probable, as an individual appeal than as a charge upon the church corporate. Still, the church in its plurality and unity has its own special enjoyments; thus :—

"*The communion of the Holy Ghost be with you all;*" there is to be a general sense of His presence, and a joyous consciousness of eternal oneness through His holy ministry. A deep and tender sympathy is to hold together in glad consent and willing service "the holy catholic church throughout all the world;" and where two or three are assembled in the name of Christ, they are to realise a bond of kinship which death cannot dissolve, and a power of mutual interpretation which will render mutual misunderstanding impossible. As distance softens the ruggedness of the landscape, so a truly spiritual view of each other throws off into perspective such unevennesses of human character as are merely superficial and temporary. By the power of the Holy Ghost we see one another in the best light; a new critical faculty (call it a faculty of verification) is brought into exercise, by which we distinguish, with something like infallible accuracy, between the outward and the inward, between the narrowness and even offensiveness which come through physical infirmity or personal disadvantage, and the inward, deep, spiritual love which is the fruit of the Holy Ghost. In a church whose inspiration is deficient, you will find strife, clamour, debate, and alienation; the members see one another in a false light; they mistake the meaning of words and the importance of accidents; they unduly project their own claims and dignities, and thus bring upon themselves penalties and annoyances which might have been escaped. But in a church whose inspiration abounds, you will find confidence, honour, love, patience, and peace like the calm of God. The whole difference lies in the degree of inspiration. It would seem as if men could not, in their natural state, live together without violence. If civilisation be pointed to in disproof of this suggestion, it should be remembered that civilisation is a system of checks and judgments specially arranged with a view to the repression of natural tendencies in the direction of social outrage and misdemeanour, and that that system is so carefully administered as to prevent men showing themselves in their real moral capacity; that is to say, they live in fear, and are good citizens only because they are timid men. In a truly Christian community, the system of repression and penalty is superseded; the church needs no magistracy; it lives in the fear of God, and is ruled by the communion of the Holy Ghost. But there are disorderly men in the church? In the visible body, truly; but not in the invisible fellowship. But good men stumble and err? Certainly; and their penitence, their humiliation, is in the proportion of their goodness. And true men fall below their vocation, do they not? Yes; and none can know the fact so well as themselves, yet they are pursued and recovered by the ministry of the Holy Ghost in proportion as their love of truth is real. "The communion of the Holy Ghost" is " with " the church when the church is pure, meek, earnest, quiet, patient, and loving; when the strong bear the infirmities of the weak; when the moral protest of the church is resented by the world as keen, cruel, relentless, and intolerable; when things not seen throw things visible into shadow and contempt. "The communion of the Holy Ghost" is a bond of union which needs no lettered law to determine its function or call attention to its dignity. And this communion is something more than secret and holy love; something more, too, than rapt contemplation or spiritual absorption: in very deed it is a revelation.

"*But God hath revealed them unto us by His Spirit;*" not unto *me* only, but unto *us*. Of what is the apostle speaking? His words are remarkable: "Eye hath not seen, nor ear heard, neither have entered into the heart of man, the things which God hath prepared for them that love Him." So much for the negative side; with this is contrasted the privilege conferred upon Christian believers: "*God hath revealed them unto us by His Spirit.*" So the Christian sees the world which is invisible to others. The horizon is the prison line of other men, but to the man who is enlightened and ruled by the Holy Ghost it is the door of his Father's higher kingdom. He has spiritual *foresight* because he has spiritual *insight*. To natural sagacity, foresight is but the result of happy conjecture and venture; but to Christian intuition everything is made plain by the Holy Ghost. John, known pre-eminently by his love, teaches this doctrine in plain words, thus: "Ye have an unction from the Holy One, and ye know all things." *Know*, *i.e.*, they have been "revealed by the Spirit." Heaven is no longer a mystery : its gates and its walls, its rivers and fountains, its thunders and storms of mighty alleluias, its harps and crowns, are made known; they, truly, are distant, but the heaven of which they are, so to speak, but the accidents, has already sent its light and joy into hearts which have known the fellowship of the sufferings of Christ. The Christian who allows himself to be darkened by passing clouds, or to be shut up within the prison of locality, is simply leaving his supreme privilege unclaimed and unexercised. "Blessed are the pure in heart, for they shall *see God.*"

But have we not gone down in the extent of divine revelation as compared with the holy men of Old Testament times ? Have we as close intimacy with the spiritual world as they had ? They had dreams and visions and many revelations of angels ; the darkness brought with it a light above the brightness of the sun, and solitude was peopled by radiant messengers ; their life had a side on which heavenly glories were poured in rich profusion,—a side that caught the morning early, and stretched far away as if to the gate of the kingdom. Where are *our* dreams, our visions of the night, our entertainment of angels, our long detentions in holy solitude ? Do we not live in meaner times,—do we not starve on the crumbs which fall from the banqueting tables of the elder saints ? These questions are all dismissed by one great answer; it is true that in our time the vision has ceased, and that the angel is no more seen, but instead of these preliminary and shadowy revelations, *God hath sent forth the Spirit of His Son into our hearts, crying, Abba, Father!* Thus we have the sufficing revelation,—" Show us the Father and it sufficeth us." Thus, too, we have an indwelling *Spirit* in place of a transient though dazzling vision. This, it should be observed, is the natural and proper climax of all preceding hints, symbols, and flashes of the hidden world. All these without a fulfilling and crowning SPIRIT would have been signs of weakness, indicating throes and agonies which ended in mere abortions. The better portion has fallen to the latter times. "God, who at sundry times and in divers manners spake in time past unto the fathers by the prophets, hath in these last days spoken unto us by His Son," and hath laid aside the awfulness of His incommunicable name that He might be known to us by the tenderer name of *Father*. The value of this revelation will be felt exactly in the measure of our spiritual mindedness. If we are yet in the flesh we shall pine for the symbol, the dream, the half-seen, whispering angel; because the carnal mind loves the spectacular, the marvellous, the outward and tangible. But if we are in sympathy with Jesus Christ we shall see in the gift of the Holy Ghost the fulfilment of the richest promises, and, even from a philosophical point of view, the most rational consummation of God's elementary spiritual training of mankind. That training, apart from the Holy Ghost, is self-concluding; if continued, it becomes

S

the gloomiest of all monotonies,—a circle whose revolutions bring repetition, weariness, and disappointment : the dreams come over again, the angels are but angels still, and thus reverence may drop into familiarity. But, on the other hand, that training, terminating itself in the Holy Ghost, as the dawn terminates in the full light, is a training towards Fatherhood, sonship, and immortal progress. Without Pentecost the Old Testament is an artificial light; with it, the Old Testament is a brightening dawn. " Have ye received the Holy Ghost ? " If so—

"*Grieve not the Holy Spirit of God.*" Grieve Him not by wishing for another ministry than His own, pining after the revelations given to the infantile world, and otherwise hinting dissatisfaction. He is all gifts in one. Let your love go out towards Him in great acts of unquestioning trust, knowing that He is " the Holy Spirit of promise," and consequently that any doubt of His power or grace will shock Him as would blasphemy itself. Neither "grieve" Him by overt sin. " Let no corrupt communication proceed out of your mouth ;" " neither give place to the devil ;" "put off all these, anger, wrath, malice, blasphemy," " and grieve not the Holy Spirit of God." The last exhortation is not thrown in as if it were directed to a mere variety of common sin ; it has a special value of its own,—it is subtler and tenderer than any of the others. Not only have we to avoid gross and abominable offences,—lying, theft, and corrupt speech,—we have to take infinite care lest we grieve the indwelling *Spirit.* Thus, as we have before seen, a severe and most jealous discipline is to be set up in the hidden world of motive, purpose, thought, and unuttered desire. As a delicate bloom requires more care than a rough bark, so a thought calls for keener watchfulness than an action. We grieve society by a *crime*, but we grieve the Spirit by a *wish*. So, we may be able to defy social judgment, yet we may be "vexing the Holy Spirit" by a rebellion of which society knows nothing. How terrible, then, in righteousness are the judgments of God, and to how sensitive a discipline are men called in Christ Jesus! Yet herein is the womanliness of the Divine nature, its infinite grace and pathos, in that it condescends to be *grieved!* Why not crush the disloyal universe, and set up Death upon the ruins of Life? Why be subjected to tears and anguish because of a few creatures who mar the beautifulness of existence? Let them be stricken down with the sword of anger, O mighty and terrible King! No: He sees Himself in them; He views them in all the possibilities of His own purpose; and He suffers the "grief" if haply there may in the long run come out of it a sweet and imperishable joy. Yet He "will not always strive;" so men are called to care and to penitence, thus—

"*Quench not the Spirit.*" This is not an act complete in itself, simple and final; it is the last point of a line that may be very long. To *grieve* the Spirit is the first motion towards quenching His inspiration. To hesitate to do that which is right ; to keep back part of the consecrated price ; to modify religious emphasis lest it should irritate worldly contentment,—to do these things is to begin to quench the holy fire. To exaggerate the tone of the voice, that the cowardliness of the heart may be disguised; to brush with more and more effusive care the garment of personal respectability, that the true condition of the spirit may be concealed from men ; to pile with lavish hands mountains of flowers upon the cruel grave of expired affections,—to do these things is to depose God from the throne of the soul! Surely, the fire cools lingeringly ; surely, it is with infinite reluctance, with inexpressible pain, that God vanishes from the soul of man! Great doctrines may be taught even in tones of expostulation and warning, as is shown with startling distinctness in this case. The sentence is so brief. It is like a sudden cry. Who could have thought it possible that God could have been worsted by His own child,—expelled from that child's holy and loving homage? When the apostle said "grieve not the Holy Spirit of God," it might have been thought that he had been giving unnecessary caution ; but when he adds "quench not the Spirit," the horror of a great darkness seems to come down upon his words. In effect he says,—You can insult God, you can mock Him, you can set His commands at nought, and banish Him from your love and reverence You cannot touch one of His stars, nor can you silence one of His winds, but you can cruelly wound His heart, and utterly exclude Him from your thought. And what can equal the emptiness and desolation of a life from which God has been expelled! "The last end of that man shall be worse than the first." It is impossible that ever more there can come to such a man the tender hopes and promises of a second spring. "It were better for that man that he had never been born." Yet with respect to other cases a very hopeful word is spoken:—

"—*renewing of the Holy Ghost*,"—as if a process of wear and tear took place in spiritual activity, and a counter process of resuscitation had been established in the divine economy. Such words seem to convey a lofty challenge, to this effect,—Give, and it shall be given to you in return; spend and be spent, and at eventide all your strength shall be recruited and increased; go out bravely into the darkest and roughest parts of the world, and sacrifice yourselves in the spirit of Christ for the salvation of mankind, and be assured that the Spirit will abound with the overflow of your love, and as your day so shall your strength be. We know what is meant by physical and intellectual renewal. A mountain climb or a journey on the sea may refresh the blood and make us young again; mental rest, or high companionship of mind, may re-establish our intellectual energy. There is something analogous to this in spiritual exhaustion. When the heart has emptied itself of its divinest elements for the good of others, it is secretly renewed, and endowed with still higher strength, by the ministry of the Holy Ghost. The athlete says that he is strengthened by exercise; so the good man is made better by his benevolence; the philanthropist enriches himself by blessing others; the liberal soul is made fat, and he who expends most of his spiritual life has most spiritual life to expend, being "strengthened with might by His Spirit in the inner man." Out of all this renewal, so constant and so abounding, there comes what is called—

"*Joy in the Holy Ghost.*" The awfulness of His presence, so far as it was merely awfulness, has passed away, and is succeeded by "joy unspeakable and full of glory." "The fruit of the Spirit is joy." "The disciples were filled with joy and with the Holy Ghost." Joy is a state in which all the powers and desires of the soul have been brought to the rhythmic point; the contentions of logic have ceased, reason has accepted its boundaries with pious grace, hope has seen lights shining afar, and doubling themselves even in the intervening stream of death, and thus heaven has been anticipated in first fruits and preliminary gladdenings and satisfactions The joy is not in mere facts or histories; it is not the happiness of momentary surprise; it is *spiritual* joy, *vital* joy, joy *in the Holy Ghost.* Why distinguish it so specifically? To show its purity, its duration, and its independence of everything artificial and accidental. This joy, too, unlike much of what commonly goes for joy, admits of analysis, and of defence on the most obviously rational grounds. It is not a flutter that has no meaning, or a throb that has no moral history behind it. If it be likened to a brilliant pinnacle which the sunlight is goldening into glory, it will be because under the pinnacle there is a solid building, and under the building great foundations of rock. Below this exultant joy lie the main facts of spiritual experience,—the fact of pardon, the fact of regeneration, the fact of adoption, the fact of sonship; and out of this solid masonry, a temple not made with hands, there rises the pinnacle of joy which flashes brightly and is seen afar. The Christian cannot but be joyous. All the elements that enter into his new personality conspire to make him the freest and gladdest of men.

We have gathered up these points as specimens of many others, without which the more continuous and formal evidence would be incomplete. The marvellous *scope* of the Spirit's work, even as thus imperfectly outlined, cannot have escaped attention. Look at it: He inspires, teaches, guides, leads, comforts, rebukes, helps, prevents; He enters human life by every line of approach; He rules human conduct by every motive that can stir the will; He throws upon human destiny every light that can make it at once solemn and glad. In this way (so profound, so wide) He fulfils every expectation created by the speciality of His mission. Great historical characters have their places and functions well defined; they begin and they end at points which admit of minute indication; their influence has an assignable range and value; even Jesus Christ, in His human and visible revelation, has His Bethlehem and Olivet, His coming and His going amongst men; but the Holy Ghost penetrates every age and every stratum of life; He goes before our very thought, and holds His light high above the secret of our heart; He inspires with gladness, and He shocks the bravest until their knees tremble. His action, like His nature, is mysterious, so sudden, so real, so deeply felt, yet neither to be measured nor expressed in words,—more delicate than thought, tenderer than love, yet mightier than lightning; present everywhere yet nowhere visible; an eternal certainty yet also an eternal surprise. All this is happily self-consistent, and is precisely what might have been (though with infinite imperfectness) predicated of the conditions. A happy sense of satisfaction comes with it all. Our sense of the necessary mystery of spiritual life is met, whilst all the pure hungerings and thirstings of the soul are appeased. We feel, as we lay hold of the realities of the doctrine, that the revelation of the Person and Ministry of the Holy Ghost is given in the best manner, with awfulness yet with familiarity,—that the Holy Ghost Himself combines the solemn magnificence and independent solitude of the *Sun*, with all the gracious universality and animating friendliness of *Light*.

At this point the expository and affirmative argument may rest for a while. We have other and less pleasant work to do; yet it must be done for the sake of those who may be undertaking the consideration of the subject from its controversial side. It must not be forgotten that Christian thinkers are called, not only to expound their Master's doctrine, but to " contend earnestly for the faith." As a matter of fact there are not a few learned and energetic writers who are doing their utmost (though often in an indirect way) to bring discredit upon Christian theology; and as their books are read by young men, it is important that some notice should be taken of the arguments which are urged upon the attention of their readers. If those arguments are sound and unanswerable we must yield to them, at all events until a teacher shall come with adequate power to disprove and overthrow them. It would be convenient to ignore all such arguments were they not troubling the minds and imperilling the faith of many,—of many, too, who only with infinite reluctance would part with anything which they had ever loved or prized for its Christian worth. How does it come, then, that in the face of highly intellectual hostility we still uphold in honour the Christian faith? Can such men as are well known in the most influential literature of Europe be wrong in their conclusions respecting religion? They are honoured as authorities in history, philosophy, logic, and general science, why are they to be discredited as theological controversialists? These are questions which are urged by thoughtful persons, or which secretly trouble them, and to their considerations we now turn.

PART II.

CRITICAL AND CONTROVERSIAL.

XVII.

THE COLLATERAL SPIRITUAL ARGUMENT.

WE may fitly approach the critical and controversial inquiry which a full discussion of this great subject necessitates, by looking at the collateral argument which is suggested by the fact that even the common objects and affairs of life have their metaphysical or spiritual side, so much so that by the exercise of our physical senses, as commonly understood, we can neither wholly apprehend them, nor wholly account for them. Things which are vividly apparent when viewed superficially, owe their existence to causes or influences which do not appear, and have round about them an atmosphere which no merely bodily sense is acute enough to analyse or explain. If this can be established we shall secure an outside standpoint from which we can look with intellectual advantage upon the higher spiritual mysteries. For the sake of illustration we shall ask for a bold assumption. Let it be granted that we can construct a world of our own: itself and all its contents shall be fabricated by human hands,—its lights, its beauties, its conveniences are all of our own invention and arrangement. Does such a world get rid of the spiritual quantity, and establish the fact of absolute materialism? We think it can be proved that it does nothing of the kind. Such a world is the creation of thought; it is the embodiment of ideas; in short, even that small and dreary world has come up out of the invisible and spiritual, and is inferior to the mind which planned its existence, and is able also to plan its destruction. Given such a world, and the power (whatever it be) which formed it shall be unto it as *God*.

The discussion will be simplified if we undertake, in the first instance, to deal with a materialist of the rudest type,—a man whose beliefs are wholly governed by what he calls his "senses," and who looks at all things in their most obvious and vulgar aspects. Even such a man may be driven to admit that the brick wall which he admires so much was thought about before it was built, and if asked why it was not twelve inches higher will probably acknowledge that the owner had his reasons for stopping just where he did, and if further pressed to explain why the wall is of brick and not of stone, he will again wander into the spiritual region to account for the fact. The vulgar man believes only in what he calls "material civilisation," in the progress of the arts, and in the cultivation of the soil;—"*that*," says he, "is *my* religion." Has he, then, in this easy manner escaped the spiritual and ghostly side of life? This ignorant man looks upon a band of workmen setting up engines, building cisterns, laying tubes, and he pronounces them, in opposition to what he calls "the philosophers," to be the true benefactors of society; he believes in facts not in theories, in the sons of labour and not in intellectual speculators and fanatics. He thinks he sees the whole case. He never dreams that behind all he looks upon there is a spiritual civilisation out of which it all comes. If he could hear "the philosophers" talking about the pressure, equilibrium, cohesion, and motion of fluids, he would be startled to find that even his admired water-supply has its hydronamic *ghost*. His idea has been limited by cisterns, taps, and sound plumbing; as for flotations, specific gravities, and capillary attractions, they are no part of *his* religion. He loves the waterworks, he loves material civilisation. But educate him a little, just far enough to get a dim glimmering of the meaning of such elementary propositions as "the densities of different substances are as their specific gravities," and "the specific gravities of two fluids may be compared by weighing the same solid in each," and he will begin to suspect that even the water question goes back into what will be to *him* something very like a ghostly and religious region. He will, too, modify and redistribute his appreciation of workers. At first, he paid homage to the men who cut the ground, then to the men who laid the tubes, and then to the skilled artisans; but now he begins to see that the mechanic is but the servant of the *thinker*, and that, after all, it may possibly be the philosophers who are the true motors and masters of civilisation. He will be hastened in this direction if he extend his inquiries into other lines of human progress. He admires the lofty and beautiful bridge which is being built over the broad river. He likes bridge-building better than praying, as it appears to him to be more sensible and useful; yet the early rudeness of his materialism is somewhat humbled when he learns that the men who planned the bridge agreed that "in all homogeneous and solid bodies, the resistances to extension and compression must be initially equal, and proportional to the change of dimensions," and that they came to many conclusions which apparently had nothing to do with putting up a bridge. Further consideration will show him that if the *thought* had been wrong the *building* never could have been right; in short, that the bridge was a spiritual conception long before it was a material fact. We are not to suppose that these discoveries will make him a religious man, but we are entitled to expect that they will lead him to admit that even outward civilisation has its invisible world, and that the arts which enrich and refine human life come up out of an abstract and metaphysical region;—these discoveries establish our right to insist that when the world of *fact* is applauded, the world of *thought* shall not be ignored.* " These

---

* "There are, I am aware, persons who willingly admit that not in articles of faith alone, but in the heights of geometry, and even in the necessary first principles of natural philosophy, there exist truths of apodictic force in reason, which the mere understanding strives in vain to comprehend. Take, as an instance, the ascending series of infinites in every finite, a position which involves a contradiction for the understanding, yet follows demonstrably from the very definition of body as that which fills a space. For wherever there is a space filled, there must be an extension to be divided."—*S. T. Coleridge.* And again :—

grand practical innovations," to quote the words of Cuvier, " are only the facile applications of verities of a superior order, not sought with a practical intent,—verities which their authors have pursued for their own sake, impelled solely by an ardour for knowledge. Those who put them in practice could not have discovered them; those who have discovered them had neither the time nor the inclination to pursue them to a practical result. Absorbed in the high regions whither their contemplations had carried them, they had hardly perceived this movement and these creations, though born of their own words. These rising workshops, these peopled colonies, these vessels which furrow the sea, this abundance, this luxury, this tumult, all this comes from discoverers in science, and all this remains strange to them. The day that a doctrine comes into practice they abandon it to the populace, it concerns them no more."

It is easy to see the next occasion of stumbling. The rude inquirer, whose case we are developing, may have advanced far enough to contend that although material civilisation has undoubtedly its intellectual or speculative side, on which the value

---

"They (Bentham and Coleridge) were destined to renew a lesson given to mankind by every age, and always disregarded—to show that speculative philosophy, which to the superficial appears a thing so remote from the business of life and the outward interests of men, is in reality the thing on earth which most influences them, and in the long run overbears every other influence save those which it must itself obey."—*Stuart Mill.*

T

of its practical expression eventually depends, yet he cannot admit any parallel between civilisation and religion, because the one is knowable and the other is unknowable; and he insists that even if there is a God, he neither knows Him nor has any power of knowing Him. Suppose we admit at once that man neither knows God nor has any power of knowing Him, what then? We believe we could justify this admission by the authority of the Bible itself; still, what then? It has not only to be proved that man has no power to know God, it has also to be proved that God has no power to make Himself known. And if the supposed proof fall short of absolute demonstration it is worthless; for if any rational hope be left that God *may* have such power, the world will build its religion upon that hope. So, the difficulty is fairly turned upon the objector; the more obviously so that there is a Book, no matter at this moment what is or is not its authority, which declares that God actually *has* made Himself known to mankind. Here, then, are two statements before us, and we are content that in the first instance nothing should be claimed on the ground of mere authority for the second of them. Let them be taken upon their respective merits, and argued without prejudice. The first statement is, that man has no power to know God; and the second is, that God has power to make Himself known to man. The supporter of the second doctrine has an immense advantage over his opponent in being able to grant what he says, and yet in having the right to demand a plain answer to a still higher proposition. The objector cannot be allowed to escape on the plea that we are resting upon the authority of a book whose inspiration he utterly denies, for we are resting on no such authority; we merely set one doctrine against another,—the one supported by A and the other supported by B, all churches and books being meanwhile ignored. Our contention is that the proposition, *God has power to make Himself known*, is presumptively true, and that as such it is philosophical, sensible, and morally satisfactory. The other proposition, Man has no power to know God, if taken as a settlement of the case, is absurd because of its one-sidedness, and immoral because of its disguised self-sufficiency: it is one-sided in confining its views solely to man, and it is self-sufficient in supposing that if man cannot know God it is impossible that God can make Himself known. Is it probable that a trick may be here played with words by a suggestion to the effect that even if God did make Himself known, man has no power to know Him? Such a suggestion is a contradiction in terms, and on that ground alone it might be dismissed with contempt. It is more, however, than a contradiction in terms; by direct implication it throws discredit upon the Christian consciousness of ages, and charges the deepest convictions of mankind with folly and superstition. We are, for these reasons, reluctant to believe that so unworthy a trick will be played, and therefore we insist that the Christian proposition be discussed and determined strictly on its own merits.

Such discussion will almost certainly involve the consideration of a difficulty proposed by the late Stuart Mill, viz.: "Nothing whatever can be known respecting the origin of things; if you teach a child that God made him, you only put the difficulty one step back by raising the question, Who made God?" Let us, for the sake of unity, suppose that the materialist whose case we are developing, has reached this point in his inquiry, and that he is willing to hear what may be said in reply. It may surprise him to be told that in this instance as in the former the Bible may be quoted in support of the doctrine that nothing whatever can be known concerning the origin of things, and that there is no answer to the question Who made God? We cannot, however, allow any man to fix "the origin of things" at a point which will suit his own argument. He cannot even be allowed to stop at the creation of the heavens and the earth; for who can say with certainty that their creation was not a trifling point in an infinite series of creations? *Our* history may begin with the establishment of the heavens and the earth, but who can tell what creations preceded them, or of what universes they may be but the outposts or shadows? Let us, then, first settle what is meant by "the origin of things,"—an ambiguous and elastic term. Probably we are agreed that on the Christian side we cannot go farther back than the point which is marked "God," and we are warned by Mr. Mill not to stop at that point, because we may be asked Who made God? But the Bible has provided

The Collateral Spiritual Argument. 277

against this very difficulty. The Bible itself declares " the incognoscibility of the Infinite "; it challenges the universe to find out the Almighty unto perfection, and declares that there is no searching of His understanding. It even says that no man hath seen God at any time; that no man can see God and live; and that consequently, in its primary and inclusive signification, nothing whatever can be known concerning the origin of things. The Christian will properly insist that he believes in the Christian revelation of God; his faith goes out in the direction of mediation; he will say that though he has not seen God yet he has seen Jesus; and as for the rest, he will walk by faith and not by sight. By the compulsion of his Christian veneration he veils himself before the essential Deity. He speaks of Him as "the only Potentate, the King of kings, and Lord of lords, dwelling in light which no man can approach unto; whom no man hath seen, nor can see;" yet his faith exults in the fact that " the only begotten Son, which is in the bosom of the Father, He hath declared Him." With such plain biblical declarations before us, we are entitled to deny all originality to the philosopher who warns us that nothing can be known concerning the origin of things, and who points out that sooner or later we shall raise the question, Who made God ? The Christian believes in God who made the heavens and the earth, and rules all things by an outstretched arm ; he has a conception of infinitude and eternity which fills his soul with satisfaction; and he will not allow his worship to be marred or suspended because there may be beyond his imagination a "thunder of power" which is yet withheld.

Even Stuart Mill himself (trifling to all appearance with his own consistency), "in reviewing the series of arguments adduced by Sir W. Hamilton for the incognoscibility and inconceivability of the Absolute," acknowledges that if for the metaphysical abstraction "The Absolute" be substituted the intelligible concrete expression "Something absolute," the most of Sir William's arguments will lose their application; and, he adds, "if I talk of a Being who is absolute in wisdom and goodness, that is, who knows everything, and at all times intends what is best for every sentient creature, I understand perfectly what I mean; and however much the fact may transcend my conception, the shortcoming can only consist in my being ignorant of the details of which the reality is composed." Now this is what the Christian student does; he knows "perfectly what he means" when he uses the term "God," though "the fact transcends his conception;" it fills him with satisfaction and thankfulness; it draws out his whole life in one trustful and loving act of worship; and, in his judgment, it sets him in a right relation to the universe, to society, and to the future. But why aim at the conception of such a Being, if it be true that when we have succeeded in realising it, we have only reached the point of asking, *Who made Him?* It appears to us that this reasoning on the part of Stuart Mill applies disastrously (if it apply at all) in other than theological directions. It discourages all high investigation, and in so many words tells intellectual ambition that when it has done its utmost there is still another question that it cannot answer. If we may not speak of *God* because we may be asked, "Who made Him?" neither may we speak of *the highest intellectual conceptions of man*, because we may be asked, "Are there not conceptions higher still?" It is on record that Ellicott set one clock going by the ticks of another, even when the two clocks were separated by a wall; but according to Stuart Mill's reasoning we must not ask, Who started the first clock? because though Ellicott may have started it, we only raise the further question, Who started Ellicott? By such verbal trifling men may be affrighted out of worship by the very question which, when properly understood, ought to invest religious homage with the charm of a profounder solemnity.

In criticising Dean Mansel's definition of "The Infinite," it appears to us that Mr. Mill too easily contents himself with a flippant answer. Having cited the Dean's definition, he exclaims,—" Here certainly is an Infinite whose infinity does not seem to be of much use to it.* Through the word "use" we see into the error which pervades much of Mr. Mill's reasoning upon religious subjects. But what, after all, if it should be proved that Infinity is *not* of much use to itself? It would appear as if this

---

* Examination of Sir W. Hamilton's Philosophy, p. 96.

were very likely to be the case, and as if it were a most gracious instead of a most lamentable fact. Suppose it should be true that infinity is of "use" to *others;* that infinity can only be revealed relatively; that infinity can only be known through condescension? Would any great disaster befall mankind if this were proved to be so? Mr. Mill himself again and again proposes to substitute for such abstractions as "The Infinite" and "The Absolute," such concrete expressions as "an infinitely good Being," and "a Being absolute in knowledge." But who knows that any Being is infinitely *good*, except by judging the public administration which he conducts? The infinity of God is one thing, and our knowledge of that infinity is another. What if God does not exist for Himself, and if infinity should be but the supreme *pain*, in the absence of channels through which it can pour the expressions of its love? Seeing that there is more or less of difficulty in every attempted solution of divine mysteries, it is not inconceivable that some minds should adopt conclusions which secure the sanction of the heart in addition to the assent of the understanding. Mr. Mill makes himself grimly merry with Dean Mansel's "Infinite," in the following manner: "Instead of 'the Infinite,' substitute 'an infinitely good Being,' and Mr. Mansel's argument reads thus: If there is anything which an infinitely good Being cannot become—if He cannot become bad—that is a limitation, and the goodness cannot be infinite. If there is anything which an infinitely good Being actually

The Collateral Spiritual Argument. 281

is (namely good), He is excluded from being any other thing, as from being wise or powerful." In the first part of this reasoning it is forgotten that one attribute may *exclude* another,—for example infinite goodness excludes evil, and infinite power excludes weakness; and in the second part of this reasoning it seems to be overlooked that a being cannot be infinite in one attribute without being infinite in all others which are of the same quality or move in the same direction : thus, infinite goodness connotes and necessitates infinite wisdom, for if the wisdom be less than the goodness, the degree in which it is less is the possible measure of its deficiency or misapplication. In like manner infinite goodness and infinite wisdom involve infinite power. Infinite wisdom must know how to resist every destructive agent or influence; if it does *not* know, then it is not infinite. As to infinite power, it must be remembered that power is more than strength; strength is but an element, or at best merely an expression, of power,—wisdom is necessary to power, so is goodness, for without them there could be nothing but misdirected and lawless force. But may there not be infinite goodness and infinite wisdom, without power to bring them to bear successfully on a definite object? Everything will depend upon the nature of the object to be secured; if it be the creation of a world the answer will be an unqualified negative, but if it be the renewal of a human heart the answer will be as unqualified an affirmative. Let us suppose that infinite wisdom can be the attribute of one Being, and infinite power the attribute of another: then we have infinite power creating a universe whose structure and appointments indicate infinite wisdom, yet the power itself cannot be infinitely wise because infinite wisdom is the attribute of a distinctly separate Being. But if there is a verbal difficulty in the proposition, Infinite wisdom involves infinite power, it will be seen to be merely verbal if we transpose the terms, and conduct the argument from the other end, viz.: infinite power involves infinite wisdom. Thus, whoever has power to create a universe, even of an extent which optical instruments have discovered, must have had wisdom in at least the same degree. That universe we know to consist of innumerable planets; those planets we know to be in many cases millions of miles distant from one another, and to revolve in orbits of inconceivable extent,—here we have at all events an approximation to the infinite, and our contention is that whatever be the degree of *power* represented by the universe, precisely the same degree of *wisdom* is logically involved.

But the materialist who has accompanied us thus far may state a difficulty: he may now admit that more importance attaches to the intellectual or spiritual side of things than at first he supposed; he may even go farther, and give the decided preponderance of importance to that side, and yet he may find it so difficult as to be almost impossible to believe that spirituality can be not only personified but deified, so that behind all things in secrecy, and above all things in power, is the Being known and worshipped as God. But, as it appears to us, he is bound to believe this, or to deny the spirituality which is known to be less than divine. He must remember that the spirituality which he has admitted to underlie the works of civilization is distinctly *personal;* he will probably find himself unable to think of it apart from personality; from this point he must give extension and elevation to his reasoning, and if he feel himself overpowered and bewildered, as undoubtedly he will, as he proceeds with the great argument, he may call in Faith, and in its exercise he will enjoy religious rest. In doing so he may honestly claim to be acting even more *reasonably* than the intellectual libertine who denies everything that cannot be certified by the senses. It may be worth while to point out in this connection that in denying the existence of God we do not escape all difficulty and put an end to all mystery. When a man says he will not trouble himself about religion farther than to deny it, has he, as a rational being, cleared the whole region of difficulty, and found his way into unclouded light and complete repose? Mark the qualification, "as a rational being," for if he please to commit intellectual suicide, and to live the life of a mere animal, he may escape all mystery and all joy by this act of madness. But let him continue to think and to reason, and mystery will follow his denial, and rest upon him as the shadow of death. *With* God there is the mystery of light; *without* Him there is the mystery of darkness. If men say they will believe only what they see, the philosophers (not only the theologians) will at once demand to know what they mean by "seeing," and will startle them with some statements which will show that all mystery does not darken around purely religious questions. Sir William Hamilton will tell them "To say we perceive by sight the sun or moon, is a false, or an elliptical, expression"! Even when Dr. Reid, so eminent as an intellectual philosopher, says, "When ten men look at the sun or moon, they all see the same individual object," Sir William contradicts him, and says, "The truth is that each of these persons sees a different object, because each person sees a different complement of rays in relation to his individual organ"; and Sir William adds that "each individual sees two different objects, with his right eye and with his left eye." Yet men talk of limiting their faith by their sight. They talk, too, of perception as if it were a simple act of the physical vision. Sir William Hamilton teaches a more spiritual doctrine: "It is not by perception, but by a process of reasoning, that we connect the objects of sense with existences beyond the sphere of immediate knowledge. It is enough that perception affords us the knowledge of the *non-ego* at the point of sense. To arrogate to it the power of immediately informing us of external things which are only the causes of the object we immediately perceive, is either positively erroneous, or a confusion of language arising from an inadequate discrimination of the phenomena." It is plain, therefore, that the man who boasts of emancipating himself from the thraldom and fear of religious mystery, will not feel himself very comfortable if he exchange the society of theologians for the society of metaphysicians. The fact is that men who walk backwards cannot feel themselves comfortable anywhere; they are out of sympathy with the spirit of the universe, and their boasted liberty soon proves itself to be but a theatrical attitude.

In accepting the doctrine of the personality of God, the Infinite and Absolute Being, we elevate human nature itself to its proper dignity. Human nature as a self-contained quantity is manifestly a failure, if regard be had to the barbarism, the oppression, the tumult, the injustice, and the confusion, which so largely preponderate in the history of mankind; it is a contest of blind forces; what appears to be virtue is but a cunning adaptation of vice; retribution is degraded into a lucky coincidence; and generosity is but an improved form of speculative investment. On the other hand, human nature as the creation of the Infinite and Absolute Being called God, is undergoing a process of discipline and education; the terrific conflicts which are apparently fraught with destruction are all under control. Weakness, poverty, and sin itself, have their great uses in the social system.

The present, with all its exaggerated proportions and furious clamour, is but a point upon an immeasurable circumference of splendid possibilities. Over all, enthroned as King and Judge of the universe, is the all-wise, the all-good, the all-powerful God, who in His own good time will bring in the spiritual summer of which we see now only the early and unpropitious spring,—this is the Christian hope; and we claim that, viewed merely as a *theory* of human life, it has an infinite advantage over every suggestion that excludes God and denies the invisible and the eternal state.

Possibly the supposed opponent in this argument may content himself by saying that whatever be the exact truth of these difficult questions, he has resolved upon a position of neutrality; he will not vex himself either with metaphysics or theology; he will do the plain work of the day, and leave everything beyond without any attempt at solution. So be it, then. There is more hope of a fool than of him. Only let it be clearly understood by others that the world owes nothing to such men, either for the healing of its sorrows or the direction of its progress. They are but consumers at best, and what good they occasion is limited strictly to their capacity as such. Possibly, on the other hand, our supposed opponent may not be unwilling to advance with us, but for the presence of certain difficulties which physical science has gathered around the distinctively spiritual argument. This is reasonable and therefore hopeful. We proceed accordingly to ascertain, as far as possible, the exact nature of those difficulties, and to inquire whether there is any sufficient answer to them on the part of Christian faith.

XVIII.

MATERIALISM AND SPIRITUALISM.

In passing still farther into the critical and controversial region of this argument, we shall endeavour to understand the anti-spiritual theory as it has been expounded by its most prominent and fearless upholders. To the utmost of our ability we shall, by careful quotation, state that theory with as much precision and completeness as if we were about to defend it; at the same time we must guard ourselves so far as to say that in antichristian writings we have often been embarrassed by ambiguities and qualifications fatal to perfect simplicity. In those writings there has been such a skilful use of parenthetic limitations that it is most difficult to bind down the writers to any specific meaning. A whole page of very definite and emphatic expression of anti-christian opinion may have a doubt thrown upon its purpose by a solitary word at the close; or an apparent tendency towards Christian conclusions may be most ruthlessly inverted by an infidel protest of unusual desperation. It is the more needful to point this out in view of our determination to use the rod of criticism in a very personal manner; in the first instance for strictly judicial purposes, and in the second by way of example to those who think that personal character and personal opinions have no connection. The reader is invited to note the consistency which marks the character of materialists from the earliest times to the present day, and to consider whether that consistency does not deserve to carry with it much argumentative weight.

Unwilling as we are to describe Epicurus as a materialist in the modern sense of the term—a term, indeed, which everybody is anxious either to modify or disown—seeing that, as Cicero asserts, he spoke of the Supreme Being in terms the most sublime, and in his letter to Menecius he defended the gods from a vulgar misconception, yet he taught that all mental phenomena are due to the properties of matter, and boldly affirmed that the soul is material. By a very remarkable forecast he laid down a great principle which Hume adopted more than two thousand years later, and for which he secured a reputation for originality, that great principle being that sensation is the only source of human knowledge. Hobbes, who used his metaphysical powers to escape the persecution which honest men would have encountered, and whose egregious mathematical errors should have tempered his partizanship in philosophy, made sensation the basis of every mental operation. In his *Leviathan* declared it to be " the sole originator of our ideas, the sole medium and test of truth." " The mind itself he viewed as wholly material, the phenomena of consciousness being the direct result of our organization." Locke was far enough from being a materialist, yet his denunciation of the doctrine of "innate ideas" seems to point to the conclusion that he was a believer in the doctrine of sensation as understood by his predecessor; this, indeed, he avows, yet he adds the word "reflection" to the word "sensation," and this is an instance of the ambiguity of which we have complained,—the term "reflection" being open to two very dissimilar uses. Hartley, a disciple of Locke, spoken of as an ingenuous and noble man, boldly struck off the term "reflection," and resolved thought and feeling into vibrations of the brain. Priestley did the same thing. As for David Hume, he has been correctly described as a nihilist; "he denied everything and affirmed nothing;" believing that such knowledge as we have comes from sensation, "he maintained that as we have no sensation of efficiency, we can have no idea of it, and no evidence of its reality. A cause is not that which produces an effect but simply that which uniformly precedes it. We are nothing but a bundle or collection of different perceptions, which succeed each other with an inconceivable rapidity, and are in perpetual flux and movement." If we inquire into materialism as understood and taught by continental materialists, we shall find that Locke's most brilliant disciple, Condillac, pronounced all thoughts, feelings, and volitions, so many "transformed sensations," though (for reasons presently to be stated) he maintained theistic principles, and, in direct contravention of his own philosophy, insisted on the necessity of a divine revelation. What Condillac was too time-serving to do was done by a bolder hand. Baron d'Holbach proclaimed that "matter and motion are eternal; thought is an agitation of the nerves; the soul is the result of our corporeal organisation; the will the strongest sensation; the ground of morals a regard to our own happiness,— there is no freedom, no morality, no future existence, no God." This is an instance in which there is no just occasion to complain of ambiguity.

The modern scientists of England who are supposed to favour these doctrines decline to be classed as materialists, their ground being that they do not degrade spirit but elevate matter. Mr. Herbert Spencer is very explicit upon this point: "Men who have not risen above that vulgar conception which unites with matter the contemptuous epithets 'gross' and 'brute,' may naturally feel dismay at the proposal to reduce the phenomena of life, of mind, and of society, to a level with those which they think so degraded. . . . The course proposed does not imply a degradation of the so-called higher, but an elevation of the so-called lower." Mr. Herbert Spencer teaches that physical forces can be transformed into chemical, and that chemical forces can be transformed into vital, whereupon he says, "Many will be alarmed by the assertion that the forces which we distinguish as mental come within the same generalisation. Yet there is no alternative but to make this concession." Professor

Huxley avows himself a disciple of Hume, and gives it as his opinion that the following words of his master contain "most wise advice":—"If we take in our hand any volume of divinity or school-metaphysics, for instance, let us ask, does it contain any abstract reasoning concerning quantity or number? No. Does it contain any experimental reasoning concerning matter of fact or existence? No. Commit it, then, to the flames; for it can contain nothing but sophistry and illusion." We shall take occasion presently to examine this "most wise advice." Before doing so, we wish to give Professor Huxley an opportunity of stating in his own words that all mental operations are due to physical forces. In his "Lay Sermons," he says: "It may seem a small thing to admit that the dull vital actions of a fungus or a foraminifer are the properties of their protoplasm, and are the direct results of the nature of the matter of which they are composed. But if, as I have endeavoured to prove to you, their protoplasm is essentially identical with, and most readily converted into, that of any animal, I can discover no logical halting-place, between the admission that such is the case, and the further concession that all vital action may with equal propriety be said to be the result of the molecular forces of the protoplasm which displays it. And if so, it must be true, in the same sense and to the same extent, that the thoughts to which I am now giving utterance, and your thoughts regarding them, are the expression of molecular changes in that matter of life which is the source of our other vital phenomena."* In strict harmony with this view, the professor continues: "I take it to be demonstrable that it is utterly impossible to prove that anything whatever may not be the effect of a material and necessary cause, and that human logic is utterly incompetent to prove that any act is really spontaneous. A really spontaneous act is one which, by the assumption, has no cause, and the attempt to prove such a negative as this is, on the face of the matter, absurd. And while it is thus a philosophical impossibility to demonstrate that any given phenomenon is not the effect of a material cause, any one who is acquainted with the history of science will admit that its progress has in all ages meant, and now more than ever means, the extension of the province of what we call matter and causation, and the concomitant gradual banishment from all regions of human thought of what we call spirit and spontaneity."†

The phrase "molecular changes," reminds us that the materialistic philosophy maintains that all mental phenomena are to be accounted for by molecular motion and molecular grouping: the brain is composed of molecules, probably too minute for microscopic detection, whose motion, combination, and electrical discharges, account for all supposed spiritual phenomena: a definite thought and a definite molecular action of the brain occur

---

* "Lay Sermons," p. 138.   † Id., pp. 141-2.

simultaneously: the growth of the body is mechanical, and thought, as exercised by man, has its correlative in the physics of the brain. It was apparently supposed by Hartley that there were little shakings of the brain accompanying every act of thought or perception: the shakings are certain throbbings, vibrations, or stirrings in a whitish half fluid substance, and this motion is thought and feeling, and precisely the same thought and feeling will exist wherever a similar motion can be excited in a similar substance. In so many words Comte (whom so many English philosophers are now anxious to disown) says, "That the positive theory of the intellectual and affective functions is henceforth unchangeably regarded as consisting in the study, both rational and experimental, of the various phenomena of internal sensibility, which are proper to the cerebral ganglia, apart from their external apparatus. It is, therefore, simply a prolongation of animal physiology, properly so called, when this is extended so as to include the fundamental and ultimate attributes." According to Stuart Mill, the mind may be a voltaic pile giving shocks of thought.

We have here, then, great names and bold statements arrayed against the Christian faith, and Christian men are bound, not only to recognise that fact, but to inquire fearlessly into the intellectual and practical value of the antagonism which such names and statements represent. From the beginning, Christianity has had a distinctly controversial side; opposition is nothing new as applied to Christian faith; it would therefore be unbecoming on the part of the Church to turn aside when its very life is threatened by culture and science. For personal and general reasons we decline the leadership of the great names which have just passed in review, and this ground we now attempt to make good. We must bespeak candid attention to the personal attack which we are about to make, because, as a general rule, personality ought to have no place in controversy. Exceptional circumstances, however, may justify a suspension of that rule. Such circumstances we now plead, and we must await the sequel for a complete justification of this course. Personality when used in argument merely for its own sake, and specially when used for the express purpose of wounding the feelings of an antagonist, is the unpardonable sin of controversy; but when, as in this case, we can only interpret the abstract by the concrete, and determine the value of an argument by its effect as seen in the life of its upholder, personality becomes doctrinal, and criticism of character is the counterpart of criticism of logic. In this sense alone we beg to be understood. We are quite willing that the Christian argument should be subjected to precisely the same tests as we are about to employ in the case of opposing creeds, so that if we give no quarter we certainly claim none.

I. Personal Reasons.

It is of course difficult to collect much information respecting an ancient Greek philosopher the most of whose works have been destroyed, but it is quite certain, in the judgment of critics, whose literary authority is undisputed by sceptics themselves, that Epicurus held opinions which, if known in the right quarter, would have secured him the honours of persecution, but which he kept so well in concealment that next to nothing was known of them until after his death. Even Cicero, whose friendly opinion we have quoted, points out, in the third book of his "Offices," that Epicurus does not always consult consistency in the maintenance of his arguments, and warns Marcus that "We are not to regard what Epicurus says, *but what it is consistent in him to say;*" showing that the crafty Greek was not unskilled in verbal manipulation. As we have pointed out, Epicurus made the belief of a god one of the fundamental dogmas of his philosophy, but in reality denied him when Anaxagoras was put to death for atheism in the city of Athens.* Epicurus had a god in his creed, yet with a controversial skill which speaks more for his cunning than his honour he so expressed his opinions respecting the functions of the gods as to render this primary dogma utterly useless; so that though for prudential motives he found it

---

* Augustine : *De Civ. Dei*, lib. xviii., cap. 41.

convenient to have a *god*, yet for philosophical reasons he had no *religion*. We should gladly give Epicurus the benefit of any doubt upon the subject if his case, as the representative of a school, stood alone; but if we find as we proceed that this subtle and selfish prudence always accompanies doctrines of the same class, we fear that a strongly presumptive case will be made out against Epicurus.

Condillac, Diderot, and D'Alembert took theistic ground in accounting for the origin of the world, but this was well known to be more a matter of prudence than conviction. A writer in the *Encyclopedia Britannica*, commenting upon Condillac, uses language remarkably suggestive: "His curious saving clause will not vindicate his opinions among the philosophers of this country, however convenient it might be found among the adherents of the Roman Catholic Church, that the dependence of the soul on the senses is one of the effects of the fall of man, and the proof of his present state of degradation." This is the man who pronounced all thoughts, feelings, and volitions, only so many "transformed sensations." What if, finding it impossible to secure immunity from trouble by a straightforward avowal and impartial application of his doctrines, he took counsel with prudence, and used the hands of Esau to pluck the blessing of personal protection from a church whose theology he contemned in his heart? If his case stood alone we might give him the benefit of a blindly charitable construction of his timidity, but we have seen that in the case of Epicurus at least he has congenial though ignoble companionship.

Hobbes presents a curious mixture of boldness, cunning, and cowardice. His vanity would not allow him to be silent upon his dogmas, but when persecution on account of them came near him, he disennobled himself by recourse to the most unmanly subterfuges. His political system was avowedly one of expediency, and so little did he care for precision and constancy of meaning in the use of words, that he actually defended himself for writing ambiguously under circumstances which exposed him to peril. He boasted, too, that his metaphysical intellect was more than a match for those who sought to expose his inconsistencies, and bring upon him penalty and disgrace. As for his power of self-contradiction, it is, we trust, unrivalled. He said that the Scriptures are the voice of God, but that their only authority is derived from the civil magistrate; he said that inspiration is the immediate gift of God, and yet he pronounced every man mad that claimed it; he said that worship was due to God, and in the next breath he declared that all religion is ridiculous. So much in proof of our introductory impeachment. This same Hobbes, quoted with applause by modern materialists, says: " It is lawful to make use of ill-instruments to do ourselves good. If I were cast into a deep pit, and the devil should put down his cloven foot, I would take hold of it to be drawn

Materialism and Spiritualism. 299

out by it." And when this valorous man came—with pitiful reluctance and dismay—to face the inevitable, he said : " I shall be glad to find a hole to creep out of the world at."

As to David Hume it will be found, on reference to his works, that he actually advised a sceptical friend to accept church preferment, and preach what he did not believe, affirming that to pique oneself on sincerity in such matters is to put too great a respect on the vulgar and their superstitions ! This is the man who, in what Professor Huxley calls "most wise advice," recommends the fire as the proper place for sundry books of divinity. We shall recur to Hume in a few pages.

We come now to John Stuart Mill, who conjectured that the brain may be a voltaic pile, giving shocks of thought. In his Autobiography (the most melancholy book of modern days) Mr. Mill says : " I was brought up from the first without any religious belief in the ordinary sense of the term ": " It would have been wholly inconsistent with my father's ideas of duty *to allow me* to acquire impressions contrary to his convictions and feelings respecting religion." (These are the men who are supposed to be unsectarian and liberal !) What follows is remarkable : " In giving me an opinion contrary to that of the world, my father thought it necessary to give it as one which could not be prudently avowed to the world." The reader will observe the word " prudently." What follows is still more remarkable. Mr. Mill having thus acted on a principle of prudence himself, and enjoyed any social advantages which might arise from its exercise, leaves a book to be published after his death in which he says : " On religion in particular, the time appears to me to have come when it is the duty of all who, being qualified in point of knowledge, have on mature consideration satisfied themselves that the current opinions are not only false but hurtful, to make their dissent known, at least if they are amongst those whose station or reputation gives their opinion a chance of being attended to."* A " voltaic battery" that could withhold this " shock" until Mr. Mill himself was secured against all personal consequences must have been a valuable property. It appears, too, to have been faithful in all its generations, in proof whereof it could summon Epicurus, Condillac, D'Alembert, Voltaire, Hobbes, Hume, and Stuart Mill, to show its wily prudence and its consummate skill in making other people its catspaw. Bolingbroke, too, could be called, for with characteristic valour he left a book which was not to be published until after his decease, in which he avowed his anti-christian sentiments in the plainest terms ; a chivalrous act which drew from Dr. Johnson's "voltaic battery" the following shock : " Bolingbroke, sir, was a scoundrel and a coward ; he loaded a blunderbuss against Christianity which he had not the courage to fire during his lifetime, but left

---

* Autobiography, p. 45.

half a crown to a hungry Scotsman* to draw the trigger after he was dead." † A voltaic battery not to be trifled with! Mr. John Stuart Mill accepted his atheism from his father, and then sneered at other people for holding fast by a traditional faith.

For these *personal* reasons we are not disposed to accept the doctrines of the materialistic school. We know the ground that will be taken, and are quite prepared to follow our opponents to it. First of all, we shall be asked, Whether Christianity itself has not had its unworthy professors; and, secondly, Whether a doctrine may not be true whatever may have been the personal character of its teachers. These inquiries follow naturally upon our criticism, and we shall therefore take care not to evade them.

Christianity has undoubtedly had its unworthy

---

* David Mallet.

† In his "Leaders of Public Opinion in Ireland," Mr. LECKY thus describes the moral character of Lord Bolingbroke :—"The son of a worthless and dissipated character who had fallen in a duel, St. John had been early thrown upon the world, surrounded by all the associations of vice, and endowed by nature with gifts almost as splendid as have ever been united in a single man. . . . He plunged with reckless impetuosity into the life of dissipation that opened before him, and, in an age of libertines, was conspicuous as a libertine. . . . The chief cause of his failure was his own character. It was the restless spirit of intrigue which led him to plot against his colleague, and to enter into relations with the Pretender. It was the notorious dissipation of his private life and the laxity of his opinions, which deprived him of the confidence of his own party, and of that of the great majority of the English people."

professors, whose hypocrisies and crimes ought in no degree to be palliated or concealed. But—and let this point be noted as carrying with it the substance of the whole answer—what they have done is in direct and shameful contravention of their professed beliefs, and is condemned with infinite displeasure by Christianity itself: this is the vital difference between them, and the skilful ambidexters whose morals we have traced. Wicked deeds have been done in the name of patriotism, but no one would think of quoting them as arguments against the love of country or the oath of loyalty. The name of truth itself has been pressed into the service of falsehood, yet the integrity of truth remains unimpaired, and the spirit of truth insists on vengeance. So with Christian profession: it has unquestionably been used for the worst of purposes, but always against its own vehement protest, and probably always with some measure of self-reproach on the part of the criminal himself. Now the exact contrary, as to morals, may logically and consistently be the case with a thorough believer in what is commonly known as materialism. Given a man who rejects all the ideas which Christians attach to such words as "God" and "Spirit"; who believes that so far as his own existence is concerned there is no world but the present; that there is neither life nor judgment after physical dissolution; that our relation to the universe is exhausted by our present sensation and consciousness; let him believe these things without a doubt, and commit himself to them without a fear, and the difficulty which other men would feel under certain moral conditions vanishes, and it is easy to see that such opinions must result in precisely the conduct of such men as Hobbes, Hume, Bolingbroke, and Stuart Mill. The materialist defends himself by what he calls "prudence," because in days of persecution it is absolutely his strongest defence : in effect he says, "Why should I expose myself to ill-treatment and suffering when by mental reservation, ambiguity, or positive misstatement, I can escape my tormentors and spend my days in quietness and ease? There is no God, no future, no judgment, no heaven, no hell,—what, then, have I to fear? There is no absolute standard of truth, no infallible authority in morals ; life is a riddle, and speculation is too fickle to be worth dying for, so why be a martyr when I can have the comfort and applause of popularity?" There is nothing in the creed of materialism, so far as we comprehend it, to point its believers to another course; this is its natural and necessary teaching in times of persecution, and its proper relief in seasons of fear. That it is so, is proved by the examples which have been cited, examples which constitute a logical and moral *propter hoc* as complete as it is self-evident. It will be understood, then, that in assigning personal reasons for declining to accept the materialistic theory, we are not influenced by the errors of men who were false to their creed, but by the conduct of men who gave that creed its proper expression under conditions which try the reality and worth of human convictions. There are circumstances in which we can most correctly interpret the doctrine through the man, and this is specially so in cases of abstract or metaphysical reasoning: a student may find himself unable to follow the dark and intricate ratiocination, yet he can form a correct opinion of its practical results as shown in the conduct of the reasoner. John Stuart Mill himself seems to admit this, for in his Autobiography (p. 159), he says that his practice, learned from Hobbes and his own father, was to study abstract principles by means of the best concrete instances he could find. In pursuance of this course we think a student might feel himself entitled to say to Hobbes, or Hume, or Stuart Mill, "I cannot give up my Christian faith at your bidding after what I have seen of your conduct in times of peril: your reasoning may turn out to be as false as your courage: you may turn upon me in the hour of danger when I point you out as my teachers, and may disown me, and abandon me to my fate. Hobbes I cannot trust, because he says 'It is lawful to make use of ill instruments to do ourselves good'; Hume I cannot trust, because he advised a sceptic to preach Christianity, and not to pique himself on his sincerity; Stuart Mill I cannot trust, because he was kept silent by prudence, and then advised other people to do after his death what he had not dared to do in his own lifetime,—as if Goliath had on his dying day told his fellow-soldiers to look for a memorandum in his helmet which would give them his mature opinion on the state of public affairs, said opinion being that on the very day after his funeral the Philistines should challenge Israel to battle. No. I decline your leadership. Intellectually you may be great men; I cannot follow all the subtleties of your *reasoning*, but when I see your *honesty* break down I begin to suspect that there may be a flaw in your metaphysics. *You* are not the men to lure me from the standard of 'the noble army of martyrs,' for it is evidently consistent with your principles to befool and victimise others, and to keep yourselves far enough from danger and pain." But it may be said that men *have* suffered, personally and socially, for their anti-christian or anti-spiritual beliefs. Possibly so; but in their cases, rare enough as to number, the reasoning has been so manifestly feeble and untenable as to deprive their mere courage of all moral value; their courage has either been the expression of bravado, or an attempt to secure notoriety by circuitous means. In the cases before us we have the most splendid natural endowments, the most consummate mental culture, and the most conspicuous opportunities of influencing public prejudice, and yet all these have been associated either with a "prudence" that was cowardly, or an attitude that was hypocritical; it will be unfair, therefore, to drag up some obscure and uninfluential

x

sufferer, and make him the pedestal on which to exalt the pretensions of men who had learning enough to bewilder the multitude, but not courage enough to take the consequences of their own opinions. Men like Hobbes, Hume, and Stuart Mill, ought to have done their own martyrdom.

But may not a doctrine be true whatever be the personal character of its teachers; as, for example, may not Christianity be true though some of its expositors are known to have been bad men? This is a mixed question, and by no means so unsophisticated as it seems to be. *Primâ facie* it calls for an explicit affirmative, but a little consideration may put another face upon it. For Christianity we must go to Christ, then the inquiry will assume this form: May not Christianity be true though Jesus Christ was a bad man? Prove that Jesus Christ was a bad man, that Peter, James, and John were bad men, and that Paul was a hypocrite and a coward, and though metaphysically it may be possible for their teaching to be true, yet any argument against Christianity must be infinitely strengthened by such glaring blemishes in the personality of its upholders. Even the delinquency of Peter is inadmissible as an argument in this discussion, because it occurred before the full development of Christianity, and was more than expiated by a life of unsurpassed devotion, and a death unparalleled in the annals of suffering. But apart from these considerations the analogy fails altogether as between materialism and Christianity. The materialist will have to be better than his creed if in any sense he be a good man at all; but the Christian professor cannot take the least departure from the strictest purity or honour without instantly incurring the severest displeasure of his creed. Materialism, either as defined or exemplified in the cases which have been quoted, acknowledges no moral sanctions, ignores the existence of God, denies the immortality of the soul, and treats the idea of a spiritual future with contemptuous laughter; thus all the forces and influences which the Christian accepts as moral guarantees are dismissed from the consideration of the materialist. Our contention, therefore, is that the creed itself is bad, and that it proves its badness by the conduct of those whose sincerity is tested by persecution. The question is, What are *the natural and proper tendencies* of materialism? not, What are some of its occasional and accidental applications? Unquestionably, as in the case of such a man as John Stuart Mill, we see an anti-spiritual creed associated with much that is really beautiful in conduct,—with benevolent interest in public welfare, with private charity, with patriotic ardour and devotion. But all this is beside the mark if used as an exhaustive argument in reply to the charge we are making. It merely shows that a man may be better than his creed; and if it proves anything more than this it proves too much, for probably there is not a creed known amongst mankind that cannot point to some of its professors as amiable and benevolent men, and consequently that could not claim to be true on that ground. With Christianity the case is different: whereas materialism is bound in deference to public opinion to provide for itself some sort of moral theory, Christianity is itself, intrinsically and necessarily, a moral creed that is under no obligation to provide a theory of the physical universe. The result is that whilst the materialist may be a bad man, without violating his strictly materialistic doctrines, the Christian professor is bound by every principle of his faith to be pure and beneficent; he is bound, too, by his professed love of Christ, to be "faithful unto death," to despise shame, and to sacrifice his life in defence of his spiritual convictions. The materialist is under no such obligation; to him (without God or immortality) shame is defeat, persecution is a reflection upon his adroitness, and death is the crowning proof of his impotence. Our conclusion, therefore, is, that whilst immorality is not inconsistent with materialism, it separates itself for ever from the very nature of Christianity; and that the question, May not a doctrine be true whatever be the personal character of its teachers? does not apply in this case, because no doctrine can be morally good that ignores morals, and no doctrine that ignores morals can be supported by men that are morally good.

II. GENERAL REASONS.

For reasons more general, the anti-spiritual theory may for the present at least be declined.

1. No man of science can object to our waiting until that theory has been more fully tested. It is almost trifling with common sense to give an assurance on behalf of Christian thinkers that they watch the progress of physical science with the keenest interest and satisfaction, yet unless the assurance be given in the plainest terms theologians will be exposed to that easiest of all literary imputations, a fear of the advancement of any knowledge that is not distinctively religious. Physicists have so often, happily for the best interests of science, contradicted and corrected each other on matters of *fact*, that it may be prudent to wait before absolutely deifying any theory which has yet been propounded. The science of one age has been the laughing-stock of the next. There was a time when "astronomers proved syllogistically that the planets could have no independent motion, because the heavens were incorruptible, and nature abhorred a vacuum."* The chemistry of the Greeks is little better than barbarism to modern Europeans. Leibnitz insisted that matter is entirely homogeneous; and, on the other hand, Sir Isaac Newton contended that its atoms are "separated by void spaces." Stuart Mill himself reminds us that "the Hindoos thought that the

---

* Macaulay, vol. v., p. 241.

earth required to be supported by an elephant; but the earth turned out quite capable of supporting itself, and hanging self-balanced on its own centre." Descartes thought that a material medium filling the whole space between the earth and the sun was required to enable them to act on one another; but it has been found sufficient to suppose an "immaterial law of attraction, and the medium and its vortices dropped off as superfluities."* Sir John Herschel once gave it as his opinion that 76° was the angle of maximum polarisation, but "careful observation" satisfied him that 90° or thereabouts is the correct angle. Newton decided "that if the density is greater in the interior of the earth than at the centre, the compression would be greater than in the case of a spheroid of equal density;" but Huygens ingeniously demonstrated that the greatest of English philosophers had fallen into a mistake. Hundreds of such instances could easily be supplied. As compared with Christian theology, science as it is now urged upon us is but of yesterday. Little more than a century ago next to nothing, in view of what is now known, was understood of heat, electricity, and magnetism. Science is young, and some of the privileges of youth may be allowed to it. It might, however, be inferred from the tone of a few living writers, that the whole sphere of scientific investigation has been exhausted, and that perfect unanimity marks the counsels of all physical philosophers whose

---

* Examination of Hamilton, 4th ed., p. 252.

opinion is worth consulting. As a mere matter of fact there are writers of acknowledged authority on scientific subjects who have successfully attacked the whole line of Mr. Huxley's anti-christian position. This should be remembered by readers who have examined only one side of the subject, for there is a danger, so familiar that it may be undervalued, of forgetting that what is a difficulty to one man may be no difficulty to another, and that a wall may appear to be very strong until the force of opposing guns has been tried upon it. Mr. Huxley's "Protoplasm" is just such a wall,—rather it is but a wooden fence, before the fire of Christian criticism. As a matter of fact there are men of science, eminent as professors and expositors, endorsed by the highest university honours, and entrusted with the gravest literary and educational responsibilities, who distinctly repudiate Mr. Huxley's doctrines, and from a Christian standpoint answer and overthrow his ill-reasoned and frivolous objections. From this it will be seen that there is not an open fight as between Christian thinkers on the one side, and scientific thinkers on the other; the Christian argument is zealously supported by men whose renown, to say the least of it, is in no degree inferior to the renown of their opponents. An eminent professor of science who has taken the trouble to inquire into the statistics of German literature, finds that out of thirty volumes published within a given period, not fewer than twenty were upon the side opposed to such teaching as Mr. Huxley's, and were, without exception, by authors of established credit and repute in Germany.

To show that such men as Professor Huxley, whose science is triumphant as delineated on his own pages, are not allowed to escape without severe reprisals, the following quotation from a vigorous book on Protoplasm, by Lionel S. Beale, M.B., F.R.S., may be taken as one of innumerable instances: " Mr. Huxley says, 'If the nature and properties of water may be properly said to result from the nature and disposition of its component molecules, I can find no intelligible ground for refusing to say that the properties of protoplasm result from the nature and disposition of its molecules.' Just as if it had been proved that the *properties* of water and the *properties* of protoplasm were properties of the same order, and properties in the same sense. Mr. Huxley's writings teem with such inaccuracies of expression. The innocent reader is of course expected to conclude, that if Mr. Huxley can find no 'reasonable ground for refusing to say,' etc., no one else can do so. The reader, therefore, thankfully accepts Mr. Huxley's opinion. If a physical writer should be in any doubt about gaining the desired number of converts to his views, and should feel a little misgiving, lest some of his readers might not be inclined to accept the conclusions upon which he desired they should rely, it would be easy for him to add to his arguments a little literary terrorism. He might remark with effect that, 'An argument like the above must indeed be convincing to any one who possesses any mind at all. He who hesitated to accept such a demonstration, would thereby prove himself to be foolish, or savage, or both"; and so forth, the metaphors being varied from time to time to suit the circumstances of each particular case. Confident writers like Mr. Huxley, who deal largely in vague assertions, sometimes express themselves as if they supposed that opponents were really attempting to extort from them a confession that they had been mistaken in some of the views they had pressed with such enthusiastic vehemence. There could not be a greater mistake. I do not believe that any one who has advanced any objections to the doctrines criticised in this work, has the faintest hope of eliciting an acknowledgment upon the part of any physical philosopher, that the slightest mistake has ever been made by a disciple of the material philosophy. It is scarcely conceivable that even Dr. Stirling, or any logician, should succeed in convincing Mr. Huxley that refutation of any of the extraordinary dogmas to which he has committed himself was possible even in thought; but, at the same time, it is perhaps scarcely probable, that every one, or nearly every one, is ready to accept Mr. Huxley's doctrines, simply because Mr. Huxley asserts them to be the only views that satisfy him, and the only conclusions he can accept."* In another part of the same discussion, Mr. Beale thus comments upon one of Mr. Huxley's theories: "I think Professor Huxley is the first observer who has spoken of the cell in its entirety as a mass of protoplasm, and the only one that has ever asserted that any tissue in nature is composed throughout of matter which can properly be regarded as one in kind. This view is quite irreconcileable with many facts, some of which have been alluded to by Mr. Huxley himself. I doubt if in the whole range of modern science it would be possible to find an assertion more at variance with facts familiar to physiologists than the statement that 'beast and fowl, reptile and fish, mollusc, worm, and polype,' are composed of 'masses of protoplasm with a nucleus,' unless it be that still more extravagant assertion that what is ordinarily termed a cell, or elementary part, is a *mass of protoplasm;* for can anything be more unlike the semi-fluid, active, moving matter of amœba protoplasm, than the hard, dry, passive, external part of a cuticular cell or of an elementary part of bone?" In view of contradictions so glaring in the treatment of purely scientific questions, it may be prudent to wait until the material philosophers have had further time for consultation upon points which ought to admit of easy definition and settlement.

---

* "Protoplasm; or, Matter and Life," pp. 103-4.

2. The anti-spiritual theory does not cover the whole ground of human consciousness. Granted, that you find in Mr. Huxley's "nettle" all that he describes; what then? There is a point at which the man and the nettle part company, and it is for that period of separation, as it appears to us, that Mr. Huxley's theory makes no provision. We are aware that this is denied, on the ground that our highest consciousness is but a variety of material change and manifestation; thought is but a molecular effect, so is feeling,—"All vital action is the result of the molecular forces of the protoplasm which displays it,"—"Human logic is utterly incompetent to prove that any act is really spontaneous." But is "human logic" the highest standard of appeal in such a case? Were we to say that human *chemistry* is utterly incompetent to prove that any man is maliciously disposed, Mr. Huxley might admit the fact, and ask, what then? What if logic have no province in such a matter? And what if *speech* itself be unable to tell in words the exact condition of the case? Speech and Logic are but instruments, imperfect and blunt enough as we all know; the appeal must be to consciousness,—that other, inner, self, which no man has seen or can see, but which is known to exist and to rule. We must know what is meant by "spontaneous" as well as by "logic": both the terms, from our point of view, are loosely employed, a fact which is the more important on account of their being high-sounding and emphatic.

Mr. Huxley has pronounced upon the utter incompetence of *logic* in a certain matter, and we have gone a step farther, and asserted the utter incompetence of *speech*, and we take our illustrative proof from Mr. Huxley himself. Possibly the term "spontaneous" may mean one thing to Mr. Huxley, and another to ourselves. Let a case be supposed, —as Mr. Huxley's words are "any act," they allow liberty enough of supposition :—A man resolves to bestow ten shillings on a poor family, and this he does without appeal or consultation,—is the resolution spontaneous or not? In what degree is it other than spontaneous? It cannot be so in a final degree, because the man altered the alms from ten shillings to five, on second thoughts; then he increased the ten to twenty, and lastly he resolved not to give anything because his inquiries were answered unsatisfactorily: how then? How did it come that the "molecules" did not settle themselves into a proper form at once? How were they influenced? Afterwards the same man was threatened that if he did not give the twenty shillings he would be made to suffer, and under the influence of this threat he gave the money: was the act spontaneous or compulsory? No; he did *not* give it, for as he was on the point of doing so, superior force came to his aid which enabled him to treat the threatening with contempt,—are the "molecules" influenced by fear or by hope? To us it appears to be infinitely simpler to believe in the immateriality of thought,—the immateriality of the moral nature; and if no act be "spontaneous," Mr. Huxley will not blame us for emphatically repudiating his doctrines as intellectually a play upon words, and morally an outrage upon truth and obligation.

We see no escape from this moral difficulty, and Mr. Huxley has not, so far as we are aware, suggested one. If all vital action is the result of molecular forces, if thoughts are the expression of molecular changes, if there be no spontaneous act on the part of man, if it be impossible to prove that anything whatever may not be the effect of a material and necessary cause, then—in view of all these scientific dogmas—where is human responsibility? If virtue is only the expression of a molecular movement, why not vice? And if vice is necessitated or induced by molecular changes, why blame the criminal? Molecular combinations in one case make a thief, and in another they make a policeman, and thus society keeps itself together with tolerable security. The man who can believe this, cannot complain of any deficiency of faith; but whether such a man ought to be trusted as a teacher, we think the most desperate molecules will hesitate to affirm. Mr. Huxley himself may justly claim to be an honest man, but that does not touch the point; his honesty (on his own theory) is a mere affair of molecular law; another man is a thief, and his dishonesty may shelter itself under the same philosophy, otherwise the philosophy is partial, necessarily and scandalously partial, because it expresses only one set of molecular excitements and combinations. Who shall say which is the correct moral reading of molecular law? Who knows beyond all doubt what is right and what is wrong? It will be difficult, too, to show how molecules come to have the power of self-correction: they pass parliamentary acts, and repeal them; they commit offences, and offer apologies; they plunge men into awful crimes, and torment them with agonies of penitence; they send men to the gallows, and advocate the abolition of capital punishments. This must be an eccentric and unmanageable law,— yet according to Mr. Huxley, it *is* a law, for all "thoughts" are "the expression of molecular changes in that matter of life which is the source of our other vital phenomena." But seeing that those "changes" are so self-contradictory, not only as between any two individuals of directly opposite character, but actually in the same individual in the course of the same process of thought, where is the inexorable law of nature, the invariable law of continuity, of which so much is made as an objection to the doctrine of influential prayer? If instead of saying "all thoughts are the expression of molecular changes," Mr. Huxley had said, "all thoughts cause or induce molecular change in that matter of life which is the source of our other vital phenomena," we could have reconciled his theory with the elements of morality,—a harmony which we cannot at present accomplish. But perhaps Mr. Huxley means no more than this, for in the conclusion of his argument, he says,*—" In itself it is of little moment whether we express the phenomena of matter in terms of spirit, or the phenomena of spirit in terms of matter. Matter may be regarded as a form of thought, thought may be regarded as a property of matter—each statement has a certain relative truth;"—and yet in the very same paragraph he tells us that " the spiritualistic terminology is utterly barren, and leads to nothing but obscurity and confusion of ideas"! This is a most extraordinary molecular change in the writer's personal protoplasm. If language is to be treated in Mr. Huxley's magical fashion, we fear it will be utterly impossible to find any common ground of human understanding; if matter and spirit are interchangeable terms, if " thought" and " molecule" are in any sense or application something like synonymous, and if the one of them is " utterly barren,"—it would seem that the other cannot be either useful or dignified. If Mr. Huxley thus allows his phrases to be read from either end, or to be inverted as the reader may think best, we shall gladly use that liberty for Mr. Huxley's own advantage, and instead of reading—" the physical basis of life," we shall read—" the basis of physical life," and then thank him, as a great scientific teacher, for much suggestion and instruction.

It has been properly pointed out that Mr. Huxley can have had no opportunity of examining other

---

* " Lay Sermons," p. 145.

than *dead* human protoplasm, and therefore he is not in a position to say what effect may be produced upon it, so as to differentiate it from all other protoplasm, by human *vitality*. That there is great similarity, not only in the basis but in many of the ordinary phenomena, of physical life is not denied; but it does not follow that because an ox and a man both have eyes, ears, bone, muscle, and skin, that therefore the one is in all respects equivalent to the other. Can Mr. Huxley be quite sure that if he could see human protoplasm under vital action he would not modify some applications of his theory? What would Mr. Huxley say to any man who took an organ to pieces to prove that there was no music in it? According to Mr. Huxley's method, there would be no difficulty in proving that an organ and a wardrobe are equally entitled, that is equally disentitled, to be called musical instruments. They could both be taken to pieces, and it could be made apparent to a business mind that a drawer is protoplastically as good as a diapason. Mr. Huxley seems to allow nothing for life in the one case, as his rival image-breaker allows nothing for combination in the other. Mr. Huxley has written upon the Protoplasm of Life; another man may write on the Protoplasm of Art, and by repeating the logic of his eminent forerunner, he may demonstrate beyond all doubt that a snuffbox and a trumpet are protoplastically the same thing. But even were it so demonstrated, what does the demonstration amount to? Things are not to be judged protoplastically altogether, that is but one view either of life or art; they must pass into combination and relationship before their real quality, uses, or value can be fully determined. One man may insist that hydrogen and chlorine never can coalesce; in proof of this he may refer to experiments made by his own hand; but it will turn out on inquiry that his so-called experiments have been conducted in the dark, and any schoolboy will tell him that if a sunbeam be allowed to get at the mixture, the hydrogen and the chlorine will rush together, and report their coalition as with a clap of thunder. Mr. Huxley seems to make no allowance for the influence of the sunbeam. Possibly some reader of Mr. Huxley's doctrines may feel himself entitled, in pursuance of Mr. Huxley's example, to reason thus :—" The Huxleys are a remarkable people: they never speak to each other; they take no notice of the world or of other men; they are blind, deaf, and dumb; they are absolutely without intelligence, sympathy, or emotion;—all this I know to be true; I have exhumed whole generations of them, and laid them out in the churchyard, where you may see them, and test my report for yourselves!" This is exactly so, from the churchyard point of view; but if the man could have seen one *living* Huxley, we know what effect the sight would have had upon his induction. It may be so in the case of Mr. Huxley's own theory We will not doubt the revelations which his microscope has made, but we must insist that until *living* protoplasm has been examined, Mr. Huxley is not in a position to dogmatise upon it. In a wider sense than was probably intended, it is yet true that a living dog is better than a dead lion.

We now come to the "most wise advice" which Mr. Huxley "enforces" in the name of David Hume, whom he terms "the most acute thinker of the eighteenth century—even though that century produced Kant." Mr. Huxley thus commits himself to Hume as an ardent admirer, but we have no doubt that the committal was mentally guarded by the strongest reservations, seeing that "the most acute thinker of the eighteenth century" gave a good deal of "advice" which is anything but "most wise." For example: the most acute thinker of the eighteenth century maintained that "there could be no evil in setting free a few ounces of a certain red fluid called blood, when the possessor of it stood in the way of one's interest"! This is the man who tells us to burn sundry books of divinity! The most acute thinker of the eighteenth century maintained that "adultery *must* be practised, if men would obtain all the advantages of life; that, if generally practised, it would in time cease to be scandalous; and that, if practised secretly and frequently, it would by degrees come to be thought no crime at all"! This is the man who, in a church, on a Sunday evening,* was described to an Edinburgh audience as "the most acute thinker of the

---

* "Lay Sermons," p. 120.

eighteenth century," and "one of the greatest men Scotland has ever produced." Now whilst it is possible that a man in whose "private correspondence the most immoral sentiments are expressed," may have given "most wise advice," it will be well probably not to act upon any of his exhortations unless they be strongly confirmed by men whose morality is at least decent. Let us once more see what Hume invites us to do :—

"If we take in hand any volume of divinity, or school metaphysics, for instance, let us ask, *Does it contain any abstract reasoning concerning quantity or number?* No. *Does it contain any experimental reasoning concerning matter of fact or existence?* No. Commit it then to the flames, for it can contain nothing but sophistry and illusion."

This so-called "most wise advice" is in reality its own Nemesis, for as it contains nothing but declamation, it must at once be committed to the flames. Shakespeare and Milton must, at the bidding of the most acute thinker of the eighteenth century, be reduced to ashes; painting, music, poetry, fiction, must all be thrown into the fire, if "quantity, number, fact, and existence," as interpreted by the materialistic school, are to be the boundaries of the new universe. It is characteristic of the gay and easy thinkers who have undertaken to banish spirit and spontaneity from all regions of human thought, that they fix the limits of creation so as to bring themselves into prominence and throw other people into remote and hazy perspective; and that they describe the cords and stakes of the universe with amazing precision and familiarity. Mr. Huxley himself gives a neat illustration of his own method of assigning limits, and chiding other people for not minding their own business; thus :—" If a man asks me what the politics of the inhabitants of the moon are, and I reply that I do not know; that neither I, nor any one else, have any means of knowing; and that, under these circumstances, I decline to trouble myself about the subject at all, I do not think he has any right to call me a sceptic," *—a pleading which shows at once the extreme convenience of every man having the right to choose his own illustrations, and the extreme awkwardness of selecting an analogy which has no bearing whatever upon the subject in hand. Suppose this same man to ask Mr. Huxley, not about the politics, but about the *astronomy* of the moon, how then? Or suppose that this same man should decline to believe Mr. Huxley's doctrine of protoplasm because Mr. Huxley cannot tell the politics of sheep and oxen, how then? Or suppose that this same man will not believe that Mr. Huxley has written a book, because he does not know in what protoplastic form or relationship Mr. Huxley existed a hundred years ago, how then? Mr. Huxley demurs to being called a sceptic when he declares the impossibility of knowing the politics of the inhabitants of the moon; but if he is thereby

---

* "Lay Sermons," p. 144.

suggesting that the special questions which Christian thinkers treat as spiritual are to be classed with lunar politics, his illustration fails both in adequacy and justice;—it fails in adequacy because no moral consequences are involved in our ignorance of lunar politics; and it fails in justice because it treats with contempt the convictions and aspirations of men of undoubted intellect and virtue. But let the question of lunar politics be imaginatively put on a level with those spiritual revelations and hopes which have secured the confidence of Christian men, and then see whether Mr. Huxley can easily escape the charge of being a sceptic: let a book professing to give the politics of the moon be published; let that book be the production of a hundred men living in different ages; let there be in that book the continuous and accumulating testimony of eye-witnesses, thinkers, sufferers, patriots, and honest, though may be mistaken, men; let that book be accepted by countless millions of intelligent and conscientious believers; let that book work its way until it becomes one of the prime factors in civilisation; in short, let it be and do what the Bible is and has done; and no man, however anxious he may be to "show a proper regard for the economy of time," can afford to treat a book which has so challenged the attention of mankind, as if it were not worthy of his inquiry or care. He may indeed be led to a rejection of it,—in which case he might be called an infidel; he might have strong doubts and suspicions of its authenticity,—in which case he would of course be a sceptic; he might accept it and honour it,—in which case he would be a believer; but in no case could he be allowed to treat the question as fit only for lunatics except on the principle that his personal omniscience had been proved.

David Hume, Mr. Huxley's most acute thinker of the eighteenth century, maintained that "as we have no sensation of efficiency, we can have no idea of it, and no evidence of its reality." But is it *true* that we have no sensation of efficiency? After what we have seen of David Hume's morals, we must have something more than his word before we can safely accept any statement made solely upon his authority, or even quoted by him without giving the most exact and accessible references. On a subject of this peculiar nature it is more than possible that bluntness of morals may imply some defect in intellectual integrity. What if it be said in reply to Hume's short and easy assumption of omniscience that we have no sensation of *in*efficiency, and therefore the theistic theory which traces the origin of the universe to the hand of Omnipotence, is presumptively true? Collating the facts supplied by astronomers, geologists, botanists, chemists, and physicists of every name, we have, as regards the structure and continuity of creation, an undoubted sensation of *suf*ficiency,—a sensation of what some persons think is best described as almightiness—a sensation, certainly, which cannot to their satisfaction be described by any other term so adequate and precise. But what is exactly meant by the words, "sensation of efficiency"? In how many directions is the term to operate? Let us try it in a direction probably not anticipated by the most acute thinker of the eighteenth century: let us doubt whether Mr. Hume produced the works which bear his name, and let us justify the doubt by saying that as we have no sensation of efficiency we can have no evidence of its reality! "But there the works are, to speak for themselves." True; but what is the use of addressing a sensation which does not belong to us? "But you can *see* the works." True; and we can see the sun and moon, the rocks and hills, and the sight does seem to call into activity, notwithstanding the most acute thinker of the eighteenth century, a sense of efficiency, and sufficiency, and confident security. The bold affirmation that we have no sensation of efficiency is probably best met by a bold affirmation to the exact contrary; certainly we have that sensation in reference to the proportion between means and ends in the common affairs of life, and we have something equal to it when we study the small portion of the universe which is at present accessible to our investigations. Mr. Hume has *said* that we have no sensation of efficiency, but he has not *proved* it. Perhaps in his case to *say* was to *prove*, an idolatry which might have tempted our faith but for what we know of the infamousness of his detestable morals. He had to make a creed which would quadrate with his immorality, or justify it at least to himself. To deny

God was equal, in Hume's case, to taking out a licence for godlessness; and to deny Him under the name of "Efficiency" was to skulk into atheism without shocking the prejudices of those to whom this application of the word was novel. Besides this, the doctrine is marked by a self-complacency at once impertinent and unphilosophical: the argument is short—*we* have no sensation of efficiency, therefore there is no efficiency. It is not supposed that the universe may be larger than it looks; it is assumed that there cannot be anything unless we have a sensation of it, and never suggested that in our own case there may be a defect in sensation. Yet these acute thinkers seem to us to contradict themselves, as will be seen from a quotation from Mr. Huxley, which we preserve from the flames in disobedience to David Hume's "most wise advice." Mr. Huxley says, "the wonderful noonday silence of a tropical forest is, after all, due only to the dulness of our hearing; and could our ears catch the murmurs of these tiny Maelstroms, as they whirl in the innumerable myriads of living cells which constitute each tree, we should be stunned as with the roar of a great city;"—but we do *not* catch these murmurs, therefore we have no *sensation* of them, and consequently, on David Hume's theory, the Maelstroms and the murmurs have no existence! We incline to think, however, that the disciple is wiser than his master in suggesting that perhaps somewhat of our ignorance may be "due only to the dulness of our hearing." This at least is modest;

it does not elevate human sensation to the throne of omniscience and infallibility; it does make some allowance for human infirmity, and by so much it makes it barely possible that "God is, and that He is the rewarder of them that diligently seek Him."

This admission as to the infirmity of our hearing suggests an important inquiry. When we are told that sensation is the source of knowledge, we have a right to ask, *Whose?* Sensation is a variable quantity. Probably no two men hear or see with equal facility; probably no two men experience precisely the same sensations; so we insist on the inquiry, *Whose?* Sensation may have only one meaning in words; but in effect, that is to say in intellectual and moral result, it may involve an indefinite number of significations. Would David Hume admit the reality of a sensation of pleasure arising from communion with nature, in the forest or on the sea? The clodhopper knows nothing of such sensation; if he has a sensation at all, it is one of weariness or disgust. Then *whose* sensation is to be trusted? It may be replied, Educate the sensibility of the clodhopper. Precisely so; but, on the other hand, does the sensibility of the philosopher admit of no education? Has it reached the highest attainable delicacy and responsiveness? Mr. Huxley says no, most distinctly; for in a tropical forest there are Maelstroms and murmurs which escape us because of the dulness of our hearing. We are content with this admission, because it limits the infallibility of man, and narrowly saves us from self-deification. Who can tell what sensations men might have were any one of their faculties increased even in an infinitesimal degree? On the theory of David Hume we are asked to find complete results by the use of an incomplete instrument, and to allow the universe to extend in exact proportion as our sensation grows in acuteness and refinement. We prefer to begin our reasoning from the other end, and consequently to believe that "we are of yesterday, and know nothing;" and that though we may have "gathered a pebble or two" of some value, yet "the great ocean of truth lies undiscovered before us."

Mr. Huxley reserves a surprise for his readers in his distinct repudiation of materialism. "I, individually, am no materialist; but, on the contrary, believe materialism to involve grave philosophical error." Mr. Huxley asks, What do we know of this terrible "matter" except as a name for the unknown and hypothetical cause of states of our own consciousness? That is to say, the question is pitifully begged by describing "matter" as a *cause*, and then implying that we know nothing about it. Mr. Huxley slips in this great word "cause" in an incidental and stealthy manner, as if it did not involve the very question in dispute. But to make things equal and comfortable in all directions, he declares that we know nothing of "spirit" either, except that "it is also a name for an unknown and hypothetical cause, or condition, of states of consciousness,"—so, then, because we know so little of "matter," he is no materialist; and because we know so little of "spirit," he is no spiritualist. On the whole, considering that he knows so little, it is remarkable how he can snub other people with so much self-complacency, and declare his views with so much dogmatic precision. This wonderful power of non-committal shows to what a state of gracious pliability molecular combination can be brought under certain conditions; and shows, too, that even when life has been reduced to an affair of molecules, we do not escape the frets and inconsistencies of speculative indecision. But Mr. Huxley cannot be allowed to make a language for himself, or to interpret common speech by a private glossary. Mr. Huxley says that thought is the expression of molecular changes in that matter of life which is the source of our other vital phenomena,—yet he adds that he is no materialist! Mr. Huxley takes it to be demonstrable that it is utterly impossible to prove that anything whatever may not be the effect of a material and necessary cause,—yet he is no materialist! Mr. Huxley says that the progress of science means "the extension of the province of what we call matter and causation, and the concomitant gradual banishment from all regions of human thought of what we call spirit and spontaneity,"—yet he is, individually, no materialist! This is something more than a mere play upon words; it is an inexcusable misuse of language, unless Mr. Huxley be the dictator of human speech and all its meanings.

We are quite sure that Mr. Huxley will not reply. He adds to unusual gaiety of expression in the treatment of serious topics, a happy consciousness that what is said by way of hostile criticism can only be accounted for by the lunacy of the critic. He says that the microscopists who have attacked his "Lay Sermons," "are ignorant alike of biology and philosophy"; he decides that the philosophers who have attacked it, are "not very learned in biology or microscopy"; his clerical assailants he simply refers to as belonging to "several denominations"; and as for the "few writers who have taken the trouble to understand the subject," he compliments their ill-spent pains by leaving his "Essay unaltered." A man whose molecular arrangements are so happily disposed can never be brought to modify or withdraw any statement he has ever made, and so his days will be passed in the quietness and serenity proper to an infallible mind. His science and his philosophy have been utterly demolished by Dr. Hutchison Stirling,* who follows him from one position to another with relentless logic; yet Mr. Huxley treats his antagonist with an incivility often indistinguishable from contempt. That Dr. Stirling has not failed in his work is clear from one sentence written by no less an authority than Sir John Herschel :—" Anything more complete and final in the way of refutation than this essay, I cannot

---

* "As Regards Protoplasm." (Longmans.)

well imagine." Yet Mr. Huxley's molecular excitement produces little beyond personal abuse by way of reply: if not "abuse" it is something very like it, inasmuch as it is enlivened by such words as "travesty," "absurdity," and "utter misrepresentations,"—harmless words, however, as they merely express a momentary uneasiness of the molecular forces of that protoplasm which men, wolves, and monkeys, possess in common.

We cannot close this review without referring very briefly to the doctrines of another deservedly eminent philosopher. It would appear from his writings that Dr. Tyndall is very far from denying the possible existence of spiritual or divine agency in the universe, but he takes special care to express his belief that next to nothing —perhaps absolutely nothing—can be known of such agency. "The mind of man," says he, "may be compared to a musical instrument with a certain range of notes, beyond which in both directions we have an infinitude of silence. The phenomena of matter and force lie within our intellectual range, and as far as they reach we will at all hazards push our inquiries. But behind, and above, and around all, the real mystery of this universe lies unsolved, and, as far as we are concerned, is incapable of solution." And again, "I walked down Regent Street some time ago with a man of great gifts and acquirements, discussing with him various theological questions. I could not accept his views of the origin and destiny of the universe, nor was I prepared to enunciate any definite views of my own. He turned to me at length, and said, 'You surely must have a theory of the universe.' That I should in one way or another have solved this mystery of mysteries seemed to my friend a matter of course. 'I have not even a theory of magnetism' was my reply. We ought to learn to wait, and pause before closing with the advances of those expounders of the ways of God to men, who offer us intellectual peace at the modest cost of intellectual life." Dr. Tyndall is evidently an agreeable man, with plenty of good healthy blood in his veins, and in the light of this happy condition we read the words "at all hazards" as a specimen of that grim pleasantry which is called irony. We really cannot allow Dr. Tyndall to surround his laboratory door with "all hazards," and to work inside as if a cruel strain were put upon his courage. There are no "hazards"; no body of Christian men is awaiting the appearance of Dr. Tyndall that they may visit him with the penalties due to confirmed and reckless malefactors; the "hazards" do not come though some men are most anxious for the honours of martyrdom. If Dr. Tyndall attaches some other meaning to the word "hazards," so be it; our only wish is to point out that no Christian thinker is likely to have any mischievous design upon his life. The concise answer which Dr. Tyndall returned to his friend in Regent Street seems to have stunned that unguarded individual, to have made him speechless, though as the brevity of the answer is much in excess of its philosophy it ought not to have ended in so decided a case of Trismus. Dr. Tyndall would find it very inconvenient to be bound down to his own methods of reasoning. If he will not meddle with generals until he has settled particulars; if he will not touch the universe until he has completed his studies in magnetism; then see how easily he will dispose of great problems. What is your theory of society? I have not even a theory of medicine. What is your theory of the destiny of the human race? I will think of that when I have found out the distinction of every Hansom now plying in Regent Street. If we have to work our way thus slowly through detail, we must know nothing about human speech until we know everything about the anatomy of the human throat; we must defer the study of latitude and longitude until we have mastered the law of parishes and the custom of party-walls; and a consideration of the disturbances of the heavenly bodies must stand over until we have comprehended the nearer mysteries of dyspepsia. Dr. Tyndall certainly drew largely upon the good-nature of his friend in Regent Street when he dismissed with such flippant conciseness the trifling problem of the universe. Consistency with his own reasoning ought to render Dr. Tyndall quite uncertain whether there is indeed any universe at all, for what right has any man who has not studied the practice of match-making, to talk about radiation or eclipses? Besides this, the principle involves the sanction of ignorance beyond a very narrow circle of inquiry and reflection. Dr. Tyndall may decline to go into theological questions because he has not completed his studies in magnetism; the tradesman may decline to read Dr. Tyndall's books, because it is enough for him to get a glance at the morning papers; and the agricultural labourer may plead that he has no time for paper reading—

> "With half the cows to calve,
> And Thornaby holme to plough."

Dr. Tyndall has, in our opinion, laid down a vicious and dangerous principle whose expression was excusable in the hurry of a walk down Regent Street, but it ought not to have been repeated at University College, nor printed as a "Fragment of Science." The simple fact is that Dr. Tyndall wishes to cast discredit upon any theory of the universe which men may suppose themselves to have found in the Bible, and to him it would appear to be quite conclusive that as he has no theory of magnetism, it is utterly impossible that the Biblical writers can have had any proper notion of the creation of matter or the origin of man.

That this is too severe a criticism will be proved, we think, by reference to Dr. Tyndall's remarks upon "the miracle by which the victory of Joshua over the Amorites was rendered complete, where the sun was reported to have stood still for 'a whole day' upon Gideon, and the moon in the valley of Ajalon." Dr. Tyndall states the difficulty of "a modern man of science" in this way: " The energy here involved is equal to that of six trillions of horses working for the whole of the time employed by Joshua in the destruction of his foes. The amount of power thus expended would be sufficient to supply every individual of an army a thousand times the strength of that of Joshua, with a thousand times the fighting power of each of Joshua's soldiers, not for the few hours necessary to the extinction of a handful of Amorites, but for millions of years." Dr. Tyndall says that " the event assumes proportions so vast in comparison with the result to be obtained by it that belief reels under the reflection." Let us say at once that if this is all that can be urged against the miracle, the Christian believer need not surrender his faith nor be ashamed of his confidence. We do not care to say one word in explanation or defence of the miracle itself, but we do say distinctly that the reason which Dr. Tyndall has pleaded against it strikes us as unjust and ridiculous. If Dr. Tyndall or any other man were to call six trillions of horses to halt, probably he would be startled if they obeyed his voice. " Six trillions" represents an astounding energy to a man who can hardly lift a body equal in weight to his own, but we have yet to learn that God and man attach precisely the same value to figures, and that a miracle looks as stupendous from a divine as from a human point of view. The ancient king well replied to an astonished beneficiary that the donation might be too much for him to receive, but it was not too much for the giver to bestow. Dr. Tyndall measures the Infinite by himself, and wonders how He could afford to expend or withhold the energy of six trillions of horses. He is not the first to remark upon instances of so-called "waste," and to point out how the "ointment" and the "energy" could have been better used; but in the latter case as in the former, probably the Lord was wiser than the critic. We are hardly surprised to find Dr. Tyndall lost amongst the numbers which he has reckoned; apparently his belief would have "reeled" less if the horses had been six instead of six trillions; it is amongst the trillions that his belief staggers and perishes. He suggests that an Israelite in the age succeeding that of Joshua would have been satisfied with much less proof of the miracle than an Englishman of average education at the present day, "for to the one the miracle probably consisted of the stoppage of a ball of fire less than a yard in diameter, while to the other it would be the stoppage of an orb fourteen hundred thousand times the earth in size;" but a miracle is a miracle whether it be wrought within the compass of a yard or within the circle of a universe, as Dr. Tyndall will admit, seeing that he quotes with approval the ancient saying that the "law which moulds a tear also rounds a planet." In standing aghast before the six trillion horse-power, he should have remembered his own words (in his paper on "Prayer and Natural Law"), "In the application of law in Nature the terms great and small are unknown. . . . The dispersion therefore of the slightest mist by the special volition of the Eternal, would be as much a miracle as the rolling of the Rhone over the Grimsel precipices and down Haslithal to Brientz,"—precisely so; hence the absurdity of Dr. Tyndall allowing his "belief" to "reel" according to the mere number of horses represented in any supposed miracle.

But Dr. Tyndall is scandalised that the six trillion horse-power should have been in any way interfered with for the sake of extinguishing a "handful of Amorites." Here is a repetition of the former vice. Had the Amorites been as numerous as the "horses" the professor would have been less disgusted; but to set six trillions of the one against a handful of the other is too much for him. Is it true, then, that the case was simply and absolutely one of a handful of Amorites? Has Dr. Tyndall stated the instance in a calm, scientific, and impartial spirit? Would he be content to have one of his own experiments or illustrations stated in the same way? Never! He would justly consider himself aggrieved and dishonoured by such a method of representation. But it is good enough for a book which limits itself to spiritual inquiries and knows nothing higher than God. Dr. Tyndall speaks of Mayer, of Heilbronn, as having "that power of genius which breathes large meanings into scanty facts," but no such power will he attribute to Moses or Joshua,—there was a handful of Amorites, and that is all, and knowing that we know everything! It is a scientific man who tells us so, and scientific men are cool, judicial, exact, not at all like theologians. Do the "scanty facts" admit of no "large meaning" being "breathed" into them? Is it not better that heaven and earth should pass away than that one word of God should fail? It may be better that the whole material universe should be consumed than that truth should be finally worsted by error. We do not always see the whole meaning of an act: even a commonplace transaction, hardly worth completing for its own sake, may be needful to the continuance of a set of influences of supreme value and importance. We do more than we think we do. The servant of Jonathan thought only of the arrows which he was gathering,—" the lad knew not of the matter." In extinguishing a handful of Amorites, God might be keeping an oath, or establishing a covenant, or laying up lessons for the ages; we cannot fix the whole measure or meaning of the deed, and as for the cost of its accomplishment it may be modest on our part to leave that with Himself.

We have said nothing about the miracle itself, yet it is an infinitely more beautiful piece of history than might be inferred from Dr. Tyndall's account of it. One circumstance in the miracle is sometimes overlooked even by orthodox expositors: Joshua was highly concerned for the name of God and the honour of Israel; he was the messenger and the representative of the Most High to the soldiers whom he led; and it was *he* who in a moment of high desire for the vindication of a just cause, exclaimed with unaccustomed fervour—" Sun, stand thou still upon Gibeon; and thou, moon, in the valley of Ajalon." By this exclamation he committed the whole cause of Israel,—probably he was as surprised at his own cry as were the people round about him,—it was a daring and even awful challenge, and from a human point of view a tremendous risk; yet, according to the narrative, "the Lord hearkened unto the voice of a man," and the miracle was accomplished. Whether the statement be believed or discarded, the grounds on which Dr. Tyndall invites disbelief are, in our opinion, altogether *ultra vires* and untenable.

That Dr. Tyndall is in the habit of making large demands upon his readers in a happily incidental and almost off-hand manner is shown by more than one memorable instance. Look at his remarks upon the growth of a grain of corn, given in his paper on *The Scope and Limit of Scientific Materialism ;*— " Now there is nothing in this process which necessarily eludes the conceptive or imagining power of the purely human mind. An intellect the same in kind as our own would, if only sufficiently expanded, be able to follow the whole process from beginning to end. It would see every molecule placed in its position by the specific attractions and repulsions exerted between it and other molecules, the whole process and its consummation being an instance of the play of molecular force. Given the grain and its environment, the purely human intellect might, if sufficiently expanded, trace out *à priori* every step of the process of growth, and by the application of purely mechanical principles demonstrate that the cycle must end, as it is seen to end, in the reproduction of forms like that with which it began." The words, "if only sufficiently expanded," will cover anything; will go far indeed towards accounting for the six trillions of horses, and explaining the "credulous prattle of the ancients about miracles." But see to what conclusions we are driven by Dr. Tyndall's reasoning, especially if that reasoning be read in the light of Mr. Huxley's molecular speculations and theories. What is true of the "purely human mind" must be true of the purely human body; therefore a body the same in kind as our own, *if only sufficiently expanded*, might play with the stars as with marbles, and run away with the sun as an exercise in gymnastics. According to Mr. Huxley, molecular movement is not confined to a grain of corn (on whose growth Dr. Tyndall's reasoning is founded), but "all vital action may, with equal propriety, be said to be the result of the molecular forces of the protoplasm which displays it ": all thought, too, is said to be the result of molecular movement. If therefore the human mind *were only sufficiently expanded* it would be able to follow the process of thought-development in the brain of every man, and thus we should be known altogether to one another. We do not object to Dr. Tyndall's theory; indeed it is so worded as to render all objection impossible; we only push that theory to its proper results to show that in proving too much he may have proved nothing, and that under high-sounding phraseology he may have palmed upon his readers a very commonplace and innocent statement. Yet that statement understood in the sense which a Bible believer would attach to it, becomes specially important and helpful. Such a believer would say, Dr. Tyndall is perfectly right within given limits; man was made in the image and likeness of God, and his mind needs but expansion and illumination to see around him a far higher universe than he has yet discovered, and to observe movements in nature which would occasion him infinite surprise and delight; towards the enjoyment of such revelations he will grow if he be faithful to the voice of God within him, and to the opportunities which arise in his daily life; God alone has the fulness of this imagined power,—the very things which Dr. Tyndall supposes possible to a sufficiently expanded mind are ascribed to the intelligence of God, almost in the very words which a modern man of science might have used—" My substance was not hid from Thee, when I was made in secret, and curiously wrought in the lowest parts of the earth; Thine eyes did see my substance, yet being unperfect, and in Thy book all my members were written, which in continuance were fashioned, when as yet there was none of them." The spiritual believer accepts this doctrine, and as to his own progression he is assured that this corruptible shall put on incorruption, and that he shall see deeply into things which now lie beyond his comprehension though they are within the sphere of his prayers.

For these reasons, personal and general, we postpone the deification and worship of physical science. It is young and therefore immature; it is pleased with its new wealth, and therefore a little boastful and off-hand; it has done wonders, and it will yet immeasurably exceed all that it has accomplished. Physical science has a friend in every theologian. Theology claims indeed to be the inclusive science; having in one hand the gold and frankincense and myrrh of physical inquiry and result, and having in the other the thought and love and worship of spiritual necessity and aspiration. The theologian has no quarrel with the scientist, but in too many cases the scientist works as if he had a natural and implacable enemy in the theologian. Where this is unhappily the case the scientist never fails (though often with avowedly contrary intention) to suggest the littleness and worthlessness of manhood; he limits its functions, impoverishes its resources, and denies its immortality. On the other hand, a sound theology identifies itself with the most vigorous investigations of science, and inspires the scientific student with the conviction that his present attainments, how numerous and brilliant soever, are but the pledges of discoveries and conquests ineffable in splendour and value. Any suggestion to the effect that theology is hostile to science is a lie. It may suit the temporary convenience of sciolists, incapable either of veneration or sympathy, to magnify themselves at the expense of others, but if they cannot be excused on the ground of immaturity they must be condemned by the example of men who to a true science have added the simplicity and dignity of Christian faith. Professor Tyndall, speaking of "the real scientific man of to-day," says:* " In common with the most ignorant, he shares the belief that spring will succeed winter, that summer will succeed spring, that autumn will succeed summer, and that winter will succeed autumn. But he knows still further—and this knowledge is essential to his intellectual repose—that this succession, besides being permanent, is under the circumstances *necessary;* that the gravitating force exerted between the sun and a revolving sphere with an axis inclined to the plane of its orbit, *must* produce the observed succession of the seasons. Not until this relation

---

* "Fragments of Science," 62, 63.

between forces and phenomena has been established is the law of reason rendered concentric with the law of nature; and not until this is effected does the mind of the scientific philosopher rest in peace." The Christian philosopher carries his inquiry one point higher. In these "far-reaching concords of astronomy" he sees benevolence as well as power, grace as well as necessity. *He* does not find "peace" where Dr. Tyndall finds it. "Gravitating force," "revolving sphere," and succeeding seasons, are appointed by a counsel and directed by an energy which the Christian philosopher believes to be personal and divine; all these things are, in his view, parts of a greater whole; and it is his joy to believe that He who gave laws to His planets has also given statutes and commandments to His children.

XIX.

THE SPIRITUAL ORGAN.

"ANY tyro can see the facts for himself, if he is provided with those not rare articles—a nettle and a microscope." These words are Mr. Huxley's. But why the microscope? Suppose the "tyro" should be provided with "a nettle" only? These inquiries point in a direction which materialists are unwilling to pursue in all its bearings and applications. The introduction of the microscope is an admission that even the keenest eyes cannot see certain substances, forms, and movements, without the aid of optical instruments. Great store is to be set by this admission, for it requires in material investigation precisely what is demanded in spiritual inquiry. Suppose that one of Mr. Huxley's students should insist upon examining the nettle without the aid of the microscope, and should declare that he is unable to verify Mr. Huxley's observations? Mr. Huxley would properly reply that the inner structure and life of the nettle could not be seen by the naked eye, for they are microscopically "discerned." Common sense would confirm the justness of this answer, and hold the student disentitled to pronounce any opinion upon the question. Now this is precisely what St. Paul does in treating the subject of spiritual investigation; he says that such an investigation cannot be conducted without an organ of which the microscope is a good emblem: "the natural man receiveth not the things of the Spirit of God, for they are foolishness unto him, neither can he know them, because they are spiritually discerned,"—the student without the microscope cannot fully or scientifically examine the plant, neither can any inquirer discern and understand "the things of the Spirit of God" without a spiritual organ adapted to the difficulty of the investigation.

It will be remembered that Mr. Huxley desiderated for the ear something equivalent in service to the use of the microscope; thus: "the wonderful noonday silence of a tropical forest is, after all, due only to the dulness of our hearing; and could our ears catch the murmurs of these tiny Maelstroms as they whirl in the innumerable myriads of living cells which constitute each tree, we should be stunned as with the roar of a great city." If Mr. Huxley could discover an instrument which could do for the ear what the microscope does for the eye, he would be entitled to claim attention to it, and to insist that no judgment respecting the air of a tropical forest was of any scientific value that was not formed by the aid of such instrument. This, again, is precisely the ground taken in the Bible; thus: "He that hath ears to hear let him hear,"—"they have ears to hear and hear not." There is hearing *and* hearing. Let two men listen to the same music; the one shall be held as by a spell, and the other shall become weary and impatient: to the one man the music is a revelation, to the other is a mere noise. In such a case whose judgment would be taken in valuing the music? An artist judging the controversy would say—This is not ordinary music; it is rich in unusual combinations; it cannot be received by the untrained or unsympathetic ear; it can be discerned only by the very spirit of music itself. Such an explanation would be allowed as valid and satisfactory, and the opposing opinion, formed without natural or scientific capability, would be held to be impertinent and worthless. It is just so that St. Paul talks upon Christian subjects. He insists that spiritual things must be compared with spiritual; that the natural man receiveth not the things of the Spirit of God; that such things are actually foolishness unto the natural man, so much so that he can neither receive them nor understand them, for they are spiritually discerned: he also explains why the gospel is not seen with equal clearness by all men. "If our gospel be hid, it is hid to them that are lost; in whom the god of this world hath blinded the minds of them which believe not, lest the light of the glorious gospel of Christ who is the image of God should shine unto them;" and as to his own knowledge of the gospel, St. Paul says, "I neither received it of man, neither was I taught it, but by revelation of Jesus Christ." So steadfastly does he stand to it that a spiritual microscope or organ is needed. He allows natural wit, sagacity, penetration, no place in this investigation: the gift is special; the power comes down from God. It will, of course, be easy to deny St. Paul's authority, but mere denial amounts to nothing. In his turn St. Paul might deny the authority of the musical interpreter, and treat with contempt every canon by which painting or eloquence is judged. If we cannot see the organism of a nettle without a microscope, can we see "the things of the Spirit of God" without special illumination? A man who will not give an opinion upon the exact structure of a grass-blade without the help of a microscope, ought to be the last man to deny the need of a spiritual organon for the interpretation of spiritual realities. Mr. Huxley will reply that the results of microscopic inquiry are self-illustrative and self-proving; but that is a mere accident of the case, arising from the fact that the thing examined is itself visible: but when did a microscope reveal a thought, or follow all the excitement of a passion? Yet thought and passion are susceptible of intellectual and moral analysis. Men understand each other by common sympathies. The mere mathematician does not understand the poet. Silence and speech may be mutual mysteries. Strangers who never saw each other may prove to be kindred in soul. Call it sympathy, affinity, spiritual faculty, or what you may, there is the fact that some kind of organon is needed for the fullest interpretation of all life that is marked by depth and richness. St. Paul gives this fact its spiritual application, or its application to the study of spiritual questions; he says there is a witness of the Spirit—a divine shining in the heart —a birth—without which no man can see the kingdom of God. What is there unreasonable in this view, or improbable? What if religion itself be the instrument through which we read the things of the Spirit of God?

Another illustration supplied by science itself will point in the same direction. There are two shining surfaces afar off; they are both equally bright: viewed by the naked eye there is no difference between them. Now examine them through the polariscope, and the one will show itself to be fire, and the other merely a reflection—not one spark of fire or ray of light in it! So much for the medium of observation. Yet when Christianity teaches that a special organ is needed for the interpretation of spiritual things, the materialist demurs and objects. Science itself being witness, the most piercing eye needs microscopic help; yet science is occasionally unjust enough to deny to others what is indispensable to itself. St. John attributes spiritual knowledge to "an unction from the Holy One," and St. Paul teaches the same doctrine in words very clear and strong: "Since the beginning of the world men have not heard, nor perceived by the ear, neither hath the eye seen it, O God, beside Thee, what He hath prepared for him that waiteth for Him" (Isa. lxiv. 4) . . "*but God hath revealed it unto us by His Spirit; for the Spirit searcheth all things, yea the deep things of God"* (1 Cor. ii. 10). Such words show that the difficulty of spiritual interpretation was felt long before modern scientists propounded their non-spiritual theories, and they show also that the difficulty was met in the only practicable way, namely by requiring a spiritual organ for the interpretation of spiritual personalities and doctrines. Christian thinkers might have been troubled if no provision had been made for the treatment of this materialistic objection, for then it would have seemed as if "the whole armour of God" was short of one weapon; but the folly was answered before the fool had spoken, that no one might imagine he had gotten an advantage against God.

It may be difficult to express in one word the nature of this spiritual organ; impossible, indeed, unless we go to Jesus Christ who came to reveal the Father. He will give us the universal term. In the Old Testament we have hints, broken and scattered lights, of which we can make little that is complete and final, but in the sayings of Jesus and the writings which grew out of them we find terms which cover all things. In the New Testament there is one answer to all the great questions which excite human thinking; thus: What is God? God is *love*. What is the greatest commandment? Thou shalt *love*. To whom will God reveal himself? He that *loveth* Me shall be loved of My Father, and I will love him, and will manifest Myself to him. Love is the universal language,—the child knows it, and the savage; it blesses earth, and is the very heavenliness of heaven. Not only so; it is the secret of all success, as it is the inspiration of all labour; and more still, it is not only true of Jesus that manifestation follows love, it is equally true of all ordinary things, and therefore presumptively true of spiritual illumination and progress. It may be helpful to the main argument to dwell upon this thought for a moment. To whom will any earnest *man* most unreservedly manifest himself? To a friend or to an enemy? To a cold critic or a sympathetic listener? Let two of his acquaintances or even kinsfolk be equally intelligent and honest, yet let one of them excel the other in tenderness or appreciativeness, in that one indescribable element which expresses itself in welcome and hospitality—not the welcome of ceremony, or the hospitality of bread—and to which of them will he manifest most of his inner life? He will in effect use the words of Jesus Christ, "I will manifest Myself to him that loveth Me." This is the testimony of universal experience. To whom will *nature* reveal itself,— the sea, the hill, the light? To the clown or to the poet? The poet gets something out of "the meanest flower that blows." Appreciation creates for itself new heavens and a new earth. The wise listener hears music in the wind, the stream, and the twitter of unfamed birds. What does the clown hear, or the sordid man? Noises without order, tongues unknown and uninterpreted. Nature says precisely what Jesus Christ says—" I will manifest myself to him that loveth me." Illustrations are afforded by every aspect of life. We get out of nature and art what we ourselves bring to them. The Royal Academy is a show of coloured canvas, or a church of lofty and sacred genius, according to the capacity, the sympathy, or the reverence of the observer; any dog may see the canvas, but only a painter or a poet can see the picture. We have here, then, a continuance of the same reasonableness that marked the use of instruments, and in addition we have a tender graciousness expressed in the fact that the organ is a simple and universal faculty, which every man holds as part of his very manhood, and which he can exercise under all possible conditions of life.

A remarkable expression, in harmony with this interpretation of love, is used by St. Paul in his epistle to the Romans:—" The carnal mind is enmity against God, for it is not subject to the law of God, neither indeed can be;" enmity is set in opposition to love, and carnality in opposition to spiritual-mindedness. The carnal mind is not only enmity against godliness, or some modification or form of religion; it is enmity against *God*,—the controversy is not with a fraction but with the whole number. But the carnal mind! is not that a remarkable contradiction in terms? Not in terms only, but also in actual life, for the anomaly is known to every observer of human nature. Mind may be so overpowered by the gratification of animal appetites as to become the minor quantity in manhood,—the body so overgrown as almost to have absorbed the soul. Where this is the case the very idea of *God* is repugnant, because that idea necessitates government, discipline, responsibility, all of which, again, are founded upon absolute and infinite holiness. Such a mind is at perpetual enmity against God : it is not subject to the law of God (carrying the ideas of government, discipline, and responsibility), neither indeed can be ; "they that are in the flesh cannot please God,"—"the world cannot receive the Spirit of truth, because it seeth Him not, neither knoweth Him." More than the gratification of bodily appetites is involved in being "in the flesh" or having "the carnal mind." Self-gratification is a wide term ; it is interchangeable with self-trust, self-sufficiency, self-completeness, or self-idolatry. Such selfhood always exists to the exclusion of spirituality ; it is enmity against God, and, properly understood, it is enmity against human nature and against society. The reasonableness of this ought to be acknowledged by scientists even of the most irreligious class; for the moment they touch any medium or instrument of observation they acknowledge their own incompleteness, and their consequent need of help. The self-satisfied mind is enmity against science as much as against religion. It declares its own sufficiency, and by so much it declines offers of illumination or advancement. St. Paul, therefore, was stating a universal truth when he said that "the carnal mind is enmity against God." Docility is one of the first conditions of improvement; but docility and self-sufficiency are incompatible; there is a controversy between them, and according to the settlement of that contention will be the spirit and character of the future man.

From these observations it will be seen that in declining the leadership of the materialists we justify ourselves by denying their qualification to judge spiritual questions. Intellectual vigour as applied in one direction accounts for nothing in such qualification: "having eyes they see not, having ears they hear not, and having hearts they do not understand." Among them that are born of women there may not have appeared men of greater intellectual capacity, but he that is least in the kingdom of God is greater than their chief or king. Evidently so, for it is a higher kingdom altogether, involving destinies and conferring advantages which cannot be described in comparative terms. The great error which scientists have committed is having, *as such*, taken upon themselves to give any opinion upon spiritual subjects; and religious men would commit a similar error if, *as such*, they undertook to pronounce judgment upon purely scientific questions. A man who has familiarised himself with the organism of a nettle is not *therefore* entitled to give an opinion upon the inspiration of the Bible, any more than is a man who can compose a sermon *therefore* qualified to criticise a painting. Scientists, too, may avail themselves of the very questionable advantage of supposing themselves able to ignore religion, whereas religious men are bound by their very loyalty to the Christian faith to encourage and applaud the progress of science, and to turn such progress into an occasion of religious thankfulness. Scientists have at present the charm of novelty—almost romance, whilst religious thinkers are reposing upon truths ripened and mellowed by centuries, yet capable of adaptation to the demands of current experience and progress. Controversy between science and religion is wholly out of place, and was not begun by religion. Science falsely so called and vain philosophy have been consistently condemned by Christian apostles, but the very terms show reverence for what is true and solid both in the one and in the other. Probably that controversy will not be allayed until the relationships (as distinguished from the dogmas) of religion and science be adjusted. Science marks but a single province of human inquiry, and (not impossibly) is as at present pursued limited to one section of one world : Religion, on the other hand, touches the whole circle of human life, and rules the spirit and habitudes of all worlds. To compare the universal with the limited is to be unjust to both; and to exalt the limited above the universal is to replace the sun with a private lamp. Religion and science has each its peculiar mystery ; and if the one is to be avoided or discredited on account of its difficulties, the other must fall by the rigour of the same law.

In his Synthetic Philosophy (First Principles) Mr. Herbert Spencer concludes an elaborate and able chapter on Ultimate Religious Ideas with a remarkable suggestion bearing upon this argument. Having expounded a good many theories, and shown the insufficiency of a good many hypotheses, he says—" Thus the mystery which all religions recognise, turns out to be a far more transcendent mystery than any of them suspect—not a relative, but an absolute mystery. . . . The Power which the universe manifests to us is utterly inscrutable." In a theologian this tone would have been regarded as dogmatic: certainly its modesty is well hidden by its decisive vigour. But is the doctrine true? So far as the Bible is concerned it is *not* true that the absolute inscrutableness of the Power was unsuspected. On the contrary it is affirmed in manifold terms, and specially declared by Jesus Christ. " No man knoweth the Father save the Son;"— ' No man hath seen God at any time;"—" No man can see God and live." A recollection of such sentences would have modified the breadth of the foregoing assertion, and brought down its argumentative value to its proper nothingness. We have already pointed out that this is a question of *revelation;* the inscrutableness is granted ("Who can find out God, or know the Almighty unto perfection?"), but the distinct revelation is also affirmed by Jesus Christ, and that affirmation has created for itself too great an influence in the world to be simply ignored. At the risk of retraversing a few steps, it may be well to recall the emphasis of that affirmation :—" The only begotten Son which is in the bosom of the Father, He hath declared Him;"— "No man knoweth the Father, save the Son, and he to whomsoever the Son will reveal Him;"—" I have manifested Thy name unto the men which Thou gavest Me out of the world;"—"As the Father knoweth Me, even so know I the Father;"—" If ye had known Me ye should have known my Father also." With declarations such as these before us, identified with a Name upon which a church is founded, and supported by a character whose purity and beneficence have excited the wonder of the world, is it fair on the part of any philosopher to dwell upon the inscrutableness of God as if no revelation had at all events been professed? If Mr. Herbert Spencer had never heard of the Christian faith he could only have stopped where he has done so; but with that faith before him, he was bound to respect it, at least on intellectual grounds. We insist that it be remembered that Mr. Herbert Spencer has not treated the Christian argument, considered as an anticipation of his own theory, and that therefore the paganism of his logic should not be taken for more than it is worth.

Looking at the whole ground thus traversed, two convictions have been strengthened by the anti-Christian argument :—

First : That the theoretical exclusion of the spiritual element, instead of diminishing the mystery of human life, greatly and painfully increases it. Viewing the whole question as lying within the province of reason, it is to us *easier* to believe that behind all visible things there is an infinite and eternal Spirit, than to believe that all things are self-existent, self-dependent, and wholly material. Our opinion upon this point has been clearly expressed by the author just quoted—" the atheistic theory is not only absolutely unthinkable, but even if it were thinkable would not be a solution : the assertion that the universe is self-existent does not really carry us a step beyond the cognition of its present existence; and so leaves us with a mere restatement of the mystery." Reason itself is more satisfied with the theory of an independent origin and a supreme rule, than with the theory of no origin and no supremacy. If any man could make good a proposition to give us a doctrine of the universe without mystery, and that would satisfy all the inquiries of reason, he would come into the discussion with immense advantage ; but instead of such a proposition, we are invited to accept a theory which treats a part as if it were the whole, and offers no answer to the wonder and the sorrow of human life. If the Bible were removed from civilisation, it would leave more mystery behind it than it would take away. With this difference, too: that whilst without it we should have mystery, cold, dark, and despairing, with it we have mystery relieved by light and accompanied by the most pathetic and comforting promises. It cannot be too constantly remembered that the Bible itself fully recognises its own mysteries, and never once asks to be accepted on the ground that it removes every difficulty from human thinking, and renders it impossible for the human intellect to confound itself by impious speculation. From beginning to end there is mystery in the Bible, but is it not just such mystery as the awfulness of eternity might be supposed to throw upon the narrow and troubled way of time ? Is not a man a mystery to a child ? And being such, is his existence to be denied or his superiority to be questioned ? The child himself is a mystery, and the man is but a continuation of the same difficulty. There is a mystery that is natural and proper, even necessary, so to say ; and there may be a mystery which is simply arbitrary, or a mystery to those only who refuse to avail themselves of proffered light. Is there any monotony so intolerable as life would be without mystery ? Every day brings its own secret, and the surprise of the coming hour is often its keenest joy. Properly understood it may be that mystery is but the longer word for mercy. We are drawn forward by the mighty and often gracious power of the *Unknown*. What is beyond the next curve on the road ? May not to-morrow open our prison-door ? By such questioning is melancholy kept at bay, and weakness preserved from despair. All our life is set in mystery, from the cradle to the grave : education, enterprise, art, wit, poetry, music, are all caught in the same cloud, a cloud often dark, yet with fringes of light and rents through which the blue is seen. Reduce the universe to a self-existent, self-ruling, and self-terminating machine, and still there will remain the mysteries:—How came it to be? By what means is it kept together? How did we come into it? What is the final appeal of right against wrong? And what is there, if anything, beyond death? Materialism is deficient in compass : it cannot comprehend the whole case : its analysis of a leaf is admirable, but it is lost amidst the secrets of the heart,—it creates more mysteries than it removes, and in the long run it aggravates itself into the greatest mystery of all.

Second: The non-spiritual argument has strengthened the conviction that any creed which discourages the pure aspirations or destroys the honourable hopes of mankind, is presumptively untrue. It will not be denied that in the human heart there is a "pleasing hope, a fond desire, a longing after immortality." This aspiration brings the most elevating and chastening influences to bear upon human thinking and human activity, and is, on that account, likely to be the expression of a profound spiritual reality. Its extinction would not only leave a great void in the heart, it would also remove encouragements and restraints which are needful to the highest development of strength and the most healthful discipline of character. Granted that goodness should be valued and pursued for its own sake, yet goodness itself is impaired alike in quality and in quantity by being withdrawn from the infinite relationships and bearings which are recognised by Christianity; it is degraded within measurable and even variable limits, and is in danger of being treated with cunning manipulation and used for selfish purposes. Not only so; immunities are granted to vice, so long as it is wily enough to escape the clutches of the law, by assuring the vicious man that when he has played out his last trick he is as well off as the man who has vainly troubled himself with a conscience, seeing that they both pass into everlasting darkness and silence. If in the common affairs of life men are moved by hope, it is but a fuller application of the same law which is found in the influence of Christian aspiration: the one being the limited, the other the unlimited term. Besides this, any doctrine that promises the universal establishment of righteousness—which asserts the coming of judgment upon every form of evil, and the raising up of every virtue that has been trampled upon—commends itself to the understanding and the conscience of man as a doctrine that is presumptively true. It is in fact the one doctrine that is needed as the inspiration of honest men and the defence of all holy and generous interests. Under its authority and consolation men can wait hopefully, and whilst they are waiting they can urge the judgments of God upon the attention of evil doers. Withdraw this doctrine, and it is impossible to deny that a great loss has been inflicted upon the human family; a loss which must be the more keenly felt, because all the arrangements of civilised society have been pointed in the very direction of its truthfulness: that is to say, society has been aiming, in all its encouragements of virtue and all its repressions of vice, to generate a social religion, and establish a commonwealth in which reprobacy shall be reduced to a minimum. But these local attempts have been founded upon what appeared to be a universal authority, and have drawn their sanctions from it. Deny that authority or impair it, and you loosen the bonds of social organization, and discourage every hope of perfect union and world-wide peace. Christian doctrine cannot be simply ignored or banished. It has wrought itself too thoroughly into the living tissue of society to be removed without necessitating the most intricate and serious consequences. Not only will there be required a reconstruction of society as it exists in christendom, but every man who has been moved by Christian aspiration will, so to speak, have to divest himself of his old consciousness, and start his whole life from a new centre; in a word, he will have to give the lie to himself, and put to silence all the voices of his own nature which have hitherto been to him as the echoes of the voice of God.

With that wonderful completeness which we have pointed out as belonging to the Bible, the very ground of scientists, so far as they dwell upon the materiality and limitations of human life, has been anticipated in the pages of revelation. It was not reserved for the microscope to find out man's weakness, or to teach him to look to the plants of the field for types of his frailty and perishableness. It might be supposed, from much that has passed under our review, that not until quite recently was it known that there is a protoplasm common to man and to the fading grass; a quotation or two will show how mistaken would be this supposition: "As for man his days are as grass; as a flower of the field so he flourisheth; for the wind passeth over it, and it is gone, and the place therefore shall know it no more;" "he cometh forth as a flower, and is cut down;" "we all do fade as a leaf." The Bible does not leave man without humiliation as to the tenure of earthly life :—" The Lord knoweth our frame; He remembereth that we are dust;" "He remembered that they were but flesh; a wind that passeth away, and cometh not again;" "What is your life? It is even a vapour, that appeareth for a little time, and then vanisheth away." Humiliation enough, long before Mr. Huxley came "with these not rare articles, a nettle and a microscope." On the other hand, the Bible never fails to magnify the inner and better life of man, thus: "The world passeth away, and the lust thereof, but he that doeth the will of God abideth for ever;" "Thou hast made man a little lower than the angels, and hast crowned him with glory and honour;" "As we have borne the image of the earthy, we shall also bear the image of the heavenly;" "It doth not yet appear what we shall be; we shall be like

Him, for we shall see Him as He is;" "We know that if our earthly house of this tabernacle were dissolved, we have a building of God, an house not made with hands, eternal in the heavens."

Dr. Tyndall, whose writings cannot be read without the highest advantage, does, indeed, allow that something more than pure materialism is needed to meet the whole circle of human want. With great beauty, he says: "The circle of human nature is not complete without the arc of feeling and emotion. The lilies of the field have a value for us beyond their botanical ones—a certain lightening of the heart accompanies the declaration that 'Solomon in all his glory was not arrayed like one of these.' The sound of the village bell which comes mellowed from the valley to the traveller upon the hill, has a value beyond its acoustical one. The setting sun when it mantles with the bloom of roses the alpine snows, has a value beyond its optical one. Round about the intellect sweeps the horizon of emotions from which all our noblest impulses are derived." Yet in the face of these admissions Dr. Tyndall would, unless we greatly misinterpret his meaning, take special care to exclude theology as a possible help to the full satisfaction of human nature. It is not to the theologian but the poet that he extends the hand of welcome: "I think the poet will have a great part to play in the future of the world. To him it is given for a long time to come to fill those stores which the recession of the theologic tide has left exposed; to him when he rightly understands his mission, and does not flinch from the tonic discipline which it assuredly demands, we have a right to look for that heightening and brightening of life which so many of us need. He ought to be the interpreter of that power which as

> 'Jehovah, Jove, or Lord,'

has hitherto filled and strengthened the human heart." Such an admission has meaning in it, and hope, nothwithstanding the dislike, latent rather than fully expressed, of theological study and suggestion. There are not wanting men, whose intellectual power Dr. Tyndall himself would be the first to recognise and honour, who believe that the "Poet" has already come with the "interpretation," and the solace. What if they be right? Dr. Tyndall is longing for a poet; other men, whom he would call great and good, think that in Jesus Christ they have found the "Interpreter" of that power which has been named "Jehovah, Jove, or Lord." Certainly, Jesus called Him by the name of Father, and spoke much of His love and care. No tenderer words were ever spoken; no deeper words ever challenged intellectual attention; and as for noble deeds His life is full of them. What the "poet" can do more than Jesus did in the interpretation of God, we cannot even imagine. When He blessed little children, and gave lost women a new beginning of life; when He brought the prodigal home, and delivered the poor from the spoiler; and did all this as the will of His Father,—it is not to be wondered at that some bruised and despairing hearts should have taken Him as their Poet, their Teacher, and their Lord. It seemed as if He was the very Refuge which men needed, and a very present help in time of trouble. His voice always sounded as if it *might* have been God's own; there was so much pathos in it, so much real loving-kindness, and such a sounding of something far-off and unknown. Possibly, too, those outcast women may have seen further than some proud thinkers, and have known through their very sin and its mortal pain more of Christ's real nature than could ever be known by self-righteousness and supposed infallibility. Shall we, then, cast off this Man thoughtlessly, and bear our sorrow in darkness until a poet come with new songs and unheard rhythms? The question is serious enough, and much may depend upon the answer. We believe that poets will come, generation after generation until the end of time, but we have no hope that any of them will call God by a tenderer name than Father, or propose a higher obedience than purity and love.

EPILOGUE.

THE theory of paganism would seem ever to have been that gods should have been as numerous as human necessities, or even human whims. It is perhaps not wonderful that polytheism should have had many believers, seeing how difficult it is on the one hand to conceive how all great and good attributes can be combined in one Personality, and how easy it is on the other hand to imagine that a distribution of such attributes might have helped to expedite and perfect the administration of universal affairs. Beyond this there is a consideration which perhaps may throw some light upon the philosophy of polytheism: human invention delights in its own fertility, and to add another god to the Pantheon must always have been peculiarly gratifying to its vanity. What a saint must he have been who descried amid the confusion and clouds of mundane and super-mundane affairs the outline of another god, yet to be named in the prayers and songs of men! To have few gods was to confess poverty of imagination; but to have many was not only a sign of intellectual vigour, it was also a delicate compliment to individual and national piety. A profusion of gods was a most *human* arrangement: manhood, wherever opportunity was afforded, has always effloresced into large establishments, and compensated for its weakness by the redundance of such displays as are possible to its limited power. Etymologically there is no polytheism in Christianized countries; but substantially there is an abundance of it: find elaborate arrangements to kill time, to make life easy, to bring good luck, to be first in the race, and to be uppermost in the fray, and you find what under barbaric conditions would have been an idol in cedar, an angel in sculptured marble, or an imaginary god lurking amid concealing clouds, and exerting a mythic influence on the life of his devotee. So we make etymological changes, and become pious by the process. In view of the naturalness of polytheism, it was very bold on the part of any religion to come into the world with only one God to offer to the attention of mankind. At this point a great controversy was inevitable. The innovating religion set itself in distinct opposition to countless hosts of gods; it mocked them with uttermost contempt and scorn; it defied their power, and shook the clouds inside out to show the world that no idol had ever climbed so high. It did not ask to be heard as if one case were to be considered equally with another, or as if possibly the idols might be able to say something for themselves. It recognised the existence of idolatry; it took notice of the workman melting a graven image, and the goldsmith spreading it over with gold and casting silver chains; and it even condescended to notice the meaner gods cut out of trees that would not rot; but argument on equal terms it never asked for, and never assumed to be possible; and in this respect at least it was singular and bold in asserting the one-ness of its God.

The original revelation of the divine one-ness had been lost, or had been so intermixed with corrupt traditions as to have been dispossessed of all authority. It is important, however, to remember that such a revelation had actually been made, so that the doctrine of the unity of God may not be classed with the impious guesses which expressed themselves in Nature-Worship, Passion-Worship, or the Olympian heavens of ancient poetry: the One God revealed in the Bible, having been dropped out of human consciousness, was thought to have reappeared in the varied forms of deification which were originated by the irrepressible religious instinct which even in the most corrupt barbarisms has interposed an infinite distance between the lowest man and the highest beast. And, strange to say, as well as most instructive to remember and reflect upon, this very variety of form, and whatever it may suggest in the direction of polytheism, may have had some colouring of truthfulness and authority in the intimations of divine plurality given in the book of Genesis. The speech of God, as there reported, is not a monologue but an interlocution, and therefore there is nothing strained, and certainly there is nothing that is necessarily profane, in the inference drawn by the religious minds of antiquity that polytheism was the true expression of divine existence. Monotheism is not a bold conjecture on the part of speculative thinkers; in no sense is it an after-thought consequent upon the excesses and abominations of idolatry: it is the original revelation, a divine statement of a divine reality.

Is this divine one-ness a doctrine or a fact so far removed from all that is known and relied upon in human affairs as to be a mystery beyond all reason, without parallel, analogue, or any manner of similitude by which we can get a hint of its purpose and meaning? Perhaps not. We ourselves may have created all the mystery by an easy misapprehension of the relative value and significance of numbers. If we have mistaken fractions for integers, and counted segments as circles, it is not improbable that we may have mistaken unity for solitude, and thought of Godhead as somehow involving the idea of infinite monotony. There is one *God;* true; and there is one *Man,* one *Heart,* one *Universe.* Fix the mind upon the fact that there is one *Humanity* as certainly as there is one *Deity*, and then the mystery of the divine one-ness will at least be seen to be not solitary in its supposed difficulty, and even some hint of plurality in unity may be suggested. A remembrance of this fact will humble men in moments of self-exaggeration and unholy self-sufficiency. To every man this doctrine says in effect—You are *human* but you are not *humanity;* you are *a* man but you are not *manhood*. Hence, everywhere in the Scriptures man is spoken of as a unity. God hath made of one blood all nations of men. It is *the heart*—the *one* heart—that is described as deceitful above all things and desperately wicked; not a heart here and there, but the *one* heart of human nature. Nor ought this consideration to be taken as detracting from the importance of the individual life, but rather as enhancing it. To be so much as a leaf on such a tree is no mean honour,—he that is least in this kingdom of manhood is greater than the highest life in the forest, in the sea, or whatsoever passeth through the paths of the sea. What is taken from the boast of vanity is added to the seriousness of stewardship : we are members one of another; each is his brother's keeper; no man liveth unto himself; as the sun shineth upon all, so the cross was set up for all, and the free gift of justification is offered to all. The *mansions* are many, but the *house* is one.

God is revealed in the Bible as having in some sense a threefold personality, which would seem to be inconsistent with the idea of one-ness. But so also is *man* himself represented in Scripture, and so also is he known to his own consciousness! Herein is it true that man is made in the image of God, and that he must look into himself if he would look deeply into his Maker. Triune Godhead is an undoubted mystery, but no greater, except in the difference of the subjects, than is triune manhood.

If the one has to be given up simply because of mystery, so must the other; but as the *fact* in the latter cases corresponds to the *revelation* in the former, the revelation is on that very ground presumptively true. As to one-ness, what if it should be found that we do not know the meaning of the term? Have we ever seen *any* life that is absolutely *one* in the popular sense of the word? A stone may be one, so possibly may be a beam of wood; but who shall say that *life* is not always and necessarily plurality, or that without plurality it is possible to have life? Here we can only stand still in wonder, in awe, yet in joyous confidence: God is three in one, so is man; as a question of consciousness and reason it is more philosophical to believe this than to disbelieve it,— something in our own nature answers to the triunity of God; we see its meaning afar; we know it to be as it is, yet we have no words that can fully tell what is in our heart.

One question there is which admits of a decisive answer. Does the Bible anywhere demand the acceptance of a plainly unreasonable doctrine respecting God? If so, it must be easy to point out the instances. We are taught that His name is I AM; that He is the Creator, Ruler, and Saviour of the world; that He numbers the stars, and binds up the broken in heart; that no man hath seen Him nor can see Him; that He will judge the world in righteousness, and allot the destiny of men on principles of equity,—these are the great features by which He is outlined in the Bible ; but interstitially there are countless hints and glimpses of purity, tenderness, and grace ineffable. Nowhere is there any attempt to satisfy mere curiosity : minuteness never fritters into pettiness, nor is the lowest condescension ever less than the attempering of infinite glory. Now, such a revelation, it is submitted, is in many respects the very contrary of what would have been invented by man ; it would seem to be deficient in precisely those characteristics which would have most gratified human curiosity, and to abound with the qualities and claims which most humblingly limit the spiritual dominion of mankind, —spiritual as distinguished from magisterial ; in his latter capacity man has charter enough, yet, though all things are put under his feet, all sheep and oxen, yea, and the beasts of the field, the fowl of the air, and the fish of the sea, and whatsoever passeth through the paths of the seas, he cannot tell what a day will bring forth, nor does he know all the meaning of his own dreams. Yet with all this limitation there is promise of wide liberty in spheres and ages to come. We are to be like the Lord, for we shall see Him as He is. We shall see God's face! Looking at all this, there is certainly no other theory respecting Godhead so simple, so reasonable, and so satisfactory, as that which is propounded in the Bible. But why have any theory at all ? Because human nature demands it,—the heart will find a God or make one. And besides this, whatever mystery may attach even to the fullest disclosure of God, such as is given in the Bible, the mystery which comes *with* Him is cloudless glory compared with the mystery which would remain *without* him.

The importance of knowing the true God will be felt all the more if we consider the doctrine *like God, like man;* that is to say, given the idea of God which is entertained and the degree of sincerity with which He is worshipped, and there can be no difficulty in discovering the moral quality of the worshippers. More dignity may be expected from a man who worships the sun, than from a man who worships a stock or stone. As is the idol, so will be his faithful devotee,—like priest like people, like God like worshipper. Find a man whose idea of God is narrow, and you find a bigot or a persecutor: find a man whose conception of God is lofty, pure, tender, loving, and you find a life ennobled and enriched with proportionate thought and charity. What, then, may be expected from the honest and constant worshippers of a God who is infinite in power, wisdom, and goodness, to whom sin is an abominable thing, and whose delight is in judgment and mercy,—a God who is angry with the wicked every day, yet who continually seeks their purification and immortality, a God who resisteth the proud but giveth grace unto the humble? What *ought* to come out of such worship is evident,—pureness, dignity, simplicity of life, hatred of evil, wholeness of noble character. But the objector will remind us, perhaps, too, with some cruelty of tone, that these results are not found in Christendom. Possibly not. Yet they are found in Christendom as they have never been found elsewhere on the face of the globe. The sneerer himself may owe the continuance of his own mean life to "the salt of the earth" which he affects to despise. And more, none will be so ready as true worshippers themselves to confess, with many bitter self-reproaches, that they dishonour the footstool at which they kneel, and grieve the Lord whom in their deepest heart they love with unspeakable tenderness.

That it is important even in Christian countries to explain clearly the true character of God as revealed in the Bible, is proved by not a few culpable instances of wilful misconception, and is rendered needful by the energetic dissemination of false and most vicious opinions. John Stuart Mill says of his father: "He found it impossible to believe that a world so full of evil was the work of an author combining infinite power with perfect goodness and righteousness. . . . 'Think,' he would say, 'of a being who would make a hell, who would create the human race with the infallible knowledge, and therefore with the intention, that the great majority of them were to be consigned to horrible and everlasting torment.'" Mr. Stuart Mill himself "believed that the time is drawing near when all persons with any sense of moral good and evil will look upon this dreadful conception of an object of worship with the same indignation with which his father regarded it." This is a fair example of the ignorance and malignity of so-called philosophical infidelity. Mr. Stuart Mill's father fabricated a monster out of his own imagination, and then called it the God of the Christian faith, which is false witness carried to the point of blasphemy. Nowhere in the Bible is there such a God as James Mill delineated. James Mill, an ex-candidate for the holy ministry, was shocked by "a world full of evil," yet he deprecated the existence of "hell," and comforted the few good people who are in the world by assuring them, though indirectly, that the universe had no Creator: as if by denying God's government we either explained the evil or got rid of it. We are asked to "think of a being who would make a hell." But this is a false view of the penal side of life. Hell was not "*made*" by the Almighty, it was necessitated by *sin;* we know this, in a measure, by the operation of moral law in society : prisons are not *made* by Virtue—they are no part of the plan of Virtue—they are made by *Vice*, and are only accepted by Virtue as a painful necessity. The father does not make the rod of chastisement, it is made by the insubordination and perversity of the child.

The theory of Mr. James Mill, as it stands in the pages of his son's autobiography, is so imperfect as to be at once morally unjust and intellectually absurd. That theory limits the case which it presumes to state, and treats the limitation as if it were inclusive and final; nothing is allowed for invisible influences; no account is taken of remote combinations: the possible range of the divine movement is either ignored or miscalculated; in short, the same theory, if applied to the form and relation of the earth, would deny its rotundity because of its mountains, and ridicule its alleged motion on the ground that no one ever saw it move. Mr. Mill's statement is either complete or it is incomplete: he gives no hint of its incompleteness, and therefore he leaves it to be inferred that it is fair and sufficient,—" Think," says he, " of a being who would make a hell—who would create the human race with the infallible foreknowledge, and therefore with the intention, that the great majority of them were to be consigned to horrible and everlasting torment." Let this theory be stated to a philosophical pagan, who has never heard of Christianity, and afterwards let the Bible, without note or comment, be put into his hands, and it would not excite surprise to find him, after due inquiry, addressing Mr. Mill to this effect: " You told me that the world is full of evil, but you said not a word about the good that is in it; you directed my attention to hell, but I did not learn from you that there is also a heaven; you told me that God created the human race with the intention that most men should go into horrible and everlasting torments, but I find no confirmation of this in the Bible;

besides, I find a great many things in the Bible, bearing upon this very point, which your statement neither expresses nor implies,—you did not tell me that God has no pleasure in the death of the sinner; you did not tell me that God so loved the world that He gave His only begotten Son, that whosoever believeth in Him should not perish, but have everlasting life; you gave a rough and vulgar account or representation of a many-sided and most intricate case, and I accuse you of having suppressed the truth, and so of having produced upon my mind all the effect of a malignant lie."

Mr. Mill did what is very generally done in the representation of the divine nature; he fixed attention upon one aspect, and treated it as the whole personality, a method which is unjust in all cases, but specially and disastrously vicious in the case before us. And this would have been not a whit the less true had he called attention exclusively to the other aspect of God, and said : " Think of a God all mercy, all pity, all condescension, and love :" that is not a full representation of God. In a very deep sense is the poet right when he says, "A God all mercy is a God unjust." The God of the Bible is righteous in His mercy, merciful in His righteousness, "just, yet the justifier of the ungodly,"—none so condescending, because none so lofty ; none so gracious, because none so terrible in judgment. God is love,—God is a consuming fire.

Mr. Mill says "the world is full of evil," but does he tell us that a scheme of redemption and purification of proportionate grandeur is at least *proposed* in the Bible? He is careful to suggest that God made hell, but does he give one hint as to the existence of heaven? He speaks broadly of "horrible and everlasting torment," but does he say that Jesus Christ tasted death for every man, that no man should die? It is important to accumulate these questions, or to set the same inquiry in different aspects, to show how utterly unworthy of confidence as a religious guide, or a guide in religious inquiry, is any man who can be so one-sided and incomplete in his statements. What if the bigotry of religion be only less than the bigotry of impiety?

From the line of this inquiry the distance is not great to other questions which have thrown candid and modest minds into temporary disquietude, and which, therefore, demand notice from earnest Christian teachers. In dealing with some of those questions we have no hope of settling them beyond all controversy, but we have a distinct confidence that they may be dispossessed of their power to keep men back from the kingdom of God. If those questions be turned into the form of objections their sharpest aspects will be seen. Thus :—

1. The Holy Ghost has been working in the name and on the behalf of Christ for more than eighteen centuries, and yet it is well known that but a small fraction of the population of the globe is even nominally Christian, and it is also well known that the fraction that is nominally Christian is far enough from being holy. How is this slowness of movement to be accounted for? You reply that the formation of the rocks was slow, but this is not a satisfactory answer; the rocks do not suffer; the rocks do not perish for lack of knowledge: I am not a rock, I am a man, and on behalf of what you would call unsaved and imperilled men I wish to know how it is that the work of the Holy Ghost is so slow in its progress, even granting that it may be said to be making any progress at all. It may be very comfortable to those who suppose themselves to be in the kingdom of God to speak of the slowness of geological formations, but what of men who are supposed to be on the way to the "everlasting fire prepared for the devil and his angels"?

Such an objection proves nothing by proving too much. By exactly the same use of it we may doubt the existence, or certainly the influence, of what is commonly known as uprightness, honour, honesty, nobleness, and magnanimity. We may even doubt the reality and power of civilisation itself. Suppose we reason thus: There can be nothing vital in the spirit of so-called *honesty*, otherwise it would make greater progress in the world; as a matter of fact the majority of mankind are dishonest, and therefore honesty has proved itself to be a failure or a mistake. Or, we may reverse the application of the argument thus: Whatever is right must make rapid progress in self-propagation; it must so commend itself to the confidence of mankind as to be instantly received with all honour and appreciation,—Dishonesty has made rapid progress; war, rapine, cupidity, oppression, are world-wide in their influence; therefore they must be right. We say (not as theologians or Christians, but simply as moralists) that "Truth is mighty, and must prevail," but facts are against that theory, for to-day, after centuries of civilised training there is more falsehood spoken by men than truth. So, if the existence and ministry of the Holy Spirit are to be called in question because of the apparent slowness of Christian progress, the existence of Truth itself may be denied on precisely the same ground, which is proving nothing by proving too much. The objector will remember the ancient confession, "I see the right, and yet the wrong pursue"; according to his reasoning, which takes progress to be the test of reality, the wrong would be the right simply because it is pursued, and has by so much ousted right from the field. But the objector need not travel beyond his own consciousness to confute his own argument. Unless indeed he be an infallible man, and therefore not a man at all, he will acknowledge that in his own life —inward and outward—the faults are in excess of the excellences, and that he has been an apter scholar in the school of vice than in the school of virtue, and because he has been such he has proved that virtue is neither divine nor supremely influential. It is not the Spirit of God that is slow, but the spirit of man, —slow to learn, slow in the direction of self-sacrifice, and in all tendencies which require self-suppression and costly discipline on the part of the scholar. If man acted fully up to his light and power in all wise and holy things, that is to say if he brought himself fully abreast of the divine movement in all things which he himself knows to be not only good but possible, then he might with some show of reason chide the divine slowness, and demand that God should not delay his progress towards perfection. But when the exact contrary is the case; when the plainest duties have fallen into desuetude, and on every hand the man is confronted by an accumulation of arrears in those very matters which lie easily within the compass of his power, he need not go far for an explanation of what he calls the slowness of spiritual progress. It may be more or less easy to him, according to the wildness of his imagination, to suggest how God could have made shorter work of the conversion of mankind, but he should humble himself by remembering that the fertility of his inventiveness is not equalled by the rigour of his personal discipline, and that there may be some things unknown to him, which, if apprehended, would prove his fancies to be idle and preposterous.

2. But has not the Holy Spirit limited His own influence and retarded His own progress by illiberal restrictions? For example, we are told that strait is the gate and narrow is the road leading to life, and few there be that go in thereat: is not the smallness of the number to be accounted for by the straitness of the gate? Can He be a God of love who thus narrows the road to His kingdom?

Everything depends upon the nature of that kingdom, and upon the destiny reserved for those who aspire to its occupancy. It is quite certain that all other kingdoms organized and defended by men themselves have before them a strait gate and a narrow road exactly in proportion to their splendour and importance. Take as an example the kingdom of *learning*,—Strait is the gate and narrow is the way, and few there be that find it. It is proverbial that there is "no royal road to learning"; the road is narrow, hard, uphill, and long, but the kingdom is worth taking. So also with the highest social *influence;* it is slowly attained. It is the expression of character which has taken long years and manifold discipline to consolidate and ripen. It is not a power to be snatched at and held by the mere charm of what men call luck; it is the result of long-continued, steady, honourable life. In short, strait is the gate and narrow is the road, and few there be that find it. What, therefore, is complained of as restricted and discouraging as to the kingdom of heaven is at all events the custom and law of all the human kingdoms which are accounted of high value. Where the honour is small, the candidature need not be keenly watched. Anybody can attach himself to a mob, but it is more difficult to find access to a reputable family. The gate opening upon social ruin is wide enough, but the gate opening upon social respectability and confidence of the best quality is guarded by a jealous discipline. To the man, then, who acknowledges the propriety and necessity of these lower laws, and yet complains of the narrowness of the heavenly road, God is entitled to say, " Thou wicked and slothful servant, *out of thine own mouth I condemn thee.*" It is interesting to remark how constantly Jesus Christ upheld this law of disciplinary entrance into the kingdom of heaven, and how He thereby discouraged such access of numbers as would have invested His cause with the noise of wide popularity. When men would have freely joined Him, He disheartened them by saying plainly—Except a man deny himself and take up his cross daily he cannot be my disciple. A rich young man, who could have made the question of church subsistence easy, and would have taken pride in helping the cause with money, was turned back to sell all that he had before he could become an acknowledged follower of Christ. Severe examinations these, and cruel pluckings! But the whole cost was calculated; the kingdom was most carefully populated; but this very carefulness was its strength, —the gates of hell could not prevail against it. This is the law which we ourselves act upon in all affairs which we reckon of primary importance, and yet we reproach God when He proceeds upon the same basis!

3. Still, having regard to the brevity of life on the one hand and its painful realism on the other, would it not be better to confine our energies within the limits of things upon which we are agreed, and to abandon all religious speculation and difficulty?

But upon what things *are* we agreed? The suggestion assumes that there is a considerable area of intellectual territory within which there are neither suspicions nor challenges, but this is the very thing which we hold to be contrary to fact. It is not true of physical science, for scientists have as much difficulty about an atom as theologians have about the metaphysics of the Trinity; nor is it true of philosophy, for its expositors are still contending about definitions, and one teacher is standing only until another is able to overthrow his supremacy, sometimes by subtler mistakes, and occasionally by louder pretensions. Where, then, is this supposed circle of agreement, this undistracted and quiet heaven of intellectual contentment? As to those things on which we are sufficiently agreed not to quarrel about them, there is nothing in their quality or claims to satisfy the inquisitiveness or aspiration of mankind; and but for this very desire, which they cannot appease, we should never have known even the few things on which we are supposed to agree. Besides this, the area of things assumed to be settled is felt to be too small for the talents and energies of mankind; by the very constitution of our nature we *must* intermeddle with things distant and unknown, a necessity to whose faithful expression we owe all that is valuable in civilisation. A standstill policy is in its very essence a blunder and a crime, and it is furthermore an impossibility in practice. Life itself is a high and solemn speculation; that is to say, its surmises, its hopes, its wonderings, and dreamings, are always in excess of its actual attainments, and that very surcharge works a discontentment which is not without a certain keen pleasure of its own. Equity would seem to require that if speculation were arrested in one direction it ought also to be interdicted in every other, in which event both poetry and philosophy and every effort which properly comes under the name of imagination, would be banished from the region of human thinking. It is evident, too, that to confine our energies within the limits of things upon which we are agreed, and to abandon all religious speculation and difficulty, is to resort to the meanest of all escapes from intellectual trouble; it is, indeed, the refuge of the suicide who is too cowardly to face the trials of life. Religious speculation need not be religious fratricide; it has no necessary connection with zealotry, uncharitableness, or pharisaism, though it may be wantonly dragged in that direction by men who excel only in obstinacy and self-worship.

4. It is not speculation, however, so much as

authority that is objected to. According to the Christian theory, the Holy Spirit is the fountain of all righteousness, and the sole arbiter in every question of casuistry, and from His decision there is no appeal. This is oppressive. Authority of this kind puts human judgment in a most servile position. Why should not every man be a law unto himself?

As a matter of fact every man is not a law unto himself even in things other than religious: then why not impeach the constitution of society, and develop the principle of *individualism* pure and simple? That "no man liveth unto himself" is clear enough, apart from New Testament teaching; it is the very necessity of life; we limit one another; beyond ourselves there is an organized authority which determines our liberty and encounters our inconsiderateness with a law of trespass and penalty. It is a very subtle authority, and often unnameable; not the will of *one* man else it would be tyranny, not the will of *all* men else it would require no sanctions; probably not the will of living men, for they may have had nothing to do with its creation, having only come under its dominion as an inheritance,— yet there it is, inexorable, indestructible, omnipotent! In religious obligation, however, the question is not primarily one of *authority*, but of *Divinity*. If *God* has spoken, there is an end of contention and doubt. Where there is any uncertainty upon this point, of course there will be disinclination to acknowledge spiritual authority; but even then that disinclination should be cautious, because every man who knows himself, knows that, even as the inspirer and director of his own thought and life, he is largely dependent upon moods and contingencies over which his control is pitifully imperfect; the consequence is, that his authority is not only variable, but often the very irony of pretended power, and so he becomes self-fooled and self-victimised. It must never be forgotten, however, that Christianity, beyond every form of religion known to mankind, has not only permitted but enjoined a high realisation of personal distinctiveness and stewardship. "Let every man be fully persuaded in his own mind:" "According as he hath purposed in his heart, so let him do:" "Every one of us shall give account of himself to Christ;" such are some of its directions, from which the tone of its dignity and condescension may be inferred,—and such, too, are some of the directions which give Christianity a unique eminence amongst the religions of the world.

5. Look at the suggestions of utilitarianism as opposed to the spiritual teaching of Christianity, and their superiority must be acknowledged. What answer can be made, that is at all satisfactory, to the theory of Stuart Mill, laid down in his book on *Utilitarianism* (pp. 21, 22), which is this:—" No one whose opinion deserves a moment's consideration can doubt that most of the great positive evils of the

world are in themselves removable, and will, if human affairs continue to improve, be in the end reduced within very narrow limits. Poverty, in any sense implying suffering, may be completely extinguished by the wisdom of society, combined with the good sense and providence of individuals. Even that most intractable of enemies, disease, may be indefinitely reduced in dimensions by good physical and moral education, and proper control of noxious influences; while the progress of science holds out a promise for the future of still more direct conquests over this detestable foe. And every advance in that direction relieves us from some, not only of the chances which cut short our own lives, but, what concerns us still more, which deprives us of those in whom our happiness is wrapt up. As for vicissitudes of fortune, and other disappointments connected with worldly circumstances, these are principally the effect either of gross imprudence, of ill-regulated desires, or of bad or imperfect social institutions. All the grand sources, in short, of human suffering are in a great degree, many of them almost entirely, conquerable by human care and effort; and though their removal is grievously slow—though a long succession of generations will perish in the breach before the conquest is completed, and this world becomes all that, if will and knowledge were not wanting, it might easily be made—yet every mind sufficiently intelligent and generous to bear a part, however small and inconspicuous, in the endeavour, will draw a noble enjoyment from the contest itself, which he would not for any bribe in the form of selfish indulgence consent to be without." What possible objection can there be to a theory so plain and sensible, and what need can there be for a spiritual or metaphysical religion to cure the wounds of human nature?

The first sentence in this extract is very remarkable as coming from one who rejects the idea of being under authority as a thinker,—"no one whose opinion deserves a moment's consideration can doubt," etc. There is something unquestionably positive in this tone, and had it been the tone of a Christian it might have been censured as haughty and dogmatic by men who boast their intellectual freedom. Let us, however, take the statement just as it stands, and inquire, If the acquiescence in the proposition be so universal as to include everybody but imbeciles and madmen, why state it with the kind of positiveness which is usually adapted to conceal the weakness of an argument? And, again, it is clear that if the opinion be so universal, the utilitarian school cannot claim it as a special "property," and possibly, therefore, even Christian thinkers may come within the circle of those "whose opinion deserves a moment's consideration"; if so, there is nothing in the first sentence of Mr. Mill's theory requiring an answer. As to the possibility of extinguishing "poverty in any sense implying suffering," and indefinitely reducing the dimensions of disease, probably there is no conflict of opinion. Still, therefore, we are waiting for the originality of Mr. Mill's theory,—so far, certainly, there is no hint of genius in it. Mr. Mill reminds us that vicissitudes of fortune and other disappointments connected with worldly circumstances are principally the effect either of gross imprudence, of ill-regulated desires, or of bad or imperfect social institutions; to which we may reply, What then? As to all the grand sources of human suffering being in a great degree, and many of them almost entirely, conquerable by human care and effort, it may suffice to say that the suggestion is so carefully limited that it is impossible for anybody fully to understand where it begins and where it ends. In the first place, the suggestion relates to "*all* the grand sources of human suffering," then it drops down to "a *great degree*"; then it comes further down to "*many* of them"; and it impotently concludes with "*almost* entirely." Who can make anything of a suggestion like this? Why does the conquest stop at "a great degree"? What *is* a *great* degree? And why does the conquest stop at "almost entirely"? And what is the meaning of "human care and effort"? Why speak of *human* care, when, according to Mr. Mill's philosophy, there is no other? This is a fair example of the theories which are avowedly or by implication set against Christianity. With apparent boldness they combine so adroit a use of qualifying words, such as have just been cited, as to leave themselves many escapes from the grave responsibilities which at first they seem but too eager to assume. If we look at Mr. Mill's theory from another point of view, we must protest against the possible insinuation that Christianity sets itself against "human care and effort" as applied to poverty, distress, and "disappointments connected with worldly circumstances." · Mr. Mill and his school do most disingenuously proceed in the statement and inculcation of their opinions as if they alone concerned themselves with the practical side of human life, and as if Christianity and its teachers were occupied with speculations and superstitions remote from the cares and sorrows of mankind. In doing so, they presume largely on the ignorance of their followers; for Christianity, as embodied in Jesus Christ and unfolded in His doctrine, is a religion of healing, sympathy, unselfishness, industry, honour, and nobleness; and to ignore this is either to be proved ignorant or criminal. But let us see how the case would stand even in Mr. Mill's own way of putting it: let every man have good health, a good income, and a good house; let poverty, weakness, ignorance, have no more place in human society: What then? With nothing to live on but Mr. Mill's doctrine, the world as thus reconstituted would be a most uncomfortable heaven. As it is to the helplessness and the ignorance of childhood that family life owes much of its mellowness and sweetest charity, so it is to the poverty and weakness of the world that society owes some of its deepest lessons of wisdom and many of its most blessed experiences of thankfulness and joy. Nor must it be supposed that poverty and weakness themselves have been utterly left without compensation. It is not unknown that the weak man has often a marvellous strength other than bodily, and that the poor man has wealth more than golden; and on the other hand it is certain that even the so-called advantages of life bring with them anxieties and responsibilities often burdensome and painful. Besides, all theories of happiness that never go beyond merely circumstantial requirements, leave unprovided for many necessities infinitely more urgent than it is possible for physical need to be. If a man's mind be thoroughly alive, he cannot be content with good health, good revenue, and good dwelling. There are heart-achings, and out-goings of love and wonder, and sighings which waste the life, which cannot be soothed or appeased by "bread alone." On the one hand you will find sad hearts surrounded by the highest personal and social advantages, and on the other you will find hearts glad with unspeakable joy in spite of circumstances the most untoward and harassing. It is, therefore, in the opinion of Christian thinkers, a superficial and mocking theory of human happiness which concerns itself mainly with circumstances. What is wanted is a principle which will put all accidental conditions in their right place, and persistently remind man that "the life is more than meat," and that apparent failure may be real success. Am I *happy?* is a mean inquiry compared with Am

I right? Christ says that the kingdom of God and His righteousness should be first sought, and that all things will be added,—where not literally so, yet so in that measure of spiritual contentment arising out of loving trust in God which is better than the technical and formal possession of the largest wealth. There is, still farther, another remark to be made upon Mr. Mill's theory, to the effect that it is heartless and cruel as bearing upon many who are in poverty and suffering. Mr. Mill says to such—This is the result either of gross imprudence, of ill-regulated desires, or of bad behaviour in some direction or other; this is, in short, your own blame, and you must devise or adopt means for your own recovery. Now all this may be true, yet for want of something else neither expressed nor implied it is most disheartening. Christianity does not shrink from inflicting just reproach upon sinful men; its judgments are keen and withering beyond all other. It steadily points to the heart of man as the fountain of evil, and emphatically declares that death is the wages of sin; but having done this it speaks a word of hope, and offers a helping hand to those who are crushed. It says, "where sin abounded, grace did much more abound;" so that iniquity may be pardoned and the life of man may be renewed; and to those who are suffering through no traceable fault of their own, it says, "All things work together for good to them that love God;" "Whom the Lord loveth He chasteneth, and scourgeth every son whom He receiveth." Place these theories side by side, and say which of them commends itself most strongly to the consciousness and the affections of mankind. But Mr. Mill *denies* the Christian theory. What of that ? Is any man's denial to have all the effect of a divine revelation ? Were this a question of mere denial or affirmation, the Christian apologist would have no difficulty in quoting names representative of intellectual power, genius, learning, and manifold human service, which would make any denial puerile and contemptible.

6. But how is it that the Bible, if inspired and dictated by one Spirit, can be taken as the foundation of theories which would seem at least to be mutually contradictory ? Calvinism and Arminianism are both in the Bible, if we are to believe their respective exponents ; what, then, becomes of the one Spirit and the one Faith ?

It may be quite true that both Calvinism and Arminianism (philosophically defined) are to be found in the Bible, but it does not follow that either of them is to be taken as a *complete* statement of Biblical truth. Great errors have unquestionably been committed by the exaggeration of special aspects or claims of revealed doctrine, and endless controversies have attended the propagation of those errors. Calvinism and Arminianism are quite as surely in human life as they are in the Bible: righteousness and mercy, government and compassion, severity and goodness, are found everywhere ; and he would be no philosopher who founded a theory of human life on one of them to the neglect or exclusion of the other. Calvinism and Arminianism are both in the Bible, as also are Adam and Eve, the strong and the gentle, the ruling and the loving. Calvinism and Arminianism are not only in the Bible but in every great-natured man,—there are times when he hardens into law, and there are times when he softens into pity, yet is he no self-contradiction or anomaly, but rather a whole-natured and many-sided man. Wherever the Bible seems to teach two opposing doctrines, it is giving the two halves of the same truth. For example, Trinitarianism is in the Bible, and so is Unitarianism—not, indeed, as these terms have often been expounded by partizans and zealots, but in a high and philosophical sense. He who says that God is three persons can quote much Scripture in proof of his statement, and he who contends that God is one can confirm his doctrine by many passages. So also with the Deity and Humanity of Jesus Christ, both of which are expressly taught in the Scriptures. Neither aspect, in all the instances quoted, is to be honoured at the expense of the other; they are mutually necessary, and are explicable by the great dual law which makes Adam and Eve one humanity, the dry land and the seas one globe.

"There is a sin unto death." "All sins shall be forgiven unto the sons of men, and blasphemies wherewith soever they shall blaspheme, but he that shall blaspheme against the Holy Ghost hath never forgiveness, but is in danger of eternal damnation." " Whosoever shall speak a word against the Son of man, it shall be forgiven him : but unto him that blasphemeth against the Holy Ghost it shall not be forgiven,"—a wide circle, yet with one tree that may not be touched! Explanation of this mystery there is probably none. It best explains itself by exciting a holy fear as to trespass. Another step— only one—and we may be over the line. One more word, and we may have passed into the state unpardonable. Life is thus infinitely delicate,—it may be destroyed by the point of a needle. Do not ask *what* this sin is ; only know that every other sin leads straight up to it, and that at best there is but a step between life and death. There are places at which we must stand still because there is no light to help us farther; our lamp goes out, so that we cannot tell what comes next,—a lion, a precipice, a grave : this is such a place,—in front of us is the *Unpardonable!* From what the merciful God does pardon, we can only infer that the sin which " hath never forgiveness" is something too terrible for full expression in words. He pardons "abundantly": He pardoned Nineveh, and Himself became their pleader and defence when His mercy was reproached ; He passed by the transgression of the remnant of His heritage, because He delighted in mercy ; where sin abounded He sent the mightiest billows of His grace ; when the enemy would have stoned the redeemed, by reminding them of sins manifold, and base with exceeding aggravation, behold their sins could not be found, for His merciful hand had cast them into the sea,—yet there is *one* sin that hath never forgiveness! As it is unpardonable, so it is indescribable. If it be too great for God's mercy, what wonder that it should be too mysterious for our comprehension? "My soul, come not thou into that secret." Yet nature has one faint ray to throw on the appalling gloom: —" There is hope of a tree, if it be cut down, that it will sprout again, and that the tender branch thereof will not cease; though the root thereof wax old in the earth, and the stock thereof die in the ground, yet through the scent of water it will bud, and bring forth boughs like a plant,"—but if the tree tear itself from the earth, and refuse the light and the dew, what can become of it, or who can cause it to triumph over God? And if man will uproot himself from the kindness and love of God our Saviour, and decline association with all the appointed channels of life and sustenance, none can save him from the second death.

www.ingramcontent.com/pod-product-compliance
Lightning Source LLC
Chambersburg PA
CBHW071436300426
44114CB00013B/1460